Quit Like a Woman

QUIT LIKE A WOMAN

The Radical Choice to Not Drink in
a Culture Obsessed with Alcohol

Holly Whitaker

THE DIAL PRESS
New York

Published in the United States by The Dial Press, an imprint of Random House, a division of Penguin Random House LLC, New York.

THE DIAL PRESS is a registered trademark and the colophon is a trademark of Penguin Random House LLC.

Photo credits: page 56: (*top*) Photo by Albert Harlingue/Roger Viollet/Getty Images, (*bottom*) Image Courtesy of the Advertising Archives; page 57: Image Courtesy of the Advertising Archives

Library of Congress Cataloging-in-Publication Data
Names: Whitaker, Holly, author.
Title: Quit like a woman : the radical choice to not drink in a culture obsessed with alcohol / Holly Whitaker.
Description: First edition. | New York : The Dial Press, 2019.
Identifiers: LCCN 2019029710 (print) | LCCN 2019029711 (ebook) | ISBN 9781984825056 (hardcover) | ISBN 9781984825063 (ebook)
Subjects: LCSH: Women alcoholics—Rehabilitation. | Women drug addicts—Rehabilitation. | Twelve-step programs. | Male domination (Social structure) | Social control.
Classification: LCC HV5278 .W55 2019 (print) | LCC HV5278 (ebook) | DDC 616.86/1—dc23
LC record available at https://lccn.loc.gov/2019029710
LC ebook record available at https://lccn.loc.gov/2019029711

Printed in the United States of America on acid-free paper

randomhousebooks.com

9 8 7 6 5 4 3 2 1

First Edition

For Mom, Heather, Samaria, Elia, Kooks,
Lidgey, Tray, Megan, Em, and Laura.
Blood of my blood.

There is nothing stronger than a
broken woman who has rebuilt herself.

—HANNAH GADSBY

Contents

Introduction *3*

1. The Lie *11*
2. Toxic Eyeliner and Goop Cocktails *23*
3. Is Alcohol Having a "Cigarette Moment"? *41*
4. There Is No Such Thing as an Alcoholic *67*
5. The Right Question: Is Alcohol Getting in the Way of My Life? *87*
6. AA Was Created for Men *106*
7. Quitting Like a Woman *121*
8. Working with Our Core Beliefs *139*
9. How to Quit Alcohol When You've Never Stuck to a Diet *170*
10. Breaking the Cycle of Addiction: Rituals and Healthy Coping Mechanisms *186*
11. Get at the Root: Learning to Mother Yourself *209*
12. Navigating the Sober Illuminati *235*
13. Hell Is Other People *256*
14. People Who Need People *277*
15. What Do You Do for Fun If You Don't Drink? *297*
16. Activism, Sobriety, and the True Resistance *318*

Acknowledgments *327*
Notes *333*

Quit Like a Woman

Introduction

Nearly a decade ago, about a year before I stopped drinking alcohol, a friend of mine showed up at my door. She lived in my neighborhood, the Tendernob of San Francisco, which is another way of saying we lived somewhere between a shithole and a fancy tourist trap. It was early on a Saturday afternoon, and my friend was carrying a Solo cup full of whiskey because some man she'd met on OkCupid had broken her heart. It seemed a reasonable solution to me at the time: to walk around the streets of San Francisco sipping Maker's Mark to dull the specific pain of being rejected by someone she met on the internets who wasn't good enough for her in the first place. Only, I would have chosen Jameson.

We called a few friends to come over, and we sat in my little studio apartment smoking pot and drinking even more whiskey and cheap wine from the corner store, when my dear, broken-hearted friend announced to the group that she was pretty sure she was going through an "alcoholic phase." *Alcoholic phase.* I looked around the room at the faces of my other friends for a hint of the same reaction I felt, which was relief. I saw not only looks of relief but also ones of deep knowing—we'd all experienced something close enough to that to empathize.

Huh.

When you're terrified that maybe *your* drinking has gone off the rails, nothing will rein in that hysterical, ridiculous thought more tightly than a group of successful, intelligent, attractive, "together" women who normalize your affliction with a new term: *Alcoholic phase!* This scenario is only one of a few hundred examples of why I couldn't figure out whether I really had a problem with alcohol, or if maybe I was just going through a little "thing" that would straighten itself out.

Around the time of this particular incident, when I was thirty-three, my drinking was escalating in a way that felt out of control. It was no longer just one or two at home, or a drunk night out with the girls, or hangovers on the weekends, or any of the things I'd done in my twenties that felt moderately in control or normal-ish. I was drinking by myself *after* going out; I was hungover more days than not; keeping it to a bottle of wine a night felt like a win; five o'clock stopped coming fast enough, and I started to leave work at 4:45, then 4:30, then 4:00 p.m. At some point, it made sense to carry airline shots in my purse— just in case. Sometimes (especially when working on a deadline) I holed up in my apartment for days on end, drinking from morning until I passed out. That kind of thing.

But (and there is always a *but* when you want to invalidate everything you've just said) I didn't drink every night, and I didn't drink any more than my friends when we went out. I'd recently made it twelve days without booze, and—perhaps most important to me—I had mastered the art of keeping my shit together when drunk in public. I was never the one being carried home, and I was never the one who got sloppy. I made sure of that.

To my mind, there was enough evidence to prove I was a "normal drinker," and equally enough evidence to qualify me for the Betty Ford. I went back and forth between knowing I needed major help and thinking if I just did more fucking yoga, I'd be fine.

My passage into sobriety was both slow and fast. Slow, in that it took me seventeen years to realize alcohol had never done me any favors, seventeen years of trying to control it and master it and make it work for me like I imagined it worked for all the other people. Fast, in the sense that once I crossed some invisible line, one I still can't retrace, I was hurtling so quickly toward total dissolution that I couldn't pretend to have the strength to stave off what was happening to me. The whole thing was like that *Price Is Right* game where the little yodeler is climbing the mountain and you never know when he's going to stop or how far he's going to make it, but you also know he has the potential to go all the way.

It might be helpful to mention that during this time I was simply killing it at work. I'd joined a start-up in 2009, and because I was a cutthroat workaholic with a habit of fucking men in charge, in a few short years I landed a director title—something typically reserved for Ivy League MBAs who favored Ann Taylor pinstripes. It was a health care company, and many of my friends were medical doctors, so I dropped in to see one of them about my "thing." I explained that I might have a teeny-tiny drinking issue and a habit of throwing up most things I ate, and when she had to google how to treat me and suggested Alcoholics Anonymous, I knew I was completely screwed. I bought wine on the way home from that appointment, because I wasn't an alcoholic and there was no way in hell I was going to AA.

But over the course of the next eighteen months, one by one, I stopped drinking, smoking pot, taking all recreational drugs, and I got over my bulimia. I started meditating and crawled out of the depths of depression, addiction, sickness, and crushing debt. Within twenty months of that afternoon with my friends— drinking room-temperature whiskey and pondering if maybe all of us are sick or none of us are—I also quit my job. I did this because I had finally become someone who (a) wasn't the kind of woman who reports to someone she's been sleeping with, and (b) had a pure reason to exist: I knew I was supposed to start a revolution around alcohol, addiction, and recovery.

What I didn't quite know was exactly how I would do that, or that this revolution would become stronger with the strands of activism and energy woven into other major social forces: fourth-wave and intersectional feminism, the reaction to the Trump election, the legalization of marijuana in several states, the Black Lives Matter movement, the opioid crisis, and the growing and vocalized dissent against a very racist, classist, imperialist—and failed—War on Drugs.

This journey has been an evolving one. At first, it was the story of a dead woman walking, of all the women in this world who try to conform to a life they are told they should want— one that looks good on paper. I drank green juice and I made the right sounds when I fucked men I didn't really like and I crushed it in the boardroom and traveled to Central America all by myself and my ass was yoga tight. I did all the right things until all the right things became so suffocating I wound up prostrate, drunk, on the floor of my apartment. It then became the journey of a woman waking up to the world and all its possibilities and wonder, her own power and voice and unique identity, the bigness that a life can be when we center it on our true desires, compared to the smallness of the one we accept when we center it on the desires we're supposed to have.

That personal awakening was followed by the part where I discovered that alcohol was not only something I could not abide, but perhaps something we *all* shouldn't, and that was paralleled by the part where I discovered that the systems in place to help me stop drinking the chemical we've been trained to tolerate—the chemical that was physically and emotionally and mentally murdering me—were archaic, patriarchal, masculine, and hence ineffective for me as a non-man. I discovered that I not only had to claw my way out of hell and construct my own system for recovery, but that also, perhaps, it was my duty to create something more so the women who come after me, women who are dying in broad daylight while we look the other way, might not have to face the same bullshit I had to endure.

We are living at a time in history where more and more women are waking up to their infinite potential and calling out the systems that hold them down and keep them quiet, submissive, sick, second-to, voiceless, and out of power. We have more socioeconomic and political clout than ever before. The movements started by women of color, the LGBTQIA community, and radical feminists have gained considerable momentum, and we've reached a tipping point—more of us are aware of the terms of our own oppression and of our complicity in the oppression of others. Words like *misogyny, patriarchy, tone-policing, white privilege,* and *gaslighting* have become common lexicon; women, now more than at any other time in history, are conscious of our collective subjugation.

And yet.

And yet: This is also the time in which women are drinking more than we ever have before. Between 2002 and 2012, the rates of alcohol addiction among women rose by 84 percent—as in, it nearly *doubled*. One in ten adult American women will die an alcohol-related death, and from 2007 to 2017, alcohol-related deaths among women rose 67 percent, as opposed to 29 percent among men. It is a time of radical progression in almost every area of our collective experience—and a time of unprecedented rates of addiction coupled with an almost gross ambivalence toward our personal and societal relationship with alcohol. Here is the time in history where The Future Is Female, the wine is pink, the yoga classes serve beer, and the death toll rises. Here is the time in history where masses of us women fill the streets to protest against external oppression, then celebrate or cope or come down from it all with a glass of self-administered oppression.

This book is about all these things—about the sickness in our society that drives us toward an unattainable perfection and lives we never bargained for and what we do to manage that impossible situation. It's about an addictive chemical that we have been fooled into believing is the answer to every problem, a healthful staple of our diet, our key to connection and power. It's about a system that limits our ability to question whether we should be consuming that addictive chemical and one that, when we do become addicted, forces us into male-centric "recovery" frameworks (i.e., Alcoholics Anonymous) that not only run counter to our emerging feminist and individualist ideals *but actively work against them*, boarding us through yet another system that requires submission to male authority, self-silencing, further dissolution of self, and pathologized femininity.

In other words, this book is about what makes us sick and keeps us sick. It's about our power as women—both as individuals and as a collective—and how alcohol can keep us from it. And most important, it is about what is possible when we remove alcohol from our lives and destroy our belief systems around it. This is the truth about alcohol, and the thing about truth is once you know it, you can never un-know it.

You will never look at drinking the same way again.

1

The Lie

Addiction begins with the hope that something "out there" can instantly fill up the emptiness inside.

—JEAN KILBOURNE

People are often shocked when I tell them that addiction was the best thing that ever happened to me. But it's true, it was. Most people go through this life living each day not much different from the next. We are born impressionless, doughy little babies into a world that carves its fear and love of conformity into us. We are told to pick the safe path, to get a job that pays well, to marry a man who provides, become a woman who provides, save our money, buy property, procreate, and die with as few wrinkles as humanly possible. We are sold the lie that if we do the things that keep us safe, we will be okay. As if it were a proven formula: 401(k) = safety = happiness.

When I was fourteen years old, my parents divorced. My mom was born with congenital hip dysplasia, and by the time I graduated junior high she'd already had both her hips replaced. (As of this writing, she's had eight hip replacements.) She'd been a stay-at-home mom for my entire childhood, and with my parents' divorce came economic uncertainty—she had to go back to both work and school. She never said it to me directly, but I knew enough to understand that we were barely making it and that our new circumstances wore her health down and her hips out. I hated the fragility of our situation, I hated the idea that we were poor, I hated how much money ruled our lives. But mostly I hated that when my mom felt pain in her hips, my first thought wasn't whether she was okay. No, my first thought was always: *I wonder if she'll have to stop working. I wonder if we'll run out of money.*

If there was one thing I wasn't going to be when I grew up, it was poor.

When I was thirteen, my family had Thanksgiving at my cousin Sarah's in Pasadena. Sarah is twenty-five years older than me, and she'd just gotten her CPA, married an oil executive, and bought a four-bedroom Spanish-style house in a neighborhood that bordered San Marino (the *best* schools). She drove a Volvo and made dinners that rivaled Martha Stewart's and was the kind of woman that kept truffles in the pantry. She bought me my first Starbucks on that trip, and I remember wanting to be her when I grew up, and her exactly. Or Amanda Woodward from *Melrose Place*. Either would do because both had everything I was supposed to have.

Not long after that Thanksgiving, my parents' marriage started to fall apart, or rather, my dad's closeted gayness outgrew the walk-in. I imagine that in his desperation to not have to come out and in my mom's desperation to not know he had anything to come out with, they thought a series of weekend getaways to reasonably priced motels on the central coast of California might do the trick. It was the summer before my freshman year of high school, and their Hail Mary attempt to save their marriage meant weekends of my sixteen-year-old sister and my thirteen-year-old self alone in our house. The first time I got drunk was during one of these weekends, and while I don't recognize myself in the stories that recovered alcoholics tell of the first sip being the answer to every prayer they ever had, I do remember trying to drink as fast as I possibly could. I wasn't hungry to feel something different; if anything, I was hungry to be someone different. Or: maybe I was just hungry to be bad.

My parents' divorce was finalized in 1994, and my dad told me he was gay around the end of my freshman year. If high school was anything, it was the letting of air out of the balloon that was my potential. I entered with a 4.0 and an eye on Stanford, and when I left I was at the height of my anorexia, a daily pot smoker, weekend partier, and giver of many blowjobs. I barely graduated, and I settled on a coastal community college that promised a social life over a future.

One Saturday night during my freshman year of college, drunk and high on meth (but let's say cocaine because that sounds way better), I was walking with my best friend's boyfriend in between parties in San Luis Obispo, and we kissed each other. I'll spare you the details, but I will tell you about the part that matters, which is how he was judged innocent by our circle of friends, and how I was judged a scheming whore. I was cut off at the knees from everything I cared about, everyone I cared about, and whatever minute fraction of self-esteem I might have had before the incident. I left town with a deficit of self-worth that was the size of me, and for the next five years I took it upon myself to warn whatever new friends I made about what I'd done, like some sex offender moving into a new neighborhood. Maybe it seems like a trivial affair, but it destroyed parts of me and made me into a woman who assumed eventually everyone would leave, or possibly turn on me, if I wasn't important enough.

Not long after that kiss, I moved back in with my mom, cleaned up my grades, and cleaned up my life. If worth wasn't something I could get socially (and try as I might, I could not), it was something I could get through success. I got into UC Santa Cruz, and at the age of twenty-three, I graduated with a degree in business management economics. Upon graduation— while most of my friends organized tree sits or went to grad school or kept the same minimum wage jobs we'd had through- out college because the tech bubble had burst and the Twin Towers had collapsed and we were at war—I secured a job at a Big Four accounting firm in Silicon Valley that started me at $52,000 a year. When I got that offer letter, I remember think- ing: *This will show them all.*

Because this is a book about drinking, this is the part where I'm supposed to explain the way alcohol showed up in my life, to paint you a picture of a woman who was destined to drink in the morning. But the thing is, my drinking wasn't notable, or spe- cific, or linear, and I didn't ever really think in terms of alcohol the way, say, Caroline Knapp did in her memoir *Drinking: A Love Story*. It was *never* a love story. The story was always about my not-enoughness and my black-sheepness and my total in- ability to not feel like an empty piece of inconsequential shit who couldn't do life. Alcohol was just part of the story of me, and it shape-shifted as I shape-shifted. There's enough of a story to convince you how entirely normal my drinking was, and there's enough of a story to foreshadow a problem.

In those dark years of high school where I forgot how to eat and study for tests, drinking wasn't what *I* did—I didn't have some sort of precious relationship with it—it was what *we* did. We drank in fields after football games and at house parties when our parents were out of town, and we took turns being the one who slept on the bathroom floor, and we spent Mondays rehashing the weekend's debauchery. And the most significant thing I can tell you about it was that I liked that it afforded me status, that it helped me to fit in and get finger-banged by soccer players, and also that I really hated it for how much it already seemed to have taken from me. It didn't feel like outlying behavior; it felt exactly like being in high school. Or: Maybe it will help to know that in certain circles and by certain parents, I was often thought of as a slut and a bad influence and a party girl, the kind of girl who might show up on a *Girls Gone Wild* clip. Maybe it will help you trace it to the beginning if I tell you that when I stopped eating food, I also learned how to drink an entire six-pack without puking.

In my first few years of college, where I learned how to eat again but also how to make myself throw up and where I got my first Fs and slutted it up with my bestie's man, drinking was still not something that *I* did but something *we* did. We drank on the weekends and sometimes during the week, and our weekends were spent piecing together the nights before and eating takeout from Gus's to cure our hangovers. It felt like extremely normal, clichéd college behavior. Or: Maybe it will help if I tell you that I ended up in the hospital for alcohol poisoning, and that I wrecked my car while under the influence not once but four times. Maybe it will help you piece it together if I tell you: This one time I was so drunk, it took me ten minutes to realize I was being sexually assaulted, and I do remember thinking that if I was ever murdered or kidnapped, people would probably have a hard time speaking about what a loss it was, or have much more to say about me than "She partied and smoked a lot of pot and loved Kenny from *South Park*."

In the years following my slut-shaming for that kiss, something shifted. I didn't want to be the kind of girl who drove her car through fences and gave handjobs to men who wore hemp chokers to Dave Matthews concerts. I didn't want to worry about how my eulogy might read, and I absolutely didn't want to end up living with my mom through my early twenties because I *failed out of community college.* I wanted what thirteen-year-old me wanted, which was money, security, status, purity, normalcy, a home with a white picket fence. Only now the home wasn't really a home so much as it was a high-rise flat in San Francisco because I'd watched *Pirates of Silicon Valley* starring Noah Wyle and decided that Amanda Woodward wasn't a high enough aim anymore—I wanted to be more like Steve Jobs.

Because I changed so much in those four years, so did my drinking. By the time I graduated college, I had also graduated to a woman who could keep the same bottle of wine or the same six-pack of beer in her fridge for a week if she wanted to, and a woman who properly kept her binge drinking to girls' weekends, bachelorette parties, and work-sponsored happy hours. I also lived in California, and because my young adult life was surrounded by wine country, my young adult drinking was shaped by it, too. I'd been doing winery tours since I'd gotten my first fake ID, I had books on wine and enology and had friends who worked at vineyards and owned vineyards and friends who curated their own wine cellars, and somewhere along the way, wine got all tangled into my conception of what "making it" looked like. If you went to a restaurant and ordered a bottle of Jordan Cab, it said something about you; if you knew how to buy a bottle of wine for your table, it said something about you; if you could tell the difference between a Syrah and a Shiraz, it said something about you. Which is to say: In my early twenties I was wine-obsessed, and not in the way where I drank a lot of wine (which I did), but more in the way where I absolutely dominated wine. It was a status symbol, something I curated like I did my taste in indie music, or my moderately priced collection of stiletto heels. And yet, the most notable thing about my drinking in my early-to-mid-twenties was that it was entirely *un*notable. I drank and got drunk. I was an asshole about wine. The same could be said about basically all of my friends.

In those early postcollege years, I took to my job like a fish to water. I didn't particularly like what I did for a living, but I did like having business cards that said Deloitte & Touche and saying I knew how to do important things, like build accretion schedules. Besides, it didn't matter if I liked my job, or if it really made me happy, because all that mattered was that it would afford me the money to buy a life that would make me happy.

Except, it didn't really happen like that. The more I worked and excelled, the more I hated what I did, how it consumed me, and how it never ended. I didn't know how to turn off or how to be less than perfect or how to not want to be better than every single person I worked with. I felt as if I had stepped onto a hamster wheel directly out of school, a life with a never-ending to-do list, credit card debt that followed me from college and somehow outpaced my raises, an inability to feel like anything was ever enough. I started out not being able to keep up with what I was supposed to be, and that feeling never really went away, no matter how great my title sounded or how much money I made. At some point, I could no longer keep a bottle of wine in my fridge for a week, or quite remember how I had once ended a day without a drink.

My work and my career trajectory were suffocating and inescapable, and they simultaneously became my escape. Work became the only place in the world where I knew how to be the worthy, together version of myself, and so work became the central force in my life. At parties in my twenties, I only knew how to ask people what they did for a living and wait for them to ask me the same. My job title and my size-twenty-five waist were the only two things I valued, because they were the only two things that had any value as social currency. I could work hard, I could starve myself, and didn't everyone want to be the girl who could pull those things off? I found that two glasses of wine—and sometimes three and sometimes the whole bottle—helped me pull those things off.

In 2009, while the rest of the world was getting pink-slipped in the aftermath of the housing bubble, I took a job at a health care start-up. I'd moved to San Francisco two years earlier, and while I drank most nights because that's what young professionals in San Francisco did, my drinking still wasn't what I'd call notable, though it was worrisome, as in I worried about how I couldn't quite keep my wine fridge stocked. Taking that job with its endless hours and promotions and potential meant somehow I gave even more of myself to my career and lost even more of my actual life. When I broke up with the man who was supposed to be my One, I stole all the wine from ~~our~~ his kitchen, which was a metaphor for how I traded my last shot at marriage and children for Russian River Pinots. I started going to bed with my laptop and wine instead of him, and my drinking finally became what I would call *notable*. I gave up on trying to be anything other than successful at work and impossibly thin, and alcohol was how I managed to both go to bed at night and get out of it in the morning. Alcohol was also how I didn't eat.

In 2011 I was promoted to director at work.

In 2011 almost every night ended with two bottles of wine.

In 2011, while my friends were buying homes and having children and my One Who Got Away went and got engaged, I was drunk-buying monogrammed sheets to replace the wine-stained monogrammed sheets I had drunk-bought as the feeblest attempt to establish some sense of having it together.

Professionally, I was everything I was supposed to be. Personally, I was a train wreck who had to borrow money from my fixed-income mother to float myself between paychecks from my six-figure job because I had entirely lost my ability to pull off life.

On a trip to Costa Rica and Panama in 2012, nine months after that promotion, three months before my first attempt at sobriety, and nine months before I finally quit, I couldn't stop thinking about how I could stay there and marry a local. One night at a wine bar in Bocas del Toro, I interrogated a young blond woman from Texas who'd come to the island in her twenties. She lived in a beach shack and had a bunch of kids and a husband, and I told my traveling companion that I wanted her life.

And I did. I wanted out, and as far as I knew then, I had three potential paths: I could find some archipelago situation like wine bar woman, I could join the Peace Corps, or I could marry rich. Only I didn't find love in Central America, the Peace Corps didn't pay off six-figure credit card debt (because I checked and that's what they told me), and the rich man I'd settled on fucked one of my friends.

The point is, I built the life *they* told me I should build (*they* being, in the words of bell hooks, the "imperialist white-supremacist capitalist patriarchy," which I didn't have words for at the time, so let's just say every piece of media and advertising I'd consumed since I'd grown ears and eyes), and all I could do was plot to escape that life.

It never occurred to me that I could just stop, that I could step off the hamster wheel, that I could walk away at any time, that I could stop running so furiously and desperately toward a future I prayed would save me. What occurred to me was that I was unlike normal people, those people who seemed to be able to do what I couldn't, which was not make messes of everything they touched. If I'd had a prayer at that time (which I didn't because no God would possibly construct the fuckery that was my life), it would have been *Why can't I be like everyone else?*

And: It wasn't as if I wasn't trying to make it, or be healthier, or live like everyone else seemed to be living. I'd been doing yoga for a decade. I ate kale before kale was Kale. I'd done the Master Cleanse and all the other cleanses. I was vegetarian. I'd been to Esalen (where Don Draper goes to find himself on the season finale of *Mad Men* and cries in a circle with rich white people who alternately wear business suits and caftans). I owned lots of Thich Nhat Hanh books. I had a debt counselor and a gym membership, and I ran along the water three or four days a week, and most weekends I would construct impossible schedules of the coming week where I'd finally nail life. I had it in my mind that if I just ate cleaner, worked out more, drank less, smoked less, lost more weight, made more money, saved more money, stopped spilling my bed wine on those monogrammed sheets—if I could just get more discipline or be more perfect— then it would all work out. It would all snap into place, and I would snap into place.

The harder I tried to be more perfect—the more cleanses I did, books I bought, and budgets I made, the more things I bought to cover up and paint over the mess that was my life— the harder it became to keep it together. The attempts to fix me only added more chaos, the chaos added more pain, and so I added more wine. And pot. And cigarettes. And food. And clothes. I was a monster who couldn't stop consuming things I thought would make me the human I was supposed to be.

Until one morning, just three months after my trip to Costa Rica, it all broke. Or rather, I broke. I woke up in my rent-controlled San Francisco apartment to the aftermath of one of my binges, one of my failed attempts at escape. My bed had no sheets. My mattress was stained with food and wine and puke. My computer was still on, so was the TV, and bags of trash and half-eaten food cartons and empty beer bottles were strewn about my apartment. My throat ached of bulimia and hangover, and I was still drunk; a pint of Jameson was in my hand. It wasn't the first time I'd woken up to this scene, but it was the first time I couldn't make myself pretend that I was okay and that this was normal thirty-something shit I'd grow out of.

Here is where I fell prostrate on the floor and asked God for help.

Here is where I stopped running.

Here is where I made eye contact with myself in the mirror again.

Here is where I finally heard the part of me that I'd tried to quiet with career and clothes and status and food and drink and drugs; the part of me that was screaming she couldn't settle for this bullshit for one more minute.

There is the life that most of us live, and then there is the life we have buried deep inside us, the life we know we're supposed to be living. Up until that moment on the floor of my apartment, the life I was supposed to be living eluded me; it eluded me so hard that it broke me into a thousand million pieces that I kept barely stitched together with Paige jeans, whiskey neats, and a really good title at work. But somehow in that moment on the floor, the jig was up. I could no longer keep it up and keep it together. Staring at the detritus in my living room that day in

October, it finally occurred to me that I had no other choice but to actually start risking everything I'd settled for in order to have the life I had buried inside me, the one that wanted to run to an island, the one that had dreams of actual happiness, the one I'm writing from today. The life I'd attempted and forced from all angles except the one that required me to look at myself in the mirror and ask the girl staring back who she was and what *she* wanted from this life.

The girl staring back did not fuck around. She knew the booze had to go first.

2

Toxic Eyeliner and Goop Cocktails

> *What we must recognize is that substance abuse is part of the patriarchy; that it is not a way out, or even a resting place. It is a lie. It is every bit a lie as sexism, capitalism, classism, racism, and homophobia. . . . There is a major difference though. Sexism, racism, and the rest are done to us; we do the substance abuse to ourselves. And we can stop.* —JEAN SWALLOW

Years ago I sent a text to my friend (and when I say years ago, I mean on my Motorola Razr). I wrote, "I think alcohol is making me fat." She sent a picture back of Paris Hilton and said, "Then how come Paris isn't?" (If you're younger, Paris Hilton was like Kylie Jenner.) I drank a bottle of Pinot in my hotel room that night (because in my logic, work travel meant whole bottles were okay), and the next morning woke up red-faced and bloated; I ran for an hour on the treadmill to fix it. Looking in the mirror on my way to work that morning, I did not look like Paris Hilton, because treadmills don't undo bottles of wine and self-disgust.

It would take many more years of denial before I went beyond *wondering* if perhaps alcohol was getting in the way of my life. That's because we're conditioned not to blame the precious alcohol, or to even worry about whether drinking it might be a bad idea, until we're certifiable fuckups. What we *are* conditioned to believe is that there are two types of drinkers in this

world, the normal ones ("normies" in AA-speak) who can tolerate alcohol, and the alcoholics who can't. And this is incredibly
convenient for the powers that be (and by the powers that be, I
mean the men—and women but mostly men—who control the
boardrooms of Anheuser-Busch and Diageo and make assloads
of cash off low-carb beer and pinked-out booze) because then
we don't spend time asking ourselves if alcohol might not be
working out so well for us or if maybe we shouldn't be including
it in our lives the same way we've come to decide we shouldn't
be eating gluten.

We just ask ourselves whether or not we're alcoholics, and
thanks to the National Council on Alcoholism and Drug Dependence's twenty-six-point questionnaire—the standard for
(self-diagnosing) Alcohol Use Disorder—we don't really qualify
for help unless we're pissing our beds, racking up DUIs, staying
drunk for days on end, or hallucinating. And if we don't qualify,
we don't really have a problem, and we can just go on free and
clear, rocking our ROSÉ ALL DAY shirts (now on sale at Target),
slamming shots at work parties, and innocently debating
whether we're heathen if we pair a red with halibut.

In other words, I didn't ask if alcohol was getting in the way
of My Best Life. I didn't ask whether maybe it was making me
sick or wasn't the best thing to do with my time. I wasn't an alcoholic, Paris was turnt up at Butter (this was a club that *Us*
magazine said Paris went to) and still kept her size-zero ass, all
was well.

ALCOHOL AND WELLNESS

In the 1950s, before we understood the dangers of smoking tobacco and nicotine, actors would pose as medical doctors in
cigarette advertisements to assure the public that smoking was

safe. *It's okay, folks. Doctors do it!* But I grew up in the 1980s. I was taught from a very young age the dangers of smoking tobacco, and my sister and I took turns pressuring my father to quit. I brought home literature from school, and Heather resorted to breaking his cigarettes in half. When we both started smoking cigarettes in our teens, at least we knew what we were doing. Cigarettes killed people, full stop. No amount of smoking was safe, and people like Debbie from the PSA ads (who smoked cigarettes through a hole in her neck that she presumably got from smoking cigarettes) reminded us of what could happen. To this day, I can't think of smoking without thinking of holes in necks, and I don't think I ever had a cigarette without considering its toxicity.

When I look at those advertisements from the 1950s, with their reassuring pictures of old white men in white coats smoking a Camel, knowing all we know now, I always wonder, *How were we ever so stupid? How did we ever buy that lie?*

Like most of us, I grew up believing that drinking was normal. There was nothing wrong with getting drunk or nursing a hangover. We are supposed to be able to handle it and incorporate it into our lifestyles. We are told if we drink moderately, alcohol will do wonderful things for us—red wine has all those antioxidants (and resveratrol!). We are supposed to be able to consume alcohol with ease, as part of a healthy and balanced lifestyle. If we can't do this, there is something wrong with us and not the substance itself.

Drinking is so normalized, and so unquestioned, that we have essentially drawn a line down the middle and put people on one side or the other. There are normal drinkers, and there are alcoholics. For the normal drinkers, alcohol is healthy! And good for you! And in the words of Cheryl Strayed (who overcame heroin addiction), "Wonderful and joyous!" For the alcoholics, alcohol is bad. Which is not unlike saying heroin is wonderful and joyous when used in moderation, but for Cheryl Strayed it is bad.

I completely bought into this. Until my life came undone, and at thirty-three I looked and felt at least a decade older than I was. Until I started to research and question. Until I realized that *oh my God, it's actually poison. We're all drinking poison.*

In conversation with my mom not long ago, about a relative dying a slow and gruesome death following years of severe alcohol abuse, I mention to her that I'm not shocked that our cousin's throat is coming apart or that her skin is falling off. I tell my mom: "Of course her throat is destroyed, she drank ethanol for decades. You can't drink the same thing we fuel our cars with and expect a much different outcome." In my mind I can clearly envision my cousin drinking from a fuel pump, but my mom is confused and says something like, "It's not the same ethanol, though. Don't we drink something different?" I tell her it's not different. My food label–reading mother—the same one who can list every health benefit of broccoli—is shocked.

From Wikipedia:

> Ethanol, also commonly called alcohol, ethyl alcohol, and drinking alcohol, is the principal type of alcohol found in alcoholic beverages, produced by the fermentation of sugars by yeasts. It is a neurotoxic, psychoactive drug, and one of the oldest recreational drugs.
>
> Ethanol is a volatile, flammable, colorless liquid with a slight chemical odor. It is used as an antiseptic, a solvent, in medical wipes and anti-bacterial formulas because it kills organisms by denaturing their proteins. Ethanol is an important industrial ingredient. Ethanol is a good general purpose solvent, and is found in paints, tinctures, markers, and per-

sonal care products such as perfumes and deodorants. The largest single use of ethanol is as an engine fuel and fuel additive.

In other words, we drink—for fun—the same thing we use to make rocket fuel, house paint, antiseptics, solvents, perfumes, and deodorants, and to denature (i.e., take away the natural properties of, or *kill*) living organisms. Which might make sense on some level if we weren't a generation of green-minded, organic, health-conscious, truth-seeking individuals. But we are.

We read labels. We shun gluten, dairy, processed foods, and refined sugars. We buy organic. We use natural sunscreens and beauty products. We worry about fluoride in our water, smog in our air, hydrogenated oils in our food, and we debate whether plastic bottles are safe to drink from. We replace toxic cleaning products with Mrs. Meyer's and homemade vinegar concoctions. We do yoga, we run, we SoulCycle and Fitbit, we go paleo and keto, we juice, we cleanse. We do coffee enemas and steam our yonis and drink clay and charcoal and shoot up vitamins and sit in infrared foil boxes and hire naturopaths and shamans and functional doctors and we take nootropics, and we stress about our telomeres (these are all real words). We are hyper-vigilant about everything we put into our body, everything we do to our body. And we are proud of this. We Instagram how proud we are of this and follow Goop and Well + Good and drop forty bucks on an exercise class because there are healing crystals in the floor. The global wellness economy is estimated to be worth four trillion dollars. *Four trillion dollars.* We are on an endless and expensive quest for wellness and vitality and youth.

And we drink fucking rocket fuel.

———

Drinking has become so ingrained in the female code, we don't even recognize the nearly endless ways it's pierced our every experience, or even stop to think about the cost of that infiltration. Wine and spirits and even beer are a celebrated, quintessential accessory to having made it as a woman. For moms—one of the most targeted demographics—alcohol isn't just something that pairs well with making dinner, it's what you do all day, every day. There are an almost endless number of greeting cards, magnets, T-shirts, *onesies,* that basically celebrate always being drunk because mothering, we kid, makes us drink. Let me repeat that: Moms are so brainwashed into normalizing what amounts to severe drug abuse, we are literally dressing our babies up in clothes to poke fun at it. There are groups like Sippy Cups Are for Chardonnay, Moms Who Need Wine, an Urban Dictionary definition of Wine Mom (#WineMom), a coloring book titled *Mommy Drinks Because You Cry,* and no one bats an eyelash; we toast and wink because we are all in on the joke. And that's just the tip of the iceberg because wine isn't just the mascot of motherhood, it's the mascot of being a young, single professional, or an old, retired empty nester, or basically being a woman at all. It is so ingrained in what it means to be a woman, we hardly even notice it's standing there next to us in almost every photograph, or showing up at every single thing we attempt to do. We have been programmed to accessorize our lives with wine to the point we can't even see it anymore, or see how the statistics that show skyrocketing rates of alcohol-related liver failure or alcohol addiction include us in them. The horror stories and damages are seen as things that happen to other people.

Recently I heard Gwyneth Paltrow (founder and CEO of

Goop, enthusiastic yoni steamer) on the *Girlboss* podcast talking about the social responsibility Goop holds for its readers. She said she couldn't in good conscience recommend a certain (not-organic, toxic, chemical) eyeliner to her readers because of the potential that it could mess with a woman's delicate endocrine system. Which would be fine and all if the Goop Health Summit weren't sponsored by Ketel One Botanical vodka (owned by the multinational conglomerate Diageo), or if she weren't promoting her preferred, anointed, all-natural, holy eyeliner next to collagen-infused martinis and CBD-spiked cocktails. Because nothing will take you down faster than toxic eyeliner, but drinking ethanol with a shot of collagen is basically snorting the fountain of youth.

What I am saying is: Booze fucks our shit up. More than most things. More than gluten *for sure,* more than dairy *for sure,* more than white sugar and tap water *for sure,* and it fucks our shit up not only because it's an addictive, toxic chemical, but because we live in a world where we haven't quite caught on to that fact just yet. Even Gwyneth doesn't know. And that—the fact that we think it's safe because it's legal and everyone is doing it, including our health icons—is what makes it even more dangerous than, say, cigarettes. Or Maybelline eyeliner.

So what *does* alcohol do to our bodies? Why should we care? And where does this "healthful" narrative even come from?

WHAT HAPPENS IN OUR BODIES WHEN WE DRINK A SINGLE GLASS OF ALCOHOL

In 1991 *60 Minutes* ran a story called "The French Paradox." It was reported by Morley Safer, a CBS correspondent, and it featured Safer in a French bistro, listing the various unhealthy, fattening culinary habits of the French people, pondering why the life expectancy, health, and weight of the French were superior to that of Americans if their diet was so full of terrible crap. The conclusion Safer alluded to? Red wine. It might sound entirely innocuous, but it wasn't—that, coupled with a number of studies that were published in the late 1990s and early 'oos, and books like *French Women Don't Get Fat,* fueled an idea the American public was all too eager to cling to: drinking wine is healthy.

A number of studies published in the last decade or so have countered this belief. We now know that alcohol is linked to at least seven cancers and a whole host of other diseases and chronic conditions, but we are pretty clueless about the smaller ways it impacts our health. Most of us are more inclined to think drinking moderately is far healthier than not drinking at all. We're also likely to underestimate how much we actually drink, without an awareness of recommended alcohol intake guidelines and serving sizes. As Keith Humphreys noted, "When you tally up all the booze that people report consuming when they are surveyed about their drinking habits, it rarely adds up to even half of the alcohol sold." Consequently, we drink a lot more than we think we do, and we often write off the amount we drink as beneficial. Further, we're more likely to think of any health risk or danger posed by consumption as extreme (addiction, cirrhosis) versus immediate toxicity.

The thing is, *even one glass of wine is disruptive.* The body is constantly seeking homeostasis, or balance, so the moment you ingest any drug, your body begins a counteractive process. Judith Grisel explains this in her book *Never Enough* as an A-B process; the effect of the drug causes an A process, and in trying to adapt to that A process, the body initiates a counteractive B process, which tends to last longer than the A process. As Grisel explains it, "The states of withdrawal and craving from any drug are *always* exactly opposite to the drug's effects. If a drug makes you feel relaxed, withdrawal and craving are experienced as anxiety and tension." Alcohol is a depressant, so if we're using it to relax, we're actually netting out with more anxiety because of this A-B process—one drink leaves us more stressed, tensed, anxious, and depressed. And this effect isn't reserved for heavy drinkers; withdrawal and craving are things we experience anytime we consume a drug. One glass is one dose.

Alcohol does so much damage to our bodies that to mention all the ways it impacts us physiologically would fill an entire book; consuming alcohol—any amount of alcohol—disrupts nearly every process, system, and organ of the body. Below is a laundry list of just a fraction of the side effects of ethanol consumption, and it reads like one of those sped-up disclaimers that run for minutes in drug commercials, or the paragraphs of fine print that accompany any drug ad in a magazine. If reading this list feels like a dive into some endless pool of health warnings, that's only because it is; the following should come at the end of every Corona commercial or winery tour.

The Short- to Medium-term Effects of Drinking Alcohol

1. Disrupts sleep. Many people think of alcohol as a sleep aid. While it does allow us to fall asleep faster by kicking us into slow-wave sleep, we aren't actually reaping the rejuvenating benefits of deeper sleep because our alpha (thinking) brainwaves are also activated; this means our brain isn't actually getting the benefit of slow-wave sleep, which is responsible for recuperation of the brain and body.

Further, we normally experience seven REM (rapid eye movement) stages during a sleep cycle; when we drink alcohol, we experience about two. Deprivation of REM sleep leads to a number of ailments, in particular an increase in anxiety, depressive states, irritability, and appetite; it also leads to memory loss. Poor sleep in general contributes to stress hormone disruption (that "tired and wired" feeling—tired during the day and wired at night) and weight gain.

The body takes three to four days to fully remove alcohol from the system, so if we are imbibing once or twice a week, we never fully reap the benefits of sound sleep. Even moderate alcohol use puts us in an almost constant state of sleep deprivation.

2. Fuels anxiety. Because alcohol is primarily a depressant, we reach for it to take the edge off. Which it does, initially. However, the counteractive process (or the B process) to the depressant nature of alcohol is a release of cortisol and adrenaline into the body. If you drink one glass of wine, you might have about twenty minutes of the desired "relaxed" effect before the drug (A process) wears off, and you're left with increased amounts of cortisol and adrenaline, which fuel anxiety. This means alcohol *causes* anxiety; it doesn't manage it. It's one of the worst drugs we can imbibe if we are prone to depressive and anxious states.

3. Impedes detoxification. The liver is the body's hardest-working organ, performing more than five hundred tasks to keep you healthy. It's in charge of detoxifying harmful compounds in everything you eat, drink, breathe, apply to your skin, and take as a medication. Since alcohol is one of *the* most toxic substances we ingest, our liver and kidneys prioritize it in the detox process. This means any other toxins waiting to leave our system are deprioritized—the alcohol cuts in line, and we are left with excess toxins.

What the body can't excrete through its own natural detoxification process, it recirculates through the system and eventually stores it in our body fat, or adipose tissue. This buildup of toxins also affects the central nervous system and mental function, exacerbates anxiety and depression, accelerates aging, and contributes to degenerative disease. All in all, this means a few things. First, losing weight becomes harder. If you've ever dieted and plateaued, this is one cause. Second, almost everything you do in the name of detoxification is entirely canceled out by the ingestion of alcohol. Body scrubbing, juice cleanses, or anything else you do to expel toxins—that's all going to serve the removal of alcohol, or the toxins left in the system after alcohol commandeered the detox process. Alcohol both flushes these nutrients and increases the need for them, eventually leading to a compromised detox function.

To put it bluntly, alcohol ruins healthy liver function, which translates to looking and feeling like shit. Fatigue, worsening PMS and hormonal issues, acne, bloating, headaches, yellowish skin and eyes, bad breath, BO, constipation or loose stools, and irritability are just some of the ways a disruption in detox shows up.

4. Causes weight gain or interferes with weight loss. Absorption of excess toxins into fat cells isn't the only way alcohol causes weight gain. Alcohol is high in sugar and calories (with zero nutritional value) and a natural appetite stimulant, and it anesthetizes the body processes that tell you when you're full. Because alcohol adversely affects blood sugar and insulin balance, it contributes to sugar and carb cravings. It's also the only beverage on the market that doesn't have a nutritional label or ingredient list. To be clear, there is nothing wrong with gaining weight or being fat, and I don't want to play into the bullshit hype that our size is reflective of our worth or that losing weight is some pinnacle of success. It's not, and diet culture, fatphobia, and the glamorization of thinness are just as choking as alcohol culture. I've included the points on weight gain for those of you who—for whatever reason—are putting efforts into losing weight.

5. Causes facial redness and broken capillaries. If you've ever experienced a flush while drinking or if you've noticed more broken blood vessels on your face, they are directly related to the process of alcohol metabolizing (or the body's reaction to a toxic, foreign substance). Because the body can't store alcohol, it first converts it into acetaldehyde, a severely toxic substance that the body then tries to rid itself of. Acetaldehyde is broken down by an enzyme known as alcohol dehydrogenase; if you drink alcohol faster than you metabolize it (and its byproducts), or if you lack the enzyme (certain populations, like East Asians, are deficient), your body is left with excess acetaldehyde, which can be released only through oxidation (or through the skin). Blood vessels dilate (expand) to release acetaldehyde, thus leaving us with (over time) permanently broken capillaries. These are often clustered near the nose. This is not limited to some people—anyone who drinks alcohol has to excrete it, and all of us do it via respiration. (This also explains that pickled smell you might have the day after a big night that you can't seem to scrub off or sweat out.)

6. Fucks up your brain. Grisel in *Never Enough* calls alcohol a "neurological sledgehammer," because it affects not just one region of the brain but *all of* *them.* Alcohol compromises the entire brain. Memory, motor function, inhibition, personality, emotional volatility—virtually nothing is untouched by alcohol, which assaults our brain on almost every known level. Again, this problem is not isolated to heavy drinking. One drink, moderate drinking, and heavy drinking all negatively impact our most precious organ.

7. Messes with blood sugar balance. Alcohol converts rapidly to sugar in the bloodstream, so it can quickly and temporarily treat shakiness, "hanger," or anxiety (which is one reason cravings for alcohol or sugar can be so intense once you've quit). This larger-than-normal dump of glucose from drinking alcohol leads to a release of insulin (from the pancreas) to restore blood sugar levels. Over time this action leads to an overproduction of insulin and results in low blood sugar levels (hypoglycemia). The pattern weakens the function of the adrenal glands, causing us to reach for more sugar, more alcohol, or other stimulants like coffee, and eventually leads to adrenal and mitochondrial fatigue and other metabolic conditions. There's also evidence that consuming more sugar is correlated to higher rates of cancer and depression, and since alcohol *is* sugar (and pretty much only sugar), there are myriad ways it contributes to depression: first through the increased sugar intake, second by nature of the drug (it's a depressant), and third through the hijacking of dopaminergic pathways (as we'll see in Chapter 5).

8. Disrupts endocrine (hormone) function. Our endocrine system is responsible for regulating our bodily functions, such as our metabolism, sex drive, sleep cycles, energy levels, menstrual cycle, and stress response, to name only a few. Alcohol disrupts the functioning of the endocrine system on a number of levels: (1) it disrupts the sleep cycle (which directly impacts the endocrine system); (2) it raises estrogen levels and depletes testosterone levels; and (3) it artificially stimulates the fight-or-flight response (release of cortisol and adrenaline, for instance), yet another cause of anxiety, depression, and insomnia. In other words, alcohol assaults the system in charge of making sure your body runs properly. The result is fatigue, low sex drive, worsening periods, mood imbalance, poor metabolic function, adrenal fatigue, and disrupted sleep cycles, to name just a few.

9. Is linked to seven different cancers. Alcohol is carcinogenic (it causes cancer). The evidence of the link between drinking and cancer is almost irrefutable. For breast cancer alone, more than one hundred studies have reaffirmed the link between drinking and breast cancer. Women who drink three alcoholic beverages a week have a 15 percent higher risk of breast cancer; that risk is increased by 10 percent for each additional drink women have daily (which makes you *really* rethink those bottles of wine with pink ribbons on them). Breast cancer is only one of the cancers linked to alcohol consumption; the others include mouth and throat, esophagus, voicebox, liver, colon, and rectum—basically, any place in the digestive system that alcohol comes into contact with. The cancer risk isn't reserved for heavy drinkers—light to moderate use puts us at greater risk for cancer, period.

10. Causes premature aging. I've already mentioned flushing (facial redness and broken capillaries) and puffiness—side effects that make us look older. But alcohol also leads to loss of collagen and elasticity. And it depletes us of the minerals, nutrients, and antioxidants that counter free radical damage (read: oxidation that ages us) and that help carry oxygen throughout the body. Alcohol also depletes us of zinc and vitamin A, two antioxidants vital for the skin and regeneration of new cells. All told, between these things and every other item previously mentioned, there's no way in hell alcohol is keeping you looking or feeling younger. If anything, the consumption of alcohol undermines every single thing you're doing to preserve your youth.

11. Destroys microbiome. Your gut is home to trillions of bacteria that help you digest and absorb nutrients from your food, regulate your immune system, and even determine how happy you are. You need a rich and diverse array of bacteria to populate a healthy gut. Alcohol causes dysbiosis, a skewed ratio of good and bad bacteria, because it kills good gut bacteria, allowing the bad kind to flourish. This adversely affects probiotic diversity and contributes to yeast overgrowth (candida) and inflammation, which may eventually cause leaky gut, brain fog, unpleasant digestive symptoms, and nutrient deficiencies. It may even increase your risk for autoimmune conditions. To add insult to injury, the gut produces 90 percent of serotonin, a neurotransmitter that promotes a positive, happy mood, and we need certain strains of good bacteria to help us produce serotonin. If these beneficial bacteria are not present due to poor bacterial diversity, your serotonin production suffers (and so does your mood). Finally, most of your immune system resides in your digestive tract. Alcohol lowers immune function in part due to intestinal inflammation and dysbiosis, which affects your ability to fight illness and even diseases like cancer.

This is the short list. There isn't a single body system that isn't affected by alcohol: it's a toxin, and our bodies regard it as such. No matter how much or how little we drink, our bodies suffer the consequences of exposure to alcohol (ethanol) and have to work overtime to counteract its effects.

The interesting thing is that while I was researching this subject, almost every article I found that described some horrific consequence of alcohol consumption included a disclaimer, some "but don't worry you can still drink!" type statement meant to reassure the reader that alcohol isn't *that* bad. The thing is, it *is* that bad, and what's worse is that even in the places where the evidence stacks up right in front of us, there's some guy in the corner trying to reassure us it's still safe to drink.

Alcohol and Feminism

At the 2017 Women's March in Los Angeles, I struggled with what to write on my protest sign. I ended up going with "I literally don't know where to start" (thank you, Emily McDowell) because no other set of words was closer to the truth—absolutely everything was fucked. More than 800,000 people showed up to the L.A. march (as did millions more across the globe), and we were protesting (for or against) all the things: the NRA, reproductive rights, diversity and inclusion, health care, the Prison Industrial Complex, women's rights. We were nasty and loud and pink and angry; our uteruses were not political objects, our pussies were not for grabbing, and our place was in the resistance. I lived in downtown L.A., the site of the march, and after it was over, I noticed something else we were all about: drinking to cap it off. The bars were full of women.

The election of Donald Trump in 2016 ruptured something

so deep and wide and vast within women that it was palpable, suffocating, raw, electric. It also ushered in an unprecedented level of cultural anxiety among Americans, especially those who aren't rich-white-straight-cis males. For the last few years, we've been in an almost constant state of outrage—developing what has been dubbed Trump Fatigue Syndrome—just trying to keep up with the news or batshit crazy tweets. We've witnessed babies being separated from their parents, families dumped into detention centers, trans folk repeatedly dehumanized on a federal scale, whole communities hunted by ICE, and a resurgence of white nationalism, to name only a few. The American Psychiatric Association in a May 2018 survey found that 39 percent of people said their anxiety level had risen over the previous year—and 56 percent were either "extremely anxious" or "somewhat anxious" about "the impact of politics on daily life." And a 2017 study found that two-thirds of Americans see the nation's future as a "very or somewhat significant source of stress." This kind of anxiety, fear, depression, despair, and unease—this sense of isolation and growing paranoia—is of course what causes women to reach for the bottle. It makes sense that we would want to drink in the face of it all, that we need a drug to cope, to turn it off, to turn down the volume for just one freaking minute.

At the same time our democracy is crumbling, our collective sense of power is erupting. Civil rights movements that have been going on for centuries, decades, years, started by radical activists on the margins of society—from Sojourner Truth to Rosa Parks to Sylvia Rivera at Stonewall to Patrisse Cullors and Alicia Garza, who started the Black Lives Matter movement—finally crashed into the mainstream. Women of privilege are finally waking up en masse to their collective oppression, and their anger has gone viral. The last few years have seen many things, from the #MeToo movement (a second wave of a movement started by Tarana Burke) to our vocalized outrage during the Brett Kavanaugh hearings to the election of our first Muslim woman to Congress, and an unprecedented number of women, people of color, and LGBTQIA folks elected to positions of power throughout the country.

We are bestirred to the many ways we are silenced, stymied, catcalled, harassed, abused, murdered, raped, assaulted, coerced, passed up, passed over. We are finally, *finally*, able to behold what a few millennia of patriarchy has done to us. We see and have words for the myriad ways racism, classism, sexism, homophobia, ableism, fatphobia, and the endless systems of injustice, discrimination, and domination take root, and we are furiously working to dismantle *all of it*. We hold every single system accountable for the ways they steal from us and keep us out of our power—except for the alcohol industry. We stop short of implicating booze as part of the system meant to keep us down.

What I want to know is why. Why are we so mad at everything and not mad at what alcohol is doing to us, or how Big Alcohol lines its pockets from our exploitation and death? Why are we not raging against all the oppressive and absolutely *murderous* ways alcohol shows up in women's lives, our kids' lives, our sisters' lives, in the LGBTQIA community, in communities of people of color or Indigenous peoples? Why do we fight so hard to transcend our collective oppression, then willingly give parts of that power back after marching for our rights, with a glass or two or the whole damn bottle?

Here is what we know about alcohol. First, it's the number-one date rape drug. Forget the roofie—booze trumps every single pill that might be slipped into a drink. Approximately half of all sexual assaults involve alcohol consumption, whether by the perpetrator, the victim, or both, and it's estimated that up to 90 percent of all college campus rape involves alcohol. It is linked to two-thirds of all reported cases of intimate partner violence and 40 percent of all violent crimes overall. Women who drink before age eighteen are eight times as likely to experience physical assault, and those who do experience sexual assault or harassment are up to 50 percent more likely to binge-drink. Alcohol is responsible for over three million deaths worldwide. No matter who takes it or how much of it they take, it leaves us worse off than before. And none of these statistics account for what happens to our self-esteem or our self-respect when we give our power over to it entirely. Spending a night out drinking is akin to dismantling every piece of protection we have—our cognition, our decision making, our reaction time, our memory, our standards, our voice. If we thought about alcohol in this way—as something that undermines our collective momentum and personal agency and vitality and self-worth—what would that mean for us? What if we all rejected the poison—then what? I'll tell you what: world domination, bitches.

Women and other historically marginalized and oppressed individuals are now absolutely ascendant in our power. My question is why, in the midst of this ascension and after all we have fought for, are we collectively and *willingly* taking ourselves down with alcohol? How are we not clued into alcohol being a women's issue, a *feminist* issue? How come *Bitch* magazine is inviting me to cocktail hours to discuss the resistance, and why is the TV show *The Handmaid's Tale*—a show about the enslavement of women—trying to market its own wine? The answer is: because we were taught to tangle drinking with liberation, and because we were taught not to question. Because very smart people with assloads of money and power and access benefit from our complicity, from our believing that drinking is an act of empowerment for women, instead of what it truly is: a drug designed to keep us down, no matter how much we drink.

3

Is Alcohol Having a "Cigarette Moment"?

It's easier to fool people than to convince them that they have been fooled.

—MARK TWAIN

It was summer and I was in Rome. The naked Francesco walked from the bedroom out to the main room of his flat. I roused myself and followed, then lingered in the doorway, watching him finger the decanters of various brown liquids. He refused to drink in front of me and resented me for this. "Let's have some glasses of fine water," he said in his perfect, Italian-flavored English as he pulled out a Chesterfield and lit it.

I hadn't smoked for nearly two years, hadn't even *thought* about smoking, but I walked behind him, picked up the pack, and gestured toward him. *"Posso?"* He shrugged and flicked the lighter.

I thought about what I was doing for a split second as I drew the cigarette to my lips. *You don't want a cigarette. You want a moment.* And it was true. *That* was exactly what I wanted: a picture-perfect Hollywood moment. The classical music, the window seat with its cold marble perch, the two of us, naked and without words, just our cigarettes and our gazes and our glasses of fine water, on a late Roman night.

It didn't taste good, and I struggled to finish it. But two days later, when I spent money I didn't have on an original Piranesi print and Francesco hadn't returned my texts, I found myself in a café buying a ten-pack of Chesterfields. This time it wasn't to complete some ideal picture I had in my head—the cigarette was not the perfect accessory to a tragically perfect moment, but instead something I did to blunt a bottomless spiral of anxiety. This is the way cigarettes always worked for me; first a prop, second a drug.

The first time I smoked was at a house party. It was 1995, I was fifteen, painfully awkward, and there was Nikki Smith—flannel tied around her waist, holding a red Solo cup and a cigarette in one perfect French-tipped hand. Nikki was a girl you didn't mess with, and I was a girl you *only* messed with, and the easiest way to be like her was to dress myself in her armor. That night I, too, held a red Solo cup of beer and a cigarette in one hand, and I never really got over the look.

Over the next seventeen years, I would try to quit cigarettes hundreds of times, and each time one thing alone would bring me back to them: the cigarette as a symbol. In my early teens, it was a symbol of how much I didn't give a shit, of my rebellion, my masculine femininity, my ability to stand strong as my world crumbled around me and to stand out from the other girls as one of the guys. Over time I learned a cigarette could demonstrate my sadness, anger, despair, or depression, as well as my sensuality, sexuality, and femininity. I lit up cigarettes after sex and I lit them up after men ripped my heart to shreds; nothing quite demonstrated the level of pain I was feeling as much as lighting a cigarette and sucking it down, except, perhaps, if I was chasing it with wine straight from the bottle. I smoked cigarettes as an extension of me; whether nursing a breakup or mourning a death, the look was incomplete if it wasn't punctuated by a drag.

The cigarette as a symbol wasn't something I accidentally stumbled on; I didn't just *make up* this idea that cigarettes gave me grit or made me tough or said fuck you to my parents or made the drama of a breakup that much more real. The cigarette is an inanimate object devoid of any meaning whatsoever that just happens to be one of the most fantastically marketed commodities in the history of America, or the history of American capitalism more specifically. Lying on the floor of my studio apartment in my underwear, hair tousled and eyes wet, staring at the ceiling, taking long, thoughtful drags off my cigarette to convey a level of pain in the mid-aughts was straight out of the 1930s American Tobacco playbook. In a letter to Hollywood producers and directors, the head of PR for the company behind Lucky Strike (and the father of modern public relations), Edward Bernays, urged them to incorporate cigarettes into films:

> A great deal can be said with a cigarette which would ordinarily require a great many words to express.... The bashful hero lights a cigarette, the better to gain hold of himself in this trying interview with his father-in-law. The villain makes hasty puffs to hide his nervousness or to ease his consciousness.

Bernays *literally* taught Hollywood how to use a cigarette as a prop, because he inherently understood that new smokers couldn't be recruited directly from a print ad. New smokers needed to believe they were choosing a behavior to define themselves; they needed to believe that they, too, could only truly convey their emotions, their individualism, their rebellion, through a cigarette.

And it worked. Through schemes like this in the 1930s, among other public relations stunts (as well as monumental expenditures in marketing), the tobacco companies took a relatively unpopular and somewhat unknown product and turned it into a staple of twentieth-century America. By 1954, 45 percent of adult Americans smoked cigarettes. It worked so well that more than eighty years after Bernays's memo was dispatched—and over half a century since we learned about the damage those cigarettes did to us—people like me still bought into the symbolism, unconsciously, religiously.

Such is the power, and pervasiveness, of Big Tobacco.

THE ENTRENCHED USE OF ALCOHOL

In order to really understand the mechanics of how alcohol came to be so entwined in American society (and recently, so deeply woven into the fabric of women's existence, from motherhood to book clubs to feminist rebellion), I set about tracing the history of the cigarette. My own recovery from alcohol addiction hinged on the realization that we, as a society, had been duped into believing that alcohol was both socially necessary and biologically normal, even healthful. Before I got sober, what I believed to be true of alcohol was exactly what most Americans believed to be true of cigarette smoking in the early twentieth century: that it was a digestive, an appetite suppressant, or an antidote to anxiousness and not at all bad for you if you partook "in moderation."

I believe that alcohol will experience its own "cigarette moment"—a reversal in public opinion and a rejection of it by mainstream culture, seen as something we *used* to do—once we remove our willful ignorance of its harmful effects on us personally and collectively. I imagine our grandchildren will one day be shocked by the idea that there was once a point in time when we drank ethanol at almost every occasion and boasted of hangovers and drunken antics, the same way I'm always shocked to see pictures of my aunts and uncles smoking indoors at family parties in the seventies.

The cigarette is not even two hundred years old, and its ubiquity is a direct result of capitalism—supply originally outstripped demand, so a consumer and a market that did not exist were created in order to directly fulfill a business objective. Alcohol, on the other hand, dates back *eight thousand years* and is ubiquitous today because it's *always* been ubiquitous, the same way bread is; colonizers carried it over on the *Mayflower*. Which is what makes the rise of Big Alcohol in the wake of Prohibition (namely, through the consolidation of the market into a few large firms or an oligopoly), and its appropriation of the tactics of Big Tobacco, almost imperceptible to us and infinitely more dangerous.

We think drinking alcohol is normal and healthful because for the most part, we always have. The builders of the pyramids were partially paid in beer, wine shows up in the Bible as the blood of Christ, and in ancient Greece they had Dionysus, the god of wine. Because of the entrenched historical and ceremonial use of alcohol since the dawn of civilization—and because governments from across the globe uphold it as a legal substance (versus every other drug with entrenched historical and ceremonial use, such as opium and peyote, which are considered illicit due to the agenda of the War on Drugs)—we are locked in a bubble of willful ignorance. Collectively, we miss how we're being manipulated into using alcohol differently than our ancestors (for instance, as a coping mechanism for parenthood), and we overlook things, like how our ancestors weren't dying from alcohol-related liver failure in their twenties at the rates we are.

Often enough, when I posit that we shouldn't be drinking alcohol at all, someone will counter that Jesus drank or assert that alcohol's been a staple of our diet since we were bands of tribes surviving on hunting and gathering. The argument goes that this is normal behavior, and we're preternaturally inclined to drink. To which I say: We've always been preternaturally inclined to do fucked-up shit. We don't sacrifice humans as offerings, burn "witches," perform prefrontal lobotomies with ice picks, pit enslaved humans against beasts to be mauled in front of a live audience for entertainment, or smoke on planes anymore. We are constantly reevaluating the way it's "always been done." But when it comes to alcohol, very few of us are ready to concede that maybe it's bad for us, or maybe we shouldn't be doing it. We are unwilling to see any other sort of truth around it *because we don't want to.* My own mother, who's lost countless family members to alcohol (and almost her own daughter), is still of the mind that alcohol is healthful and joyful in moderation, no matter how many articles I send her explaining it's really not.

The point is, while Big Tobacco had to convince the public to smoke cigarettes in order to grow its business, Big Alcohol didn't have to convince anyone to drink—we were already drinking. Consequently, the alcohol industry is even more dangerous, more pervasive, and more deadly than Big Tobacco because of alcohol's entrenched historical use. If that sounds like hyperbole to you, consider that at the height of cigarette consumption, the percentage of American adults who smoked was around 50 percent. Today nearly 70 percent of American adults drink. It is a $1.5 trillion industry, made up almost entirely of sixteen companies (all run by men). It kills over three million people a year globally, treats women, children, and citizens of nations with developing economies as "emerging markets," and escapes mass critical judgment (and criminal prosecution) because we are all too happy to point out that alcohol is a ritualistic superfood that predates Jesus; because *we* defend its pervasiveness and innocuity.

STEALING BIG TOBACCO'S PLAYBOOK

Three key factors led to the blockbuster success of Big Tobacco throughout the twentieth century and kept us smoking despite mountains of evidence that it was murdering us: (1) consolidation of the market, (2) engineered consent, and (3) engineered controversy. In other words, (1) a large corporate engine was created in order to make an obscene profit from a product that ritualistically killed off its most loyal customers, causing the need to constantly indoctrinate new smokers and to operate above the law and beyond reproach; (2) in order to expand its business and make up for the death of its users, it had to manipulate the public through engineering an idea of consent; and (3) in order to keep consumers from discovering the adverse health consequences of smoking, it had to keep the general public in a confused state over whether the product was lethal. These same exact tactics were co-opted by what we'd now call Big Alcohol, to allow it to grow unchecked and without consequence at the cost of millions upon millions of lives. Here's how they did it.

CONSOLIDATION OF THE MARKET
(WHAT MAKES THEM "BIG")

> We've opened seven markets in sub-Saharan Africa in the last six or
> seven years. Historically, we'd only been present in South Africa, since
> 1993. Now we operate in Namibia, Angola, Nigeria, Kenya, Ghana,
> and more recently, in Mozambique. We have a clear vision—Africa is
> Asia 15 to 20 years from today. That's because of demographics,
> urbanization rates, and economic growth.
>
> —ALEX RICARD, CEO, PERNOD RICARD, 2019

> The Chinese domestic tobacco industry is a major frontier for interna-
> tional tobacco companies.
>
> —PHILIP MORRIS INTERNATIONAL, 1994

The history of the cigarette is fascinating and short—it was invented in 1865 during the Civil War. While many of us today
might easily imagine it as always lodged in American culture, by
the early 1900s it accounted for only 2 percent of all tobacco consumption in the United States. (The mainstay of tobacco consumption was via chew, pipe, and cigar.) The cigarette started out
as a stigmatized, cheap product associated with the "lower
classes." Its rise to popularity was meteoric—by 1952 more than
80 percent of all tobacco consumption in the United States was
via cigarettes, and by 1954, almost half of all American adults
smoked them. This total shift in both the pervasiveness and popularity of the cigarette was brought about by a number of things,
most notably developments in business organizations, mass
marketing, rejection of Victorian moralism, and astonishingly
brilliant maneuvers in the manipulation of the public.

When all was said and done, it took about sixty years for the
cigarette to become de rigueur—a symbol of rebellion, sexual-

ity, masculinity, and femininity, and the defining habit of idyllic midcentury America. It took another sixty years for it to become what it is today—a reviled habit, practiced mostly at the fringes of American society, in the few remaining places we're allowed to smoke.

The Tobacco Industry Consolidates

In the late 1800s, few people smoked cigarettes and few tobacco companies bothered to manufacture them. It wasn't until the head of American Tobacco, James Duke, encountered the first effective rolling machine (the Bonsack) in the 1880s that the cigarette—and Big Tobacco as we know it today—was born. The gist of the story is that Duke's business savvy and vision for a smoking future first led him to mass-produce cigarettes at American Tobacco. That mass production led to an oversupply of a relatively unknown commodity, which then led to the necessity of creating new cigarette smokers. In other words, supply had to invent demand. The easiest targets in the early 1900s were boys. World War I played a significant role in market expansion as soldiers were plied with free cigarettes and came home with both a habit and a brand preference.

In 1890, to gain even more market share and power, Duke formed the American Tobacco Company, a trust built of the five largest tobacco companies, and by 1907 it was one of the three largest companies in the United States, right alongside Standard Oil and U.S. Steel. As part of the trust-busting efforts of the early twentieth century, in 1911, the U.S. government broke up the Tobacco Trust, leaving us with four of the five firms that became what we know today as Big Tobacco—American Tobacco, P. Lorillard, R. J. Reynolds, and Liggett & Myers (Philip Morris came into play later), each of which settled on a flagship brand of cigarettes.

A monopoly became an oligopoly, and five firms were left with one identical product, vast amounts of capital to spend, and a nation (and later globe) of uninitiated consumers to hook.

Because these five corporations were each fighting for the same exact market, with the same exact product—a product that killed their customers—their only chance to differentiate was to drive a sense of identification with their brands, and their only choice to grow the business was to recruit new smokers to replace the dying ones.

The new recruits were women, children, and—when the American market plateaued—citizens of nations with undeveloped capitalist economies (or LMICs, Low- to Middle-Income Countries), all three of which came to be known as "emerging markets." The land grab for these uninitiated smokers would come in the form of an unprecedented marketing spend, and the deployment of cutting-edge techniques from the nascent field of public relations.

This was entirely new to American capitalism and became one of the deadliest capital pursuits—and crimes—known to history. Today, because of this market consolidation and sprint to hook consumers, 7.1 million people die a tobacco-related death worldwide annually, 100 million people died in the twentieth century, and it's projected that nearly 1 billion human beings will die a tobacco-related death in the twenty-first century.

The Alcohol Industry Consolidates

Consolidation of the alcohol market tipped after Prohibition, when the chemical processing of water (which allowed for a homogenous product) and advances in packaging (allowing for longer shelf life) made mass production and national brands a possibility. Today nearly every brand of spirit, beer, malt beverage, or alcopop that you are familiar with is owned by one of the sixteen conglomerates that dominate the global alcohol trade. While in 1938 the alcohol industry spent $6 million on advertising and around $50 million in the 1950s, in 2016 the alcohol industry spent $2.3 *billion* on marketing and advertising in the United States alone.

Just like Big Tobacco, consolidating the alcohol industry into a few small firms with an identical product means that competition for our dollars is taken to a whole other level and all kinds of tactics are deployed: they don't just want our money, they want our lifelong dedication to their brand. And just like Big Tobacco, Big Alcohol has to factor in replacements. Since the industry is losing 3.3 million of its most loyal customers every year (due to the unfortunate side effect of death), its sustained growth depends on indoctrinating new drinkers: children, women, and citizens of LMICs.

Though the tobacco industry insisted for years that its marketing was focused on converting existing smokers to their brand, and not on seducing new, underage customers, the introduction of Joe Camel—a cartoon camel that smoked its namesake brand, Camels—was incontrovertibly aimed at kids. A 1991 study found that children between the ages of three and six recognized Joe Camel almost as widely as Mickey Mouse. And though the alcohol industry insists the same—that it is focused on getting existing drinkers to switch brands and not on generating new recruits—there's evidence to the contrary. Anheuser-Busch introduced a series of Spuds MacKenzie ads in 1987, featuring a bull terrier that acts and dresses like a human; one study showed that 88 percent of fifth and sixth graders could match Spuds with Budweiser. Was that just Anheuser-Busch doing a public service to provide children's entertainment, or was it perhaps exactly the same scheme R. J. Reynolds used to snag a generation of loyal Camel smokers?

We've already established the consequences of pursuing the emerging market of female drinkers. As a result of pink booze, Rosé All Day, alcopops, Mommy's Time Out wine, and Ketel One–sponsored Goop events and podcasts, our livers are failing, our rates of addiction are doubling, and women are the new binge drinkers. But the female market in the United States, Great Britain, and Canada can get Big Alcohol only so far, so the focus of Big Alcohol has grown to include LMICs in order to expand its market share.

It's worth noting that fewer than 100,000 of those 3.3 million annual alcohol-related deaths occur in America; the rest are found throughout the world, not just in countries where alcohol has been a ceremonial and cultural staple, but in those that are adapting Western values and Western drinking practices. Some countries with these surging death tolls—such as India—historically shunned the consumption of alcohol. (India's alcohol consumption per capita more than doubled between 2005 and 2016, rising from 2.4 liters to 5.7; in 1961, the per capita alcohol consumption was less than 1 liter.) But because of Big Alcohol's need to exploit for gain, the continents of Africa, Asia, and South America have seen a rise in alcohol distribution, marketing, and public relations, as well as a resultant surge in alcohol addiction and alcohol-related death. The big sixteen profit from these deaths and brag about these untapped growth opportunities; while in countries such as Uganda, where alcohol is consumed like a street drug—sold in little baggies in portions that those at the margins of society can barely afford—children are growing up in a new generation marked by a wave of alcohol addiction never before seen, in places with no system of recovery, rehabilitation, or addiction medicine.

Big Tobacco consolidated in the early 1900s, while the alcohol industry remained mostly decentralized. It wasn't until the latter half of the twentieth century that Big Alcohol consolidated (and is in many ways still consolidating), so it is still in its infancy, which means the damage from it is also in its infancy. If we thought Big Tobacco was a murderer, we haven't seen anything yet.

THE ENGINEERING OF CONSENT (WHAT GOT US HOOKED)

> We are governed, our minds molded, our tastes formed, our ideas
> suggested, largely by men we have never heard of.
>
> —EDWARD BERNAYS

In order for Big Tobacco to initiate new cigarette smokers, it deployed never-before-seen manipulations of public behavior. One of the first large-scale influencer campaigns came from American Tobacco's quest to get new women smokers, and this publicity stunt is why the cigarette became the emblem of feminist rebellion. Big Tobacco played us into believing smoking was symbolic of our liberation, the same way alcohol interests later played us into believing our drinking symbolized this, too.

The type of marketing that sold the cigarette to us as a political statement (and a fashion accessory) is known as "engineered consent"—a spectacular feat of public relations or *propaganda* that tricks us into believing our behaviors, tastes, and preferences are chosen not by the machinations of men in boardrooms, but of our own volition. Engineered consent operates on the premise that as consumers, we simultaneously want to maintain our individual preferences and gain acceptance for our choices when adopting a new set of behaviors—which explains a lot of things, like how some of us ended up wearing wedge sneakers, dressing in millennial pink, or drinking asstons of rosé. We think we're making a decision based on our own preferences, when we're actually being manipulated into that decision because of someone else's.

"Torches of Freedom" Become Glasses of Liberation

In the late 1920s, the tobacco industry realized women weren't smoking as much as men. This was due in part to the hangover of American Victorian morality (where, for instance, women were once arrested for smoking in public), and in part to Big Tobacco's lack of focus on its lady consumer. In 1929 George Washington Hill, the CEO of American Tobacco and peddler of Lucky Strikes, called in Edward Bernays and asked, "How can we get women to smoke on the street? They're smoking indoors . . . if they spend half the time outdoors and we can get them to smoke outdoors, we'll damn near double our female market. Do something." Bernays did something.

After doing some research with psychoanalyst A. A. Brill, Bernays concluded that women who smoked did so to signify their rejection of feminine sensibilities and to assert their (increasing) equality with men. When Brill said, "Cigarettes, which are equated with men, become torches of freedom," a light went off in Bernays's head, and a PR stunt was born that would forever connect the images of women's liberation, feminist rebellion, and smoking.

It went like this: During the 1929 Easter Sunday parade in New York City, between Forty-eighth and Fifty-fourth Streets on Fifth Avenue, women would smoke (Lucky Strikes) en masse during the procession to protest inequality. Ruth Hale, feminist and founder of the Lucy Stone Foundation, was enlisted (on behalf of American Tobacco via Bernays) to place advertisements for the protest in New York papers; invitations were sent to prominent socialites (from American Tobacco via Bernays's female secretary and Ruth Hale). The copy read: "Women! Light another Torch of Freedom! Fight another sex taboo!"

The stunt didn't just go over well—it created a media shit-storm. Images of the new liberated woman smoking a cigarette *in public* on *Fifth Avenue* during the *Easter Parade* sent shock waves through society—inviting women across the nation to smoke a Torch of Freedom in public as a fuck-you to the patriarchy and a nod to their increasing liberation. The Easter Protest, along with innumerable other campaigns directed to ensnare women smokers, changed the course of cigarette use among women forever. Within not so many decades, women would close the gap with men in terms of cigarette consumption and tobacco-related deaths.

Bernays knew that while marketing campaigns are good for brand awareness, direct advertising isn't so great at influencing any large social change. To change behavior, you have to go deeper. Americans aren't stupid. We are, however, preternaturally disposed to herd behavior (FOMO), with a strong desire to preserve a sense of individuality and maintain control over our decision making. We're joiners and don't want to be left out of fads; we're also fiercely independent and don't want to be told what to do. We are a people constantly balancing our need to belong with our need to maintain individuality and control over our decision making. When Bernays—a nephew of Freud—coined the term *engineered consent,* he was speaking to this tension.

If Bernays's early writings show anything, it's his total contempt for the general public's ability to think for themselves. He believed that every behavior that people adopt is based not on free will but on rules, fashions, and beliefs that could be strategically engineered by a small group of men and imposed on a generally pliant public through imperceptible maneuvers. When American Tobacco approached Bernays about ensnaring more female smokers, women were an easy target. All it took was a calculated manipulation of our social fabric through what we'd now call an influencer campaign—and almost overnight, cigarette smoking became not just something women could do in public, but the very symbol of their feminist revolution.

It didn't take long for alcohol to get wrapped up in that symbolism, too.

This . . .

becomes this . . .

becomes this.

The work of Bernays and American Tobacco eventually fanned out across the entire tobacco industry; soon all of Big Tobacco was targeting female smokers with ad campaigns and even cigarettes made especially for them (like Virginia Slims, a dainty, slender cigarette appropriate for a dainty, slender female). The result was fantastically successful. By the 1950s, it was entirely normalized for women to smoke; the rates of men smokers peaked in the 1960s, while the rates of women smokers continued to climb, peaking in the late 1970s. The trend with alcohol isn't much different. Currently, men are drinking less, while women continue to drink more.

We Become the Marketers

It's not hard to draw parallels between the tobacco industry and the alcohol industry when it comes to this type of marketing scheme. Big Alcohol used the same liberated imagery and co-opted the same feminist ideals, and women like me lapped it up. I may have started out with sweet pink drinks like wine coolers and Strawberry Hill, but the goal was always to be one of the guys, or the cool girl. When I came to associate my alcohol consumption directly to my parity with men, I moved to microbrews—strong IPAs and lagers. And when that wasn't enough, I turned to the drink that ultimately reflected how much I drank like a man: a whiskey neat. I marveled at my own ability to pull that hard-edged, bad-bitch, whiskey-drinking look off, and I was definitely the kind of woman who taunted men who could not keep up.

The alcohol industry didn't have to convince women that alcohol was the elixir of women's lib like the tobacco industry had to convince women that the cigarette was a Torch of Freedom; all they had to do was put a drink in her hand right next to her cigarette and exploit the fruits of a labor done for them. They also didn't have to instruct Hollywood that drinking fast, or by yourself, or from the bottle might demonstrate a range of human emotions; by the time the alcohol industry was big enough to rival the tobacco industry in marketing spend, Hollywood already knew.

In this way, Big Alcohol benefited freely from the labor of Big Tobacco, but that wasn't the only way it got a free ride in terms of social influence: With the emergence of social media, meme culture, and influencer campaigns that began to dominate our society post-Facebook, *we* became the marketers of alcohol.

Because the tail end of my drinking career coincided with the emergence of influencer culture, I don't have vivid memories of rosé being shoved in my face as the elixir of life. I have vague memories of a friend calling her wine "mommy juice," or a kitchen towel embroidered with a pithy saying about drinking a fuck-ton of wine. But it wasn't until I stopped drinking that these things came into focus, and their increasing pervasiveness became glaringly apparent. It wasn't just Goop normalizing alcohol with its sponsored cocktails, Hoda and Kathie Lee getting on their morning swill, Courteney Cox on *Cougar Town* with her bottle-sized wineglass, movies like *Bad Moms* (and *Bad Moms 2*!) where a group of overworked and underappreciated moms claim their due reward by getting shitfaced, or even the introduction of a feminist whiskey, Jane Walker. Alcohol was all of a sudden an accessory to every product, service, and event *everywhere:* wineglass holders for my bathtub, wine yoga for my nerves, pro-wine onesies for my baby, wine wipes for my wine-stained teeth, wineglass holder necklaces for my aching arms, wine sports bras for my runs, an article in *Cosmo* that instructed me on how to hide two bottles of rosé on my person, a viral video of a woman's barbell strapped with wine bottles to show me how to work out *and* get wasted, entire Facebook pages and Instagram accounts dedicated to showcasing memes that promote binge drinking and drunkenness. If there's one thing I know for sure, there is a lot of effort going into promoting alcohol consumption, and even more of an effort to normalize abuse. And it's only getting worse.

We started this story at the beginning of the twentieth century, where in order to get more American women to smoke, Big Tobacco infiltrated our movement toward liberation, put a cigarette in our hands, and told us that smoking symbolized our feminism. We end the story here in 2020, when Big Alcohol has not only appropriated the fundamental message sold to us by Big Tobacco—wrapping alcohol up into another symbol of liberated feminist disobedience—but also recruited *us* to do its bidding. In 1929 the ace up American Tobacco's sleeve was Bernays, a man with connections to *The New York Times;* today, the ace up Big Alcohol's sleeve is a woman with an Instagram account.

THE ENGINEERING OF CONTROVERSY
(WHAT KEPT US HOOKED)

There are some individuals who cannot use tobacco, there are some who should not use it, there are some who use it to excess and who suffer in consequence. There is on the other hand a large army of moderate tobacco users, who indulge for years without appreciably bad physical effect and good mental effect.

—AMERICAN PHYSICIAN (1920)

The first studies showing the causal links between smoking and lung cancer emerged as early as the 1940s, but it wasn't until the mid-1960s that the dangers of smoking became generally known and affected the consumption of cigarettes. For almost two decades after those first reports indicating that cigarettes were addictive and carcinogenic were published, cigarette use continued to rise (it wasn't until the mid-1970s that the health effects had any appreciable effects on smoking). It seems almost impossible to believe that we were kept from the truth for so long, but we were, because of another brilliant public relations move by Big Tobacco: the establishment of the Tobacco Industry Research Committee (TIRC), a lobbying group funded by the tobacco industry, disguised as a public interest research institution, headed by a number of scientists.

As the evidence mounted that cigarette smoking was toxic, carcinogenic, and deadly, the TIRC held to one line that kept the public from believing the piles of evidence, the surgeon general's warning, even their own increasing rate of sickness: "There is not enough research." In other words, the TIRC succeeded in concealing the dangers of cigarettes by stoking an idea that we didn't have enough proof and couldn't rely on the research. To every study published, their response was that nothing could be proved beyond reasonable doubt. It was a completely effective tactic—people ate it up as reassurance and continued to smoke because there appeared to be conflicting reports. This "engineered controversy" is what Allan M. Brandt in *The Cigarette Century* describes as the effort to "produce and sustain scientific skepticism and controversy in order to disrupt the emerging consensus on the harms of cigarette smoke." It was a public relations move, a midcentury version of fake news, designed to keep the public locked in debate, and it was how Big Tobacco continued to control the positive narrative of the cigarette long after science more than adequately proved it was deadly.

If you've heard the phrase "Drink responsibly," I imagine it makes sense to you, that it even sounds sane, thoughtful, perhaps something your parents might tell you. A quick internet search for the term will take you to the site Responsibility.org, where the banner message reads "EMPOWERING adults to make a lifetime of responsible alcohol choices as part of a balanced lifestyle." If you look a little closer, you'll notice that the site is run by the Foundation for Advancing Alcohol Responsibility, and if you dig a little deeper on the site, you'll find that this organization is sponsored by the kindhearted, well-meaning folks at Bacardi USA, Beam Suntory, Brown-Forman, Constellation Brands, Diageo, Edrington, Jägermeister, Moët Hennessy USA, and Pernod Ricard USA.

Whereas the tobacco industry's refrain "Not enough research" kept the public confused and willfully ignorant of the dangers of cigarette smoking, Big Alcohol's slogan "Drink responsibly" posits that the drug isn't the issue—the issue is that some unfortunate, irresponsible people can't use it right. "Drink responsibly" and "Not enough research" are the exact same sleight-of-hand tactic; the only difference is the alcohol industry has a boon that the tobacco industry didn't—an entire organization dedicated to the treatment of irresponsible drinking. The alcohol industry doesn't really need that "drink responsibly" PSA, because Alcoholics Anonymous echoes the lie Big Alcohol wants you to believe: the problem is not the drug, the problem is the people who can't use the drug.

Blaming the People, Not the Substance

Clarence Cook Little, a Harvard-educated geneticist, became the first head of the TIRC. He was also a staunch eugenicist who believed that cigarettes were a mechanism to thin the herds. Eugenics is the "science" of breeding for desirable characteristics in order to "improve" the human race. While it is best known as the philosophy that underwrote the Holocaust, it was also a massive influence in early 1900s America. Eugenicists like Little believed that only those with bad genes and a predisposition for addiction—aka "weaker" people—were vulnerable to the effects of cigarettes, and that natural selection would weed out those unfit to survive smoking. Eugenics was a philosophy that helped remove some of the early indictments against tobacco: it said the product wasn't to blame, the people were.

Just as Big Tobacco evaded early mass criticism and thus stymied public health efforts to control cigarette smoking and its related diseases (*It's the people, not the substance*), Big Alcohol does the exact same thing today with alcohol: *It's not the substance. It's the people who can't handle it.*

I argue that the term *alcoholic* and the disease *alcoholism* are inherently eugenicist. If you think that claim is outrageous, it might help you to know that in 1935 in Nazi Germany, 41 percent of the "biologically defective persons" sterilized by the SS (sterilization was the precursor to genocide) were alcoholics, and that alcoholics were affixed with a black triangle in concentration camps (not unlike the pink triangles that labeled someone a homosexual).

Prohibition was one of the few exceptions, during the period of eugenics, where the people weren't blamed as much as the alcohol was. The temperance movement didn't assert that there were some normal people who should drink and some sick fucks who couldn't; it asserted that all drinking was demonic, and therefore all drinking had to go. When Prohibition was repealed a decade after it became law, plenty of groups, or "drys," still believed alcohol was the root of all evil. One such group on a mission to bring back Prohibition was the Research Council on Problems of Alcohol, or RCPA, which hoped to prove the inherent toxicity of alcohol. In *US of AA*, Joe Miller describes how at its inception, the RCPA couldn't find funding and ended up taking money from the alcohol industry to further its anti-alcohol research. In order to avoid conflicts of interest, the RCPA turned its efforts from researching the dangers of the drug alcohol to something the alcohol industry was keen to investigate: the "disease" of alcoholism.

In 1940 a story in *The New York Times* chronicled the work of the RCPA under the headline "Alcoholism Seen as a Major Ailment: Medical Science Must Study Fundamental Causes." It was a turning point in the framing of alcohol addiction as a disease. Due in part to the efforts of the industry-backed RCPA, and the efforts of Alcoholics Anonymous (at that point an organization in its nascency, the history of which we'll get into later) over the next few decades to get the American Medical Association to recognize alcoholism as a disease, the attention was no longer focused on the drug but on the people who used it "incorrectly," who had some yet-to-be-discovered genetic mutation that made them react poorly to a substance that normal, healthy people consumed without bad effect. No one was talking about alcohol as a drug—they were talking about alcoholism as a disease.

Here the alcohol industry and the recovery industry converged, settling on the inherently eugenic belief that asserts humans are to blame for their alcoholism, not the toxic substances marketed to them in ways that subvert their rational thinking. If I had a dollar for every person in recovery who told me I needed to take responsibility for my actions and stop vilifying poor alcohol—or worse, ruining it for the people who "can" drink—I'd be a rich woman. We love to protect alcohol and our right to consume it, and to vilify people who can't handle it. We venerate the substance; we demonize those who get sick from using it.

BELIEVING THE LIE

The engineered controversy born of Big Tobacco's need to keep the public trapped in cognitive dissonance—first over whether the cigarette was to blame, or a few unfortunate people with bad genes, and eventually over whether the mounting scientific evidence could be believed, or if we needed more proof—is the same mechanism that's being applied to alcohol today. Because of this co-opting of Big Tobacco's strategy, we hold on to ideas that alcohol is bad for a fraction of the population instead of all of us, or that it's a matter of drinking responsibly versus drinking irresponsibly. We are focused on the narrative we've been sold that tells us alcohol brings joy, connection, and happiness, more than we are on the actual narrative, which tells us alcohol brings death, sickness, and rape. Ask anyone who drinks whether the first thing that comes to mind when they hear Chardonnay is sexual assault or drinking around a patio table. We are more likely to believe that alcohol keeps us heart-healthy than that it increases our risk of breast cancer; we are more willing to believe it will get us dates and sex and love and a life than we are willing to believe it destroys all those things.

Meanwhile we overlook the statistics proving the overwhelming role that alcohol plays in sexual assault and violent crimes. Instead we say, *This is my choice!* and *This is how I take the edge off!* or *This is how I get my edge!* And so we lead with choice feminism, which says anything a feminist does is inherently feminist because she does it, and we pay for those hard-earned glasses of wine with our health, our lives, our dignity, our power, and our liberation.

This is how capitalist patriarchy works. It depends on us drinking the Kool-Aid, or in this case the rosé, and not questioning it. It depends on willful ignorance born of confirmation bias. We see images of our icons and idols drinking, from Gloria Steinem to Oprah Winfrey to Gwyneth Paltrow, so we don't question, we just follow their lead.

In an article by Leandra Medine, "Tell It to Me Straight: Is Wine Ruining Me or Saving Me?" that appeared on her site Man Repeller in June 2018, Medine got to the crux of where most of us are these days with booze. If moms are drinking in order to make it through homework with their kids, if Oprah can spend her precious few Weight Watchers points on a glass of white wine, if there is such a thing as YogiWino (and there is), what are we to make of a 2018 study published in *The Lancet* that suggests that literally no amount of alcohol is healthy and that we should avoid it altogether?

With the benefit of 20/20 hindsight, we're able to watch Betty

Draper on *Mad Men* and know she shouldn't be smoking with her kids in the car, or in her home, or in her bed. When she's diagnosed with lung cancer in the final season, we're not surprised at all, because we now know, without a doubt, that smoking causes lung cancer and death (among many other terrible, horrible things). Consequently, the final season is set in 1976, the year American women's cigarette consumption peaked, then began its decline—nearly a century after its introduction, and hundreds of thousands of cigarette-related deaths later.

Given what we now know about cigarettes, we might think Betty was just a dumbass who ignored reality. But Betty wasn't dumb; she was *typical*. We are *typically* a believing, trusting public when it comes to massively trendy conspicuous consumerism. Sure, Betty had access to twenty-five years of published studies that confirmed the lethality of cigarettes, but mostly what she had was a cigarette-soaked lifestyle and enough shrugging doubt of tobacco's harm to push through any perceived dangers. She was manipulated, like everyone else who smoked was manipulated. Although it's 2020, in terms of what and *how* we know about alcohol, it's really 1976, and we are Betty. We think this manipulation is so obvious, so easy to spot, because *hindsight makes it obvious*. When we're pressed up against the glass and caught up in the illusion, it's almost impossible to see any of it clearly.

4

There Is No Such Thing as an Alcoholic

Our deep collective denial is strange.

—JUDITH GRISEL

On a summer vacation at some resort in Mexico, about nine months before I stopped drinking, I swam up to the pool bar. It was eleven a.m., and I ordered two shots of tequila and two Coronas. My buddy G, whose birthday we were there to celebrate, waved away the shot. "I can't." He had a stomachache, which he'd already told me about at least ten times. I was annoyed, and not because I felt like he was being a pussy, which I did, but because somewhere in the back of my mind I was wondering why it was that *I* could never pass up a shot when *my* stomach hurt.

I took both shots, and we nursed our beers, he more slowly than I, and because I had never met anyone in his life in the four years that we'd been buddies and roommates and work-married, he took his time pointing out each of his friends and connecting them to the stories he'd told over the years. I don't remember most of this trip because somewhere in the last three years I'd lost time and my ability to be in it, but I do remember the part of this conversation where G mentioned the one friend who wasn't there, the one with the problem, the one who could no longer drink: Tragic Alcoholic Friend.

This part comes faster than I can digest but it's also in slow motion, like a train wreck in a pudding cup, and I start to ask questions because I've had a growing suspicion it's also *my* train wreck. G explains that Bob* (*I have no idea what his name was, but Bob feels right) was always the one who took it too far, did things like ruin weddings, including his own. Bob's wife almost left him at some point so he had to give up the booze, and apparently that was very hard for him because G tells me he had to take pills to do it. Other things I learn about him include: he pounds nonalcoholic beers to get the smallest high, he can no longer go for long weekends to resorts in Mexico that have pool bars, or do anything, really, that every single one of his friends still gets to do.

Then it's over and G is on to the next story, the next friend in the lineup, some other white bro from the Midwest with a corn-fed name like Dan who's done well in private equity and drives an M3. But I am gone, sinking, paralyzed by the recognition of myself in Bob's story. At the same time, I am also entirely absorbed in counting the ways I am absolutely nothing like Bob. For instance: I have never peed myself while drunk, and I think *Bob for sure wet many beds in his day.*

This is the moment that alcoholism is no longer an abstract condition that other people suffer, because this is the moment someone who runs in the circles I run in has caught it. It's closer than it's ever been, swimming right next to me in an infinity pool in Mexico, and because of that, I can't help thinking that one day soon I'll be the story of a woman who can't make it to the party, too. A ghost.

On my last day in Mexico, G's stomach is feeling better and

he's running around our hotel room in my big, black, floppy hat. He's shitfaced, and I know he wants to kiss me because he always wants to kiss me when he's drunk, and I am genuinely turned off; not by him—by his sloppiness, his intoxication. I *loathe* the drunk version of G, drunk versions of anyone, really. I can't get away from him fast enough, and with this in mind, I pass up the airport bar, pass up the drink on the plane, and I don't drink that night when I get home. I don't drink the next night either, and none of this requires any restraint. I just don't *want* to drink sometimes, and this—exactly this—is what keeps me trapped. *Bob would never pass up airport drinking.*

This is important: My drinking problem—or lack thereof—was qualified by comparison to other people's drinking. It never occurred to me that people who don't have problems with drinking don't run around comparing their drinking to people who do have them. What did occur to me back then was that I would rather die than be an alcoholic.

Four months after that Mexico trip—four months of asking myself that same mindfuck of a question (*Am I an alcoholic?*) and the period of time where drinking in the morning starts to make sense—I find a clue. I'm babysitting the young kids of a doctor friend of mine, and before he leaves for the evening, we get to talking about a colleague who he thinks is exhibiting signs of Borderline Personality Disorder (BPD). As soon as these three words leave his mouth I recognize myself in them, just like I recognize myself in the word *alcoholic*. I put the kids to bed, pour myself a whiskey neat, and google BPD. By the time my friend and his wife come home, I have (mis)diagnosed myself as Borderline and bought two books. One was *The Borderline Personality Disorder Survival Guide: Everything You Need to Know About Living with BPD.*

You would think this would be one of the darkest moments

of my life, all of a sudden realizing that I'm thirty-three and bordering on psychosis. But the weird thing is, it isn't that dark, or even dark at all. It's actually a *relief,* and for the first time in forever I am hopeful. There's a reason I'm so fucked up, and it isn't alcoholism. It's just severe mental illness.

The second book I bought was Allen Carr's *The Easy Way to Control Alcohol,* and I bought it because what was clear from my three hours of ~~whiskey-fueled googling~~ extensive research was this: Having BPD means I am not supposed to drink alcohol, whatsoever. Here's where it gets even weirder: I am not upset about this, or even sad. I am double relieved. Turns out, I was desperate for anything and anyone to tell me I had to stop.

Much later, well into my sobriety, three different therapists would tell me that in no way, shape, or form did I have Borderline Personality Disorder. Each of them would confirm that what I had was alcohol addiction, which can mimic other mental illnesses, especially BPD. I wonder, if I had not found that third door but had been told from the start that I was just an alcoholic, how much longer would I have denied it? Why the hell was being diagnosed with a mental illness so much more hopeful than being diagnosed an alcoholic?

I don't open the BPD survival guide, but I start reading *The Easy Way* immediately, because by the second paragraph, the author, Allen Carr, tells me that he's about to give me an enjoyable, painless, EASY way to control my drinking. All he asks of me is that I keep drinking and read his book. This sounds like the most fantastic way to quit drinking; I immediately fall in love with him and do as he says. I pour a drink, I read. His promises and his process feel safe.

Carr argues that alcohol is a trap—an ingenious addictive trap—and that we are lemmings who have bought into a marketing scheme that tells us that the only way to be happy/relax/

eat fancy dinners/celebrate/date/do anything worth doing as adults is to drink alcohol (ethanol). His book reveals a truth I never even thought to entertain, which is that it isn't about not *getting* to drink, but about not *having* to drink. There are many other salient points in his book, but the most important one of all: there is no such thing as an alcoholic, just as there are no such things as cigarette-aholics. By Carr's logic, there are smokers and nonsmokers, and there are drinkers and nondrinkers.

Over the next few weeks, I slowly pick through *The Easy Way*. It's short, less than two hundred pages in all, but I'm afraid to finish it because I'm afraid it won't work on me, that I am the single exception to the hundreds of thousands he's claimed to help stop drinking. Except it *is* working, because as I am going through the motions of my alcohol-centric life—going to weddings and baby showers and happy hours and nights out with my friends—I am all of a sudden acutely aware of how entirely pointless it is that we drink. It was like: noticing you've lost ten pounds without trying.

Two weeks after diagnosing myself with BPD, I'm out with a friend in the Mission District of San Francisco, when over my protests she picks up two men. They are Canadian, and the one she guns for loses interest in her by the second bar; the one I am stuck with—who can't stop talking about the fucking Lumineers and rubbing his pierced nipples—basically wants to marry me. This is not a situation I'm particularly winning at, but it's also a situation my friend can't abide. Because I'm not sure how I feel about alcohol anymore, I've had far less to drink than I usually do; I am sober-ish. She is absolutely the opposite, and when her Canadian starts talking to another woman while my Canadian asks me how many kids I want, she runs from the bar.

And then there I am, sober-ish, running down Valencia Street through crowds of people, chasing my irrational, drunk friend who hates me because some guy who *genuinely loves the Lumineers* is interested in me. She's screaming names at me and I am letting it slide because girl code explicitly states you don't leave your slobbering-drunk vagina-owning friend alone on dark streets after midnight. After some cajoling, I finally get this bitch into a cab, and right as we are about to flee the scene, she jumps out in a hail of fuck-yous and middle fingers. We drive past her walking into another bar on our way out of the Mission, the cabbie and I both staring as if we're on safari: we are carefully watching the tiger. I can't believe what's just happened, and I wonder if I can't believe it because I'm sober enough to see how goddamn ridiculous it all is, or if it's because Allen Carr has brainwashed me. All I know is, I'm thirty-three, and this is the exact moment I know I am done with alcohol. I think: *Is this so much fun? AM I LIVING MY BEST LIFE?*

The next day I get on Amtrak and head to Fresno to watch my cousin get married. Even though 1 "only" had four or five drinks the night before, I am hungover and bloated and my face is impossibly red. I am in the period of my life where hangovers physically deform me. My anxiety is high, my depression is swallowing me, I am shaky, and nothing I do makes any of it better.

At the reception I run into a friend from high school; he's married and his kids are in tow and I am a loser who is wondering if he can smell my whiskey-scented sweat. I drink one glass of wine and my fingers swell almost immediately and my self-loathing is so thick I can barely swallow. I get home to my mom's house that night and continue reading Allen Carr as fast as I can; I am desperate for the book to deliver on its promise. On Monday morning, on the train ride back to San Francisco, I finish *The Easy Way*. The punchline is: The only way to control alcohol is to not imbibe at all.

The combination of reading Carr and just a few weeks of witnessing the pointlessness of alcohol and the way it was *actually* showing up in my life has officially convinced me that I don't *want* to drink. I am sold. I am ready for my transition to nondrinker.

Carr instructs me to drink my last alcoholic beverage, and so I go to the train snack bar and buy a tiny bottle of terrible red wine. It is something that maybe weeks before would have scratched an itch or delivered me something I thought I wanted; this time I don't want it. I take the wine back to my seat, I pour it into a clear plastic cup, I drink it, and I observe what it does to me: I note it makes me depressed and tired. I take a picture of it, I recycle the bottle and the cup, and then I read the final pages of the book. Carr's parting orders are: *Make a decision to never drink again, and never question that decision.* I write the words NEVER QUESTION THE DECISION in big bold letters in my work notebook, and I am done. Just like that, I am done with alcohol, and I'm not sad, or ashamed, or deprived, or any of the things people are supposed to feel when they stop drinking. I am proud. Happy. *Giddy,* even. I never have to drink again, and life is—quite suddenly—filled with possibility.

I get to San Francisco around noon and go directly to work. I want to shake people and tell them I am born again, but I refrain. That night I go to a happy hour for work, and because I have a reputation for shaming people into taking shots, the fact that I'm pounding Diet Cokes is slightly obvious. When people offer me a drink, or ask me why I'm not drinking, I joyously explain I've stopped drinking, that I'm a *non*drinker now.

For some reason, I expect applause; instead, hardly anyone I tell about my decision can get past what my not drinking means about *their* drinking. For the next two months, the same scenario will repeat itself over and over again. People not only aren't happy for me, they are confused and threatened. They want me to drink. One night I light up a joint, and a friend dramatically bows in relief: "Oh thank God you still get fucked up." "Of *course* I do," I assure her. She, like everyone else, is not okay with me not drinking for no particular reason. I'm not an alcoholic, I am someone who has broken our social contract.

In December, nearly eight weeks into my nondrinking life, I am getting ready for my company's holiday party. I'd been in an on-again, off-again relationship with the head of the company since my One That Got Away got away, and the relationship was currently off. I want it back on, at least for the night, and the only way I know how to do such a thing—and by "such a thing" I mean screw someone who wants absolutely nothing to do with me anymore—is drunk. I do exactly what Carr warned me not to do: I question my decision to not drink. Which is another way of saying, I reopen the whiskey floodgate.

At a pre-party I join a circle of friends for a shot of Jameson. I expect there to be some resistance to it, some encouraging admonishment, "But you're doing so well!" from at least one friggin' person. That doesn't happen, but my friend G does express a sentiment I won't forget. We are planning on going to Italy together that June with his family, and he tells me he's been thinking of asking someone else to go with him—someone who drinks. It's as if until that moment I'd forgotten the extent to which drinking is a qualifier for belonging. Or: being invited to Sicily.

I imagine I'll just have one or two drinks at the party, enough to numb the part of me that knows she shouldn't be sleeping with the person who broke her. I also imagine that after two months without drinking, I'll have the tolerance of a high schooler drinking her first Zima and that I'll make jokes about it, maybe say, "I'm just a cheap date!" as I wobble on the dance floor. But my tolerance hasn't budged; I need just as much as I always did, which is a lot. When I wake up the next morning in my ex's bed, I am in a worse hell than I've ever been. I think to myself, possibly for the first time, *I have a drinking problem.*

In January, in the throes of depression, I throw myself into fixing the problem. I start meditating and I read more spiritual books. I begin going to church on Sundays, and I find a better therapist. I start dancing in the mornings to "Gangsta's Paradise"; I get stomach massages and acupuncture; I hang Post-it notes with affirmations scribbled on them all over my apartment. I do yoga in the evenings. I write in my journal that I don't want to die; I think I am going to die. I tell people I am trying not to drink, and I try not to drink, and while sometimes this works, for the most part it doesn't—my binges are more extreme than they've ever been.

I am tempted to read *The Easy Way* again, to be transported back to that place where alcohol was just something I used to do, but that feels more terrifying than anything else. I think, *What if it doesn't work this time?* I finally do read it again, and on a Saturday in March, I once again follow Carr's instructions and have my ceremonial last drink. This time it works for two weeks, but at yet another company event, for the same reasons as at the holiday party, I find myself wanting to get naked with the same ex-boyfriend and don't know how to do such a thing without being half-conscious. That night I drink again, and the next day I quit again, and this time I quit for good. My sobriety date is April 14, 2013.

On that first day of sobriety, desperate for just one person to tell me it would all be okay, I asked my friend if her father—a twenty-something-year veteran of AA—might talk to me. We chatted on the phone later that night about my alcohol addiction. Toward the end he asked me, earnestly, why I hadn't once in our entire conversation mentioned "my alcoholism," and because I had run out of answers, I took his advice and found an Alcoholics Anonymous meeting close to my office.

I went to my first meeting the next day, the day of the Boston Marathon bombing, during lunch. When it was my turn to talk, I told them all my name, and I told them I was an alcoholic, and I told them it was my first time saying that word. It went exactly like it does in the movies, and after the meeting I was given business cards from genuinely kind and helpful people.

This was the culmination of everything I'd feared happening in my life.

While I stopped going to meetings not long after that first one (AA wasn't my scene, which we'll get into later), I did absorb the label *alcoholic* for a time, and I did find identifying as one made sobriety easier. At least it ended the questions and pleas to drink. Not drinking was no longer something cute I was trying on, but something serious, because now I had a life-threatening disease: *alcoholism*. A one-word answer that explained everything, and a definition that had been desperately lacking in my previous attempts to quit drinking.

Shortly after that first AA meeting, I took a group of friends to dinner to come out with it. Over *quartini* of Italian reds and one very obvious mocktail, I explained my alcoholism and promised that nothing would change; I was still me. I could still sit down in a restaurant and inhale the fumes of a Nebbiolo without imbibing, my sickness would not impede our good times, I would not ruin the party. After dinner, we walked to a friend's apartment up the street to smoke pot before going out to a bar. My friend C, who was on her third or maybe fourth glass of wine (the same one who months earlier had swooned in relief upon discovering I still smoked pot), sat next to me on the couch. She leaned in close and, with her hot, alcohol-soaked breath, explained how she wasn't like me, how she could take alcohol or leave it. What was odd was that in the five years of our friendship, I'd never seen her leave it.

There was something jarring and humiliating about the conversation, something I couldn't put my finger on then but can now because the same scenario would repeat itself time and again: *Alcoholism* was a word that invited other people to use me as their own personal navigation system. The word helped people make sense of my shitty relationship with alcohol so they could make sense of their own shitty relationship with alcohol, or at least know what their shitty relationship with alcohol was not. The thing was, the term *alcoholic* didn't do much for me except eat away at the things I'd spent the last six months trying to build, like being a woman who could be trusted with herself.

Nearly a year later, in February 2014, driving in a tiny rental car in Oahu with C, I called myself an alcoholic because somewhere along the way I'd forgotten I had a choice in the matter. I didn't use the word often, but whenever I did, it felt wrong, or maybe not true, or maybe like a machete to my throat. We had stopped at a light, and the word hung in the air until C said I didn't have to call myself that if I didn't want to. I don't know why it took someone else to point it out to me, or why someone else's permission felt more reliable than my own, but that was the last time I identified as an alcoholic. Which is another way of saying that was the last time I carried that word around with me everywhere to explain who I was, or what I was not, or why my suffering and my sickness and my recovery were valid. I left it on the side of the road in Oahu, near Kualoa Ranch, where *Lost* was filmed.

———

This isn't a chapter on Alcoholics Anonymous, or its effectiveness as a program. But this *is* a chapter about the word *alcoholic* and, by extension, *alcoholism*. The word wasn't created by AA, but it was placed into common lexicon by AA—and strapped with a load of baggage. A load of baggage I understood even as a young girl, before I took my first drink, and a word I knew was one of the worst things you could become, before I ever contemplated becoming it.

Before I stopped drinking—*before I even started*—I understood that admitting a drinking problem meant alcoholism, and alcoholism meant a life sentence. I didn't have to crack open *The Big Book* to believe that there are only two types of drinkers and that no one wants to be the alcoholic type. I didn't need to search the web to know that only alcoholics seek treatment. I just had to live in America to know these things, because here we look at and measure our relationship with alcohol through the word *alcoholism*.

You don't need to know my story to understand how this affected me or how it affects anyone who drinks in our culture. Drinking is a rite of passage that nearly everyone is expected to go through, and most of us do—about 70 percent of adults eighteen and over in the United States drink. We are given a set of mixed messages of what is good, bad, normal, unacceptable, and worrisome. There is no magic number of drinks per day or perfect delineation of what an alcoholic is. There are qualifiers, and it's best understood that alcoholism is what happens when our lives become intolerable, or resemble Nick Cage's in *Leaving Las Vegas*. We know what happens to people who can't control their drinking, and we know it will happen to only a small percentage of us.

I can't tell you that I spent every single day between April 2013 and February 2014 struggling with the label and what it meant. But I can tell you that at some point, on this side of surrender, I forgot Allen Carr's logic: that what made sobriety so full of wonder is the fact that I didn't have to negotiate a word that implies a life sentence or a chronic, relapsing disease or a condition that 64 percent of people believe should bar an individual from employment. What made the label *nondrinker* downright magical was that it wasn't synonymous with *drunk, inebriate, junkie, addict, lush, wino, liar,* or *cheat.*

I can also tell you that from that day in Oahu forward, I got enraged at how much the word *alcoholic* in and of itself had cost me. Not from using it to define myself (which it did), but from the years I'd spent trying *not* to use it to define myself. The years I'd spent trying not to be a word no one wants to be instead of just evaluating whether alcohol was something I should be consuming. It was like: watering the lawn while the house was on fire, or maybe while I was on fire. For two decades.

Not long after I left the word by Kualoa Ranch, I came to the conclusion that not only did *I* need to ditch the label entirely but that *we* do. That the words *alcoholic* and *alcoholism* need to burn.

To be clear, I believe that alcohol is addictive, that alcohol addiction is progressive, that some people are wired a bit differently and are more vulnerable to alcohol addiction. In fact, I don't just believe these things, *science tells me these things.* I'm not refuting that alcohol addiction is an actual thing, because it is an actual thing—a thing *I* had.

What I am saying is, alcohol is addictive to everyone. Yet we've created a separate disease called *alcoholism* and forced it upon the minority of the population who are willing to admit they can't control their drinking, and because of that, we've focused on what's wrong with those few humans rather than on what's wrong with our alcohol-centric culture or the substance itself.

Instead of looking at how insane it is that we consume the amounts of alcohol we do in this country (the beer industry alone makes up 2 percent of our GDP), we've systematically labeled anyone who can't hang as having the problem and washed our national hands of any responsibility. Alcoholism is a *you* problem, a *them* problem, a thing that happens to people with shitty self-control and bad genes. Alcoholism is not a *we* problem. (In contrast, the opioid epidemic, which claims about half as many American lives as of this writing, is a *we* problem.)

The label *alcoholic* and the disease *alcoholism* keep us focused on a construct and distract us from the real problem at hand, which is our cultural and individual relationship with alcohol and addiction. We should be able to ask ourselves these simple questions and answer honestly: *Does alcohol negatively impact my life? And if so, should I take steps to address my relationship with it?* Instead we are conditioned to ask one question, which is whether we *might be* alcoholic, and only then, only if we qualify, are we supposed to do anything about it.

Ten Reasons the Labels *Alcoholic* and *Alcoholism* Should Die

1. They assert that it's normal to consume an addictive substance with ease, and abnormal not to be able to. One time a dear friend who had stopped drinking some ninety days previous posted on Facebook that she "has a body that cannot handle alcohol." I replied, "*No*body has a body that is meant to handle alcohol." And that is 100 percent true. Alcohol is a drug, a carcinogenic neurotoxin, and no human body is designed to tolerate it with ease. Just because we as a society believe that relaxing with a glass of wine (or two or three) is "normal" doesn't mean it's what we are designed to do. It means we accept it without question, just like we accepted doctors recommending smoking in 1950s advertisements.

2. They prevent all drinkers from observing their own relationship with alcohol and provide a false sense of security. We tend to think in black and white: there are normal drinkers, and there are alcoholics. We are one or the other, and as long as we are not alcoholics, we are okay. I found that by identifying as an alcoholic, my friends began to draw lines between my behavior and their own, justifying their alcohol consumption and abuse as "normal" against the depths of my "abnormal." They wanted to know how bad it got in the end, so they could benchmark their own relationship with alcohol. My response came as a relief to most of them. A free pass—*I never did that, so I'm okay.* They failed to remember that once upon a time I was just binge-drinking, too. Or that once upon a time I limited myself to a glass or two of wine after work, just like them. They failed to take notice of the progressiveness, or that they occupied the same space on the spectrum as I did for most of my drinking career.

My friend, the author Annie Grace, once recounted a conversation she had with a friend—who identified as an alcoholic and attended AA—nearly six years before Annie herself got sober. Annie asked her friend what her drinking was like and what it meant to be an alcoholic. Annie didn't recognize her own behavior in her friend's story, and her friend confirmed that what was happening to Annie "wasn't alcoholism," so Annie went on drinking. It would take another six years for her own drinking to match her friend's. She was given just enough confirmation of "not a problem" to keep on drinking, and enough room for her drinking to get worse.

We are trained to ask ourselves only if we are alcoholics, because that is when we are supposed to get help and challenge or change our relationship with alcohol. We are not trained to ask if we are just not particularly okay with how alcohol shows up in our life or whether we should do something about it. If we aren't like "them"—if we aren't alcoholic—we don't have to worry.

3. They suggest the problem lies on the extreme end of the spectrum—full-blown addiction. And that's not where the majority of problem drinking lies. Ninety percent of "heavy drinkers" (defined as women who drink more than eight alcoholic beverages per week and men who drink more than fifteen alcoholic beverages per week) are not addicted. Let me repeat, nine out of ten people who struggle with alcohol are *not* clinically addicted, *not alcoholics.* A 2014 study published by the Centers for Disease Control reported that 29 percent of adult Americans eighteen and over met the definition for problem drinking. This means that 51 million abuse alcohol and are vulnerable to developing a chemical dependence, but only 5 million qualify as clinically addicted. And because we have come to accept that only those who are addicted truly need help, we don't have adequate prevention or treatment programs for the population that is most at risk—problem drinkers who are not formally addicted. We wait until people bottom out. We fail to address those who are not addicted but simply struggle, which is akin to waiting for a heart attack to check cholesterol, and then treat it.

4. They scare the shit out of people. The term *alcoholic* and the "disease" of *alcoholism* create fear—fear that you will always crave alcohol, forever have to use willpower to resist it, spend the rest of your life just trying not to drink. Who wants to be an alcoholic? I'll tell you who: no one. *No one.* And why is that? Because we have been told it's an incurable disease. Because our idea of an alcoholic is someone who attends Alcoholics Anonymous for the rest of their life, assumes a lifetime label, and is stuck in perpetual craving— one drink away from being a drunk, one day at a time. Because our concept is that alcoholics are different, they're outcasts and social pariahs and weak-willed and a whole host of other things no one wants to be.

I can't begin to tell you the number of times someone who struggles with alcohol has said to me, "I'm not one of them," or "I'd rather keep drinking than suffer that fate." The truth is that anyone who consumes alcohol and can't live without it is to some degree hooked on it, regardless of whether it's a glass a week or a bottle a night. Adding a label with a heavy stigma does nothing but keep us in a fear state about our own drinking, preventing us from being able to observe our own drinking as it shows up in our lives.

5. They assert that the majority of drinkers drink "normally." Alcohol is an addictive substance. End of story. There are no "normies" who don't have to control their drinking and "alcoholics" who cannot—everyone who consumes it to some degree has to exert control over it. I'm not asserting that everyone who drinks has a problem, I'm absolutely not. There are people, like my mother and her one or two glasses of wine a week, who have no degree of difficulty managing or controlling it. But that doesn't mean my mother doesn't exert control over limiting it to that one or two, or isn't in some way reliant on it. There are degrees of ability to control that are unique to each one of us, to our genetic makeup, our exposure, our trauma, our other coping mechanisms, the age at which we started drinking, our environment, our level of anxiety, our degree of depression, our peer groups, and so on. There *is* no normal, and the only way to have 100 percent control over alcohol is to eliminate it entirely.

6. They are (largely) self-diagnosed. One thing that confounds me the most is that we are often left to self-diagnose based on a loose set of judgments. One of the most common tools to determine alcoholism is from the National Council on Alcoholism and Drug Dependence (NCADD), the "Am I Alcoholic Self Test." If you answer affirmatively to eight or more of the twenty-six questions, you may be an alcoholic. In other words, if your tolerance has increased since you first started drinking, if you can't remember things you have done, if you drink heavily when you are disappointed or under pressure, if you sometimes feel uncomfortable when alcohol is not available, if you regret things you've done drunk, if you have been advised to cut down by a doctor, if you sometimes feel guilty about your drinking, and if you have felt depressed after it, then you might be an alcoholic. If this quiz can be relied upon, then everyone I went to college with and perhaps 90 percent of San Franciscans are alcoholics.

7. They keep us stuck in a story. In 2014, on the phone with a guy I'd met on the internet who also didn't drink, I mentioned casually that I was stressed about not accomplishing enough in my day. He quickly replied, "That's your alcoholism talking." I rolled my eyes so hard they groaned into the receiver. No. Just, no.

The story is that alcoholics are different; that we struggle more than others; that we are a certain way, will always be a certain way; and that minding the truth of "who we are" and being hyperaware of our "faults" will keep us out of trouble and in check. Even if we stop drinking, even if we are sober for years and do more work on ourselves and spend more money on self-improvement than the entire GDP of some small nations, we can't get out from under our alcoholism. We still have it, and not only do we still have it, but it extends to every area of our life. It's why we are [insert every shitty human behavior here].

In other words, it limits us. *I'm just this way. I'm just fucked as a human being, and I guess I always will be because I'm an alcoholic.* It also ensures we will live in an infinite hellish loop. If our alcoholism is running the show from the dark corners of our soul, and all our shortcomings are products of this chronic, incurable condition, then, well, fuck us.

The truth is we *can* change. From what we now know of neuroplasticity, we can rewire our brain with meditation and chanting and yoga and food and CBT and DBT and a whole host of other evidence-based modalities, practices, and treatments. Epigenetics tells us we can even change our gene expression and the predeterminants of addiction. Our absolute nature as human beings is that we are always evolving and growing and changing—in fact, over the course of seven years, *our entire cellular structure* changes. But when we hold tight to an idea of "I'm just this way," we settle for being *just this way.* "Hi, I'm Holly, and I'm an alcoholic," ensures that I will remain in the mind-space of something I don't even do anymore. "Hi, I'm Holly, and I'm a writer, speaker, CEO, meditator, daughter, auntie, sister, friend, and addiction advocate, who speaks terrible Italian," works a lot better for me.

8. Alcohol is the only drug in the world where, when you stop taking it, you are seen as having a disease. Because alcohol is the only socially accepted drug, because most of us consume it, because we have come to believe that there are "normal" drinkers and there are "alcoholics," and because alcoholism is self-diagnosed, it is literally the only drug in the world where you get a label and a lifetime disease once you admit you need to, want to, or do stop.

I never had a problem when I was out three or four nights a week drinking the same amount as my friends. I never had a problem when I was doing ski shots with my co-workers or when I stayed out drinking until four a.m. on a weeknight. But when I tapped out—*when I stopped drinking alcohol*—was when I qualified for a drinking disease.

Let me be clear on the insanity of this. When I drank (and clearly abused), I did not have alcoholism. When I said, "I can't drink," I became an alcoholic. Because we believe everyone "should" be able to drink ethanol, and those who can't are somehow defective, we assign them a label and a lifetime disease.

9. Alcoholism is supposedly an "incurable disease." The need for alcohol is perpetuated by the consumption of alcohol. Pure and simple. You were not addicted before you imbibed, the same way that you were not addicted to cigarettes before you smoked. Further, it has been shown time and again that after people ditch their addiction to the substance entirely, they go on to not want it at all. People like me. I'm not one drink away from alcoholism or addiction. I'm beyond the need to get intoxicated in order to get through life or have fun at a party. Not because *it has to be this way* but because *I prefer it this way*. I *like* life without a crutch. I *like* not having hangovers or forgetting parts of the night before or living in a fear state. I *like* not having to think about alcohol.

We think that being "cured" means being able to drink again without going overboard or our life going to hell. We think it means being able to imbibe like the "normal drinkers." Bull-cocky. Cured means *never having to drink again*. Cured means enjoying life without needing to reach for a glass of wine to unwind each day or to enjoy a celebratory event. Cured means being able to remain present and to ride the ups and downs without having to numb or escape them. Cured means not having to keep the beast of alcohol at bay, but being free of it altogether.

10. They grant impunity to Big Alcohol. If you will, imagine a world that treats cigarettes the same as alcohol—they are fine and healthy for the general population to consume, but toxic for some folks: cigarette-aholics. Not only that, but we are expected to smoke; as soon as we turn twenty-one, we are inducted into this precious ceremonial rite, with an understanding that only some of us will become addicted—those of us with a genetic predisposition, or an allergy, to cigarettes. In this world, the cigarette companies are no different from the food industry. They are absolutely not at fault for a disease that develops not from the use of the substance, but from the person's unfortunate genetic makeup.

The War on Drugs spun out of the agencies responsible for policing alcohol Prohibition; after Prohibition, drugs other than alcohol were made illicit, and policed by an outgrowth of the establishment meant to police alcohol. At the height of the War on Drugs, during the Nixon and Reagan administrations, capital punishment was considered a reasonable sentence for a drug pusher. In 1984, New York City mayor Ed Koch, commenting on David A. Kennedy's suicide (by overdose on illegal drugs), said, "I believe the person who sold him these drugs is guilty of murder," and said he wanted to see capital punishment for such crimes on a national level. The Clinton administration was the first to carry out the death sentence against a drug trafficker. Today around 20 percent of the prison population is incarcerated for a drug-related crime. According to the World Health Organization, around 3.3 million people died alcohol-related deaths in 2018. In contrast, around 450,000 people died worldwide in 2015 from a drug-related death.

With every single other kind of drug use and addiction, we blame the drug, to the point of prosecuting individuals for trafficking, distributing, and possessing them—even though drugs account for less than 14 percent of the deaths caused by alcohol. When it comes to alcohol, however, we blame the people, which means the alcohol industry doesn't just profit from our death, it gets away with it as an innocent bystander. The industry has absolutely no liability, because how could it possibly be accountable to a disease that some people just have?

5

The Right Question:
Is Alcohol Getting in the Way of My Life?

I'd say the most common thing to do in the year before quitting booze is to hunch over a laptop and miserably type Am I an alcoholic? *into Google at 1 a.m. (in Incognito Mode, of course). I did it many, many times. Sometimes the internet told me I was, sometimes it told me I wasn't.*
— CATHERINE GRAY

I once went to an AA meeting where the speaker got up to tell how she came to recovery. She was young, just twenty-three, and she hadn't started drinking until she entered college. Her slide to the bottom came fast: she moved from binge drinking to drinking by herself to entering rehab before she graduated. She was beautiful and funny, and I remember thinking how I wished *I'd* figured it out that early. The part that caught my attention the most, however, was when she explained that she now knew she was an alcoholic as early as five: "I would stay in my room for days on end, isolating myself from the world, journaling about my fantasies, making up stories and self-aggrandizing to numb my feelings. I was insecure and full of my ego; I thought only of myself." I looked around and saw a sea of nodding heads, agreement from people I could only suspect remembered being alcoholics in kindergarten, too.

There was something so reductive about the entire story and the simple explanation of it *always* being about the alcoholism.

Here was a normal human being who had done normal human things to survive and adjust to a painful, confusing world. How were we uniformly convinced that her problems—like our own—were rooted in the condition of alcoholism *fifteen years* before she ingested alcohol? It sounded like brainwashing, like total bullshit.

At the time of that meeting, I was less than a year sober from alcohol and still calling myself an alcoholic. I was also entirely consumed with the etiology of my addiction, and addiction in general. What caused me to drink the way I did, or eat the way I did, or smoke the way I did? What made me an endless pit of hunger? What drove me to consume alcohol and pot and food and cigarettes and men and work until I hurt? What made other people *not* do this kind of shit? And why are we so attached to using one word to describe it all?

We are supposed to consume alcohol and enjoy it, but we're not supposed to become alcoholics. Imagine if this were the same with cocaine. Imagine we grew up watching our parents snort lines at dinner, celebrations, sporting events, brunches, and funerals. We'd sometimes (or often) see our parents coked out of their minds the way we sometimes (or often) see them drunk. We'd witness them coming down after a cocaine binge the way we see them recovering from a hangover. Kiosks at Disneyland would sell it so our parents could make it through a day of fun, our mom's book club would be one big blow-fest, and instead of "mommy juice" it would be called "mommy powder." There'd be coke-tasting parties in Napa and cocaine cellars in fancy people's homes, and everyone we know (including our pastors, nurses, teachers, coaches, bosses) would snort it. The message we'd pick up as kids would be *Cocaine is great, and one day you'll*

get to try it, too! Just don't become addicted to it or take it too far.
Try it; use it responsibly. Don't become a cocaine-oholic though.

Now, I'm sure you're thinking, *That's insane, everyone knows*
that cocaine is far more addicting than alcohol and far more dan-
gerous. Except it's not. In 2010 the former UK drug czar David
Nutt and a team of researchers assessed twenty licit and illicit
drugs on two criteria: harm to users and harm to others. Alcohol, with a score of 72, came in on top as the most dangerous
drug (in the UK), followed by heroin and crack cocaine. Regular old cocaine came in at 27, just above tobacco, which had a
score of 26. Even when we take out the societal harm scores, we
still end up with a harm-to-user score of 26 for alcohol, well
above the harm-to-user score of 18 attributed to cocaine. In his
2014 book *Clean*, David Sheff says that 40 percent of people
who consume alcohol abuse it, and 15 percent become addicted;
whereas 45 percent of those who consume cocaine abuse it, and
the same exact number—15 percent—become addicted.

The point is not that alcohol is worse than cocaine. The point
is that we have a really clear understanding that cocaine is toxic
and addictive. We know there's no safe amount of it, no such
thing as "moderate cocaine use"; we know it can hook us and
rob us of everything we care about. If we do use it, we go into it
(hopefully, theoretically) with our eyes wide open. We don't
have a story around cocaine that some people can use it safely
(normies) and some can't (cocaine-oholics). We know we are
better off not tangling with it at all.

The same goes for cigarettes—we don't split up smokers into
categories of "normal smokers," who smoke the safe and socially acceptable amount, and "cigarette-oholics," who take it
too far; there are smokers, on a spectrum of smoking addiction,
consuming a drug that we know to be toxic, addictive, and
deadly.

But with alcohol, it's different. We *do* have categories of "normal drinkers" and "alcoholic drinkers," and often we don't know which we are. We are given messages through advertising, movies, TV, our parents, our peers, and social media that alcohol is this magical, life-giving substance that will work wonders for us (if we're normal, which we are assumed to be). We are *supposed* to be able to tolerate it, and when we can't, when it doesn't feel good or things start going to hell for us, it's not the substance that's the problem—it's us. We are damaged, weak-willed, defective, and totally fucked.

So we're supposed to drink alcohol, but we're not supposed to become addicted to it. We're trained to ask one question of our drinking—*Am I an alcoholic?*—and to keep drinking if that answer is no. We're conditioned to believe it's normal to imbibe, abnormal to abstain, and because of this, we are not conditioned to ask the most reasonable questions of all: Is alcohol getting in the way of my happiness, my life, my self-esteem? Is it getting in the way of my dreams, or maybe just not working for me? Does it cost more than it gives, does it shrink more than it expands, does it cut pieces out of me I can't reclaim? Does it make me hate myself, even just a little bit?

THERE'S NO STAGE IV ALCOHOLISM

If alcoholism is a ride, it's one that starts at birth, since the likelihood that somewhere along the way a celebration of your birth will include a toast or a drink, or your mom pumping and dumping. It's there all along, sitting in the back of the refrigerator, or associated with that one uncle, or all your uncles, or everyone who's ever existed in your family. Alcohol shows up throughout our lives, so alcoholism, by proxy, does too. When you take your first drink, no matter what age, it's there as a potential, and when you wake up hungover one too many times, or forget one too many things, or drink more than you used to, its potential expands. It ebbs and flows; it takes down friends. It's a bigger threat if you lose your partner or your job, it's less of one if you're newly in love. For certain, it is abstract, but then it comes into focus when, say, your liver hurts one morning, or maybe your soul does.

If you're concerned about your drinking, you're likely to at some point ask yourself the age-old question of whether you're an alcoholic. You might do a google search, or buy a book, or—most likely—take an online multiple-choice test. The multiple-choice test will tell you not to worry, to worry a little, to worry a lot, or to check into rehab immediately.

Sometimes the test is all we need, or sometimes we don't even take the test but leap right into the diagnosis: *I am definitely an alcoholic.* A doctor will sometimes qualify all this for you, confirm it is true—that is, based on your anecdotal evidence, a doctor will agree it sounds like alcoholism. A doctor will also basically tell you there's no hope, no cure; that alcoholism is a chronic, relapsing brain disease. When you ask your doctor for their recommended course of treatment, they might tell you that there is none, or that you could try some pills to help with cravings, or they might recommend a twelve-step fellowship and peer support. They might suggest therapy. Your doctor might also, as has happened with countless people I know, tell you that you have no problem at all, that your multiple-choice test is wrong, that you're making this up and you don't need to be such an ascetic or extremist. A doctor will sometimes tell you that you're not an alcoholic—you just like booze.

Either way, there is no certifying alcoholism. There is no blood test for it, no gene test. No one in a white coat can quantify or print out your level of alcoholism on a scale or show you what stage of alcoholism you have compared to other people with alcoholism. There is no Stage IV alcoholism with a 7 percent survival rate. There is no pricking yourself a few times a day to measure your resting alcoholism. There is no remission. There is no shortened life expectancy. You just can't drink again, you just will always want to drink again, you just keep going to meetings, you just remain vigilant against it, because alcoholism can get you at any time, but especially when you get lazy about remembering you have it.

None of anything I just wrote is helpful; it is a secret handshake more than a diagnosis. But we are a people who need definition—we need to know what is broken so we can fix the broken. With alcoholism, we essentially say the broken is that you are a person who wants to drink alcohol and unfortunately you are a person who cannot drink alcohol. Which ultimately means, we're trying to solve for alcohol rather than trying to solve for our lives.

Looking back on that meeting where the young woman was preaching to the choir about being an alcoholic at age five, I realized that what was so infuriating about the whole thing is that we're lost in a vortex of what doesn't matter, instead of looking at what does. I spent a year chasing down the question *Why am I an alcoholic?* before I started chasing down the questions that matter, like *Why can't I be with myself at all?*

THE DEFINITION OF ADDICTION

There are numerous definitions of *addiction*. The National Institute on Drug Abuse (NIDA) defines it as a "chronic, relapsing brain disease that is characterized by compulsive drug seeking and use, despite harmful consequences." Marc Lewis, author of *The Biology of Desire*, contends it's not a disease, and points out that "like all habits, addiction quite simply grows and stabilizes, in brain tissue that is designed (by evolution) to change and stabilize." Lewis argues that addiction is the brain reacting to a motivating experience *the way it is supposed to* and that addiction is the product of a brain that learns and adapts to repeated experiences, and that because the brain is doing what it is built to do, addiction can't be a disease—it's a pathological overlearning, a feedback loop with dire consequences.

In his book *The Globalization of Addiction*, Bruce Alexander identifies four definitions of addiction. Alexander asserts the closest and truest definition is an "overwhelming involvement with any pursuit whatsoever that is harmful to the addicted person, to society, or to both." He stresses that addiction must not be limited (as it often is) to alcohol and drugs but must encompass the wider set of behaviors, habits, chemicals, and pursuits (gambling, work, power seeking, internet porn, sex, tech, etc.) that can come to dominate an individual's world. Alexander also reminds us that addiction can be healthy—Gandhi, for instance, was addicted to his cause for liberation.

Tommy Rosen, author of *Recovery 2.0*, says addiction is the opposite of awareness, and I've heard Johann Hari explain that addiction is the opposite of connection. More often than not, I've heard it explained as something one does repeatedly, despite negative consequences. In an interview on The Fix, addiction specialist and author of *In the Realm of Hungry Ghosts*, Gabor Maté, said, "My definition of addiction is any behavior that a person finds pleasure or relief in and craves, but suffers negative consequences and can't give up."

Did any of this help, or are your eyes blurring from bore-

dom? Notice there's no scale here, no number of drinks or number of hours spent watching porn that specifies whether you are
just fucking up a little or are actually, legitimately caught in addiction.

The questions I would ask instead: *How many times have you
suffered a hangover, regretted something you said, kissed someone
you didn't want to, because of booze? Does drinking feel like it
takes more than it gives? Do you feel like you'd have a better life if
you never had to drink again? Do you need a definition to answer
these questions?*

THEORIES OF ADDICTION

There are also plenty of theories of addiction, if you're looking
for them—or rather, ideas of what causes addiction or how we
find ourselves in addiction.

The **choice theory** is precisely what it sounds like: one makes
a choice to be addicted. It's the moralistic theory, and the cruel-
est of all, because while indeed we have choice in whether to
face our addiction, and choice comes into play as we work our
way out of it, no one I know chooses to struggle with addiction.
We don't vote ourselves into it—we slide.

The **self-medicating theory** is also exactly as it sounds; we
are in pain, we find something that relieves that pain, that something worsens our pain, we use it again—it provides enough
temporary or instant relief to keep us coming back, even if it
leaves us worse off.

The **disease model** is the theory most generally accepted
both by Alcoholics Anonymous and by the medical community.
It posits that there is something fundamentally wrong, different, and diseased with the brain or biological process of the addicted person. It also concludes there's no cure: once an addict,

always an addict. The disease model was made popular in the 1960s, most notably with the publication of *The Disease Concept of Alcoholism* by E. M. Jellinek, and the classification of alcoholism as a disease in 1967 by the American Medical Association. The disease model has been upheld by recent advances in neuroscience and is what the National Institute on Alcohol Abuse and Alcoholism (NIAAA), NIDA, and the National Institutes of Health (NIH) endorse: addiction means the brain is diseased, chronically.

The **learning model,** proposed by Marc Lewis, asserts that addiction is the brain doing what it's supposed to be doing. Addiction isn't pathological, it's normal and adaptive. The learning model basically says: If you go to the gym every day, your brain and organism will change, if you use alcohol every day, your brain and organism will change; and neither of these is an example of disease—they are both examples of *learning.* The learning model of addiction uses the same science that the disease model does and makes no counterarguments to the data—both models acknowledge changes in the brain. The qualifying difference between the two is that the learning model assumes curability and adaptability (we unlearn addiction the same way we learn it), while the disease model assumes we manage it into perpetuity (we are always an addict the way a diabetic is always a diabetic).

The **dislocation model,** as proposed by Bruce Alexander, asserts that addiction is wholly driven by a free-market (capitalist) system. Alexander, the researcher of the Rat Park experiments, argues (in a very, very long book) that addiction stems from an increasingly dislocated capitalist society—not from medical pathology. In other words, addiction is a direct or indirect outgrowth of society; humans are becoming increasingly addicted not because some mutant addict gene is flooding the pool or because alcohol or addictive chemicals and behaviors are increasingly available, but because we are becoming more disconnected from our purpose, nature, culture, and each other.

Taken together, these five theories assert that addiction is (1) a pure choice; (2) an attempt to soothe pain; (3) an unavoidable sickness that can't be cured; (4) a learned behavior that can be unlearned; (5) a response to being reduced to chattel in a capitalist society. The only thing the different theories really have in common is that all were developed by white men with lots of letters behind their names, and they all seek to explain one of the most common and complicated aspects of the human condition in grossly reductionist terms.

When I first started down the path of untangling my own "what the hell happened to me" story, I was hungry for these definitions and theories of addiction. I wanted a simple explanation to a simple problem. I wanted clarity and hard lines and answers and to trace back to the moment the addiction started growing, the same way someone might want to trace back to the minute a cancer started growing. I once heard a man explain his decade-old tumor as something that was always there; there in a picture of him standing in front of the Colosseum, there at his daughter's birth, there at every Christmas. I wondered, was my addiction like that, too? Could I just not see it like he couldn't see the tumor? Was it inevitable like that?

I couldn't decide if it was just the way I was born or the way I was raised, or the people who raised me. I was fascinated by twin studies where one twin became addicted and the other didn't, and I was equally fascinated by some accounts asserting that only "10 percent of humans have the constellation of genes that predisposes them to addiction," a statistic that can be rendered meaningless by observing any two-year-old with a smart-phone. I read anything and everything I could get my hands on: medical studies and books on neurobiology, *The Big Book* and memoirs and blogs and textbooks. I read from people who believe addiction is the devil's work and people who believe it is God's work and people who believe it is simply the will of fully participating humans who want to be addicted. As I read, I returned again and again to the question I could not seem to answer: *How and why did this happen to me?*

I wish I could tell you there was a click, but really there wasn't. It was more like making a stew over a period of years. I drew conclusions of my own, threw out other people's conclusions entirely or took only the parts that made sense. I didn't believe things just because they came from a medical doctor or scientist's mouth or because we'd "always" believed them. I took pieces of what others had mapped together and repurposed them into my own map.

The five theories of addiction didn't *not* make sense to me: I could see how choice played a role in my becoming addicted and in my recovering; I could appreciate the concept of self-medication, and I could appreciate the importance of calling addiction a disease (for instance, because diseases get medical attention and insurance coverage). Lewis's explanation that addiction is learned and can be unlearned was deeply resonant; and Alexander's work was a breath of fresh air (I mean, of course we are sick because of our fucked-up society). It was just that, for the most part, those five theories and the mountain of other information published to explain the etiology of addiction seemed to want to find a unified theory of addiction, or a tidy explanation. As with everything else that ails us, we want to boil addiction down to something a pill can fix; we want it to be a question with a simple answer. But I wanted something bigger than that. I wanted something that felt less like a diagnosis and more like a treasure map, or at least something where all these different ideas could exist together.

Ultimately, what helped me understand addiction and how I came to be ensnared was first realizing that we all suffer some degree of addiction. While not all of us give our lives over to it as much as I did, or get tangled up in chemical addictions, the fact remains that all humans suffer, all look outside themselves to manage that suffering, and all get stuck in feedback loops that run through the same wiring in our brain that alcohol addiction runs through. The second thing that helped me pull apart my own addiction, and thus understand how to approach it and overcome it, was breaking it up into two distinct parts: the root causes, or the things that drive us out of ourselves to cope, and the cycle of addiction, or what happens to us biologically, spiritually, socially, and psychologically over time when we use an effective but addictive substance or behavior in an attempt to regulate ourselves. I call it the Two-Part Problem, and in order to heal, we need to address both parts.

THE TWO-PART PROBLEM

Addiction is almost universally looked at as the root issue that needs to be eradicated. We isolate it as if it existed in a vacuum, and we celebrate abstinence as a marker of success. But isolating addiction as the problem doesn't actually consider how it takes hold of us or why it persists; addiction doesn't just bubble up out of nothing. It's a response to something, an outgrowth, a *symptom;* addiction says, *Something is wrong over here.* Therefore just tending to the cycle of addiction or to the addictive behavior—or saying "Just quit drinking" or "Just quit using"—is like cutting out only part of a cancer or putting a Band-Aid on a broken bone. In order to truly heal, we need to first look at the root cause.

The Root (What Causes Us to Reach Outside Ourselves)

Until quite recently, it's been generally accepted that the root cause of addiction is our genetic makeup. We were just born this way, and from the moment we met sugar/alcohol/drugs/sex/food/whatever we find ourselves addicted to, it was game over. But we now know that while, yes, some of us are more susceptible than others to addiction or more vulnerable to specific substances, what determines whether and how much we will struggle with addiction has far more to do with what happened to us in life than anything else: the traumas we've suffered (from being bullied or sexually assaulted or going to war), our feeling of safety in our lives and our homes and our bodies, the example our parents set, the environment we live in, the age we came into contact with a chemical substance (if a drug or alcohol is the addiction), our peer group, our ways of coping with anxiety, our degree of power in society, the presence of strong support networks, our feeling of belongingness, the oppression we've endured (poverty, racism, sexism, homophobia, ageism, classism, ableism, all the *isms*). All these elements—in conjunction with our genetic makeup and biology—set the stage for whether we will turn to a substance or behavior to escape.

What pushes us to want to escape and so engage in addictive behavior is the state of our lives and how we deal. We drink and drug and eat and smoke and shop and reach outside ourselves for so many reasons. We fear we aren't good enough, and we're terrified of failure. We're stressed and don't know how to unwind. We live on the margins of society without access to opportunity. Our parents perpetuated a cycle of addiction or abuse or just didn't hold us enough when we were babies. We have no purpose or connection to something bigger than ourselves. We're bored, unhappy, angry, depressed . . . and on and on and on. If we hope to heal, we must address these primary wounds that make the home that is our self unlivable.

Genetics plays a role, but not the one we typically think. To date, scientists have not discovered an alcoholism gene or an addiction gene. What they have found is genetic predisposition: a genetic makeup that will make some of us more vulnerable to addiction, or more vulnerable to certain substances and behaviors. Genes determine how we metabolize the substances we ingest; in the case of alcohol, for example, a low responder has to drink more before feeling its effects. Genes determine how resilient we are, or how much the world impacts us, and how long it takes us to stand back up when we get knocked down. Genes determine our baseline brain chemistry and hormonal makeup. They determine comorbid conditions like depression. But gene expression is only one small part of a very large story that has countless inputs, and the presence of certain genes doesn't necessarily mean we'll become addicted—it simply makes us more susceptible.

The Cycle of Addiction (What Keeps Us Stuck)
The cycle of addiction, the second part of the Two-Part Problem, is a *response* to what's happening at the root—that brings with it its own set of problems. Addiction is essentially a symptom of those root issues that becomes its own "disease"—when we use any substance or behavior to manage our underlying pain, and use it repeatedly, we enter into a cycle, or a feedback loop. To understand what the cycle of addiction is, or in the case of alcohol what would be classified as Alcohol Use Disorder (AUD), we need to look at how alcohol dependence is formed.

When we consume alcohol, our body reacts to the substance

by releasing artificially high levels of dopamine. Dopamine is the neurochemical of wanting and motivation, and it lives in the midbrain—the part of our brain that is tasked with ensuring our survival. Typically, our midbrain releases dopamine when we encounter something that keeps us alive or that aids in procreation, like when we eat a piece of chocolate or have good sex. Dopamine is released in order to tell our brain that some activity or substance is good for survival, and the higher the levels of dopamine that are released, the more we are programmed to repeat the activity. When dopamine floods into the brain, it sends a signal that the activity is good for survival, and in order to make sure we repeat the behavior, our brain releases another neurochemical called glutamate to lock in the memory of the event, so that we are wired to do it again.

When we drink alcohol, artificially high levels of dopamine are released into the brain—a glass of wine will release more dopamine than good sex, good chocolate, or good coffee. The above-normal level of dopamine tells our brain that alcohol is *really* good at keeping us alive, and so the brain sends out higher levels of glutamate to lock in the experience. We remember the experience of drinking a cold glass of Chardonnay on a hot summer day more than we remember eating a slice of apple pie, or drinking a kale smoothie, because of this neurobiological process.

If we drink enough alcohol over a long enough period of time, this cycle locks in, and our brains identify alcohol as necessary for survival. When the midbrain is working properly, it will normally prioritize fighting, procreating, and eating. But over time and with enough exposure, the midbrain will begin to identify alcohol as necessary for survival. If we drink enough alcohol, our midbrain will eventually elevate drinking alcohol above other survival behaviors. Alcohol becomes more important because drinking it excessively tricks a primitive, unconscious part of our brain into believing it's more critical to our survival than it actually is.

The artificially high levels of dopamine that flood the brain when we ingest alcohol begin a cascade of other reactions and responses. The brain has a hedonic set point (a term coined by Dr. Kevin McCauley), which means that it both needs a certain amount of dopamine to register pleasure, and is programmed to downgrade levels of dopamine when we receive too much pleasure. Our bodies are constantly trying to find stasis, or balance, and the hedonic set point is an example of that. When high levels of dopamine are regularly released into the system from chronic use of alcohol, the dopamine is down-regulated (or balanced) by something called corticotropin-releasing factor, or CRF—a hormone that makes us feel anxious or stressed. If we flood our system with higher-than-normal levels of dopamine, we also flood our system with higher-than-normal levels of CRF, or anxiety.

Over time, when our system is assaulted by surges of dopamine, our hedonic set point goes up (requiring more dopamine to feel good), and things that used to register as pleasurable (like warm hugs or our children's laughter) don't release enough dopamine to hit that raised baseline. To boot, activities that normally relieve stress, like a bath or a brisk walk, also lose their effectiveness. Alcohol becomes the quickest way our body learns to handle anxiety (which begets more anxiety because alcohol is a depressant, and the body reacts to it by releasing cortisol and adrenaline, which means the net effect of a glass of wine is more stress, not less). Our bodies are adaptive, and they adapt to an environment that expects the effects of alcohol.

So here we are: we start using alcohol because it gives us more pleasure than sex and does more for stress management than chamomile tea. Over time it gets wrapped up in our survival response, so we are motivated to drink with the same force that motivates us to eat—only the force is stronger than the desire to eat because our midbrain, which ranks everything based on dopamine, thinks we need alcohol more than food. That seems like enough fuckery to contend with, but there's more to the story.

Humans have what is called a triune brain, or a three-part brain. The midbrain or reptilian brain is the oldest part of our brain, where our survival instinct lives; the limbic or mammalian brain is where our emotions live; and finally the neocortex is our thinking brain. Adult humans with a fully developed neocortex are typically operating from the top down, from the neocortex down to the midbrain. This basically means we (normally) don't bang each other on the sidewalk or resort to fistfights to settle disagreements at work because our moral, rational, thinking brain—the neocortex—asserts control over our base survival instincts. The neocortex, and specifically the prefrontal cortex, is where our judgment, personality, willpower, inhibition, social skills, morality, decision making, planning, and loads of other functions live. If the brain is a car, the survival response (midbrain) is the gas, and the prefrontal cortex is the brake.

In alcohol addiction, the top-down control gets flipped, and the survival, animal instinct overrides the rational, thinking brain. This is due to two different causes. First, the prefrontal cortex loses its strength and volume; it's like a muscle, and the chemical component of alcohol (it's a neurotoxin, as in it attacks gray matter or the regions of the brain involved in sensory perception, memory, emotions, speech, decision making, and self-control), along with the consistent deferral to the survival instincts, weakens its function. So the part of our brain that is

responsible for inhibiting actions (willpower), making decisions, moderating social behavior, constructing our personality,
upholding our ethics, and planning our future goes offline. At
the same time, the midbrain—which thinks only about the next
fifteen seconds, not tomorrow or next year—becomes more
powerful. It believes alcohol is necessary for survival (again,
more than food, more than sex), and it's on a mission to get it. If
you've ever woken up hungover and resolved to never drink
again, and at five p.m. found yourself standing in line with a
bottle of red in your hand, this is the flip. Your top-down
controls—which made promises to not drink, which are horrified by your perceived weakness, which know that alcohol does
you no favors, which want a social life and a future and a sober
night with your kids—are weakened, and the part of you that
thinks in terms of the next fifteen seconds, which is concerned
only with your survival, is running the show and telling you to
fuck it, the wine is what matters.

This is the cycle of addiction. It doesn't matter how much we
want to quit or hate that we haven't; we feel compelled to ingest
a substance or engage in a behavior we think will provide relief,
or make us feel good, and whatever relief or goodness we get in
the short term always leaves us in a place worse off than when
we started.

To properly heal from addiction, we need a holistic approach.
We need to create a life we don't need to escape.

We need to address the root causes that made us turn outside
ourselves in the first place. This means getting our physical
health back, finding a good therapist, ending or leaving abusive
relationships, learning to reinhabit our bodies, changing our
negative thought patterns, building support networks, finding

meaning and connecting to something greater than ourselves, and so on. To break the cycle of addiction, we need to learn to deal with cravings, break old habits, and create new ones.

To address all of this is an overwhelming task, but there is a sane, empowering, and balanced approach. But before we discuss *how* to implement solutions to the Two-Part Problem, we need to address one of the bigger issues that women and other historically oppressed folks need to consider, which is how patriarchal structures affect the root causes of addiction, how they dominate the recovery landscape, and what that means for how we experience recovery. If we are sick from sexism, homophobia, racism, classism, microaggressions, misogyny, ableism, American capitalism, and so on—and we are—then we need to understand how recovery frameworks that were never built with us in mind can actually work against us, further pathologizing characteristics, attributes, and behaviors that have been used to keep us out of our power for millennia. We need to examine what it means for us individually and collectively when a structure built by and for upper-class white men in the early twentieth century dominates the treatment landscape.

6

AA Was Created for Men

*The path of renunciation described by certain mystics
is women's daily lot.*

—LUCE IRIGARAY

A couple of years ago, I attended a symposium called She Recovers, where I sat among five hundred other women in recovery listening to a keynote speech by one of my first teachers, a woman who is in recovery herself. In her talk she repeated some of the central tenets of Alcoholics Anonymous to a roomful of women—most of whom were in the earliest stages of recovery, most of whom were still on their knees. She said that we needed to remember our humility. She said that three or four years in recovery was no time at all, that we still knew nothing, that to heal we needed to *get over ourselves even more,* to get more *right-sized than we already were,* to mind those egos of ours that were out of control and ever scheming, that we needed to *be humble in our recovery.* It was standard AA stuff, and because AA has been more or less the only game in town for nearly a century, I'm sure to enough women in the room it sounded familiar and correct—comforting even. But I had to do everything in my power not to stand up and scream.

I don't know how you're coming to this book, but if you're a woman, you're most likely not wielding an ego so big it can't fit through the door or suffering from a pathological lack of humility. If you're anything like me, you don't need to be told what "right-sized" is because you've been trying your whole life to be impossibly small. You don't need to figure out what the hell a character defect is (or search deep to find the entire list of defects, as Step Four of the Twelve Steps instructs) because you are already the QUEEN of cataloging all the crap wrong with you— just ask your journal, your mom, any ex, your boss, therapist, friends, and cat. And asking God to take it all away (Step Six)? Nope, you've done that, too. Every day of your life you've asked God to not be what you are, to be different, to be perfect, because ever since age five (or four or three or two), you've been told you were wrong.

You don't need to be told not to trust yourself, because you've always been told not to trust yourself. You don't need to be told how to apologize, because you've already been apologizing for everything you are and everything you do to everyone forever. You aren't coming in too big and too proud, you're coming in cratered, and you don't need to be broken the fuck down because you're already broken the fuck down. In other words, the Twelve Steps aren't some radical new way of being; they are your daily lot.

Since the beginning of my recovery, I'd felt that there was something about the AA message that didn't work for me, although I didn't start out with the words to describe my opposition. Way back at the start of all this, I would have told you it didn't appeal to me or I didn't need it. I did eventually attend meetings for a short period of time—*after* I got sober—and it did have a meaningful place in my journey, but I never got rid of the feeling that there was something more to my refusal than, say, not identifying with the word *alcoholic*. Attending AA felt like heading in the direction opposite of where I was going; or like having my head held under water.

It wasn't until I heard that speech at She Recovers that it came to a head. I was mad at that woman's words, and mad that a lot of my newly sober friends felt obliterated by them. Just a few months later, on a walk with my friend Cath Gray, I mentioned to her, "I fucking hate the word *humble*." She asked me why, and I couldn't really explain it. All I could say is, I suppose because it's one of those words we use on women to keep them in their place.

I'm getting ahead of myself, though. Let me back up a bit.

A VERY BRIEF HISTORY OF ALCOHOLICS ANONYMOUS

In order to understand how we view alcohol consumption patterns, addiction to alcohol, and recovery from addiction to alcohol—not just practically, but also societally and culturally—we have to go back to the origins of Alcoholics Anonymous, the substratum of American (and thus global) addiction treatment.

AA was the brainchild of Bill Wilson (aka Bill W.), a white stockbroker from Brooklyn with a drinking problem. It was co-founded by Wilson and Bob Smith (aka Dr. Bob), a white proctologist from the Midwest. The story (and now legend) goes like this: In the early 1930s, Wilson struggled heavily with his drinking and found no help through the methods that existed at the time. Then one day in late 1934, a former drinking buddy of Wilson's showed up at a bar and told him he'd found relief from his own addiction to alcohol by finding God via the Oxford Group, an evangelical Christian organization. The story made a huge impression on Wilson and not long after, he attended meetings of the Oxford Group, checked himself in to a hospital for detox, took some hallucinogens (belladonna), saw a bright light/God, and was freed from his addiction.

For a time, Wilson tried to carry the message of the Oxford Group and worked to free others from their alcoholism within the organization's infrastructure, but he found no success. It wasn't until Wilson met Dr. Bob and was able to help *him* get sober that Alcoholics Anonymous was born—first from within, and eventually outside the Oxford Group. Wilson took the framework being used in the Oxford Group at that time (six steps that eventually grew into the Twelve Steps) and birthed the framework for what we know of today as the fellowship of Alcoholics Anonymous. AA was founded on June 10, 1935—Dr. Bob's sobriety date.

What is important to understand here is not so much *how* AA was formed, but *who* it was formed for, and *why* the program worked for its members. These were not women or some other marginalized class of people; these were upper-middle-class white Protestant men in 1930s America. This was ten years after women's suffrage, at the height of the eugenics movement, and thirty years before the dismantling of Jim Crow. The basis of AA's program is the same one that asserts Eve grew from Adam's rib; it's one where God is a white-haired white man who men talk to directly and women talk to through their husbands. None of this framework has been addressed, changed, or altered since—it remains intact, as it first appeared eight decades ago.

When it was founded, women were not admitted into AA or even considered capable of being alcoholics; they were the *wives* of alcoholics. Being an alcoholic was an inherently masculine thing, and women who drank alcoholically were not only denied the alcoholic title, they were seen as having failed at womanhood—they had committed the cardinal sin of female selfishness by prioritizing their drinking above their lady-duties of child-rearing and vacuuming and wife-ing.

It is well documented that the role of women at the organization's inception was narrowed to that of the long-suffering housewife. A chapter in *The Big Book* called "To Wives" was actually penned by Bill W. under the guise of his wife, Lois. The chapter reduces women to servants of their husband's healing. It instructs them to "never be angry," to be patient and of good temper, to not be a "nag or a killjoy." It warns that an unsupportive wife might find her man turning to another woman. The original title of *The Big Book* was *Alcoholics Anonymous: The Story of How More Than One Hundred Men Have Recovered from Alcoholism.* The first woman admitted to the fellowship was Marty Mann in 1937; the first Black group was formed in 1945.

What I am saying is, This was an organization that began before almost any oppressed person's rights were won. It was created by the oppressing party *for* the oppressing party: for men who were sick from an overdeveloped sense of owning the world, from believing they were God. A 1979 history of AA, *Not-God* by Ernest Kurtz, derives its title from this concept as the basis of AA: "The fundamental and first message of Alcoholics Anonymous to its members is that they are not infinite, not absolute, *not God*. Every alcoholic's problem had *first* been, according to this insight, claiming God-like powers, especially that of *control*" (Kurtz's emphasis).

But women in 1935 America—even privileged white women—had no illusions that they were God. No woman in the history of the patriarchy has that illusion. We are second, always second, if not third or fourth or fifth depending on other intersections of identity. If being reminded of how much we are *not*

God, how little control and power we have, or claiming our fallibility and insignificance and humility was the antidote to a drinking problem, women wouldn't have drinking problems. From Charlotte Kasl's *Many Roads, One Journey:* "If we take Bill Wilson's idea of deflating the ego to its extreme we would have a crushed, nonexistent ego. That's what lots of women and minorities already have, which is not functional."

THE TWELVE STEPS AND TWELVE TRADITIONS

If you're not familiar with the Twelve Steps, they are guiding principles that outline a course of action to recover from alcoholism, first introduced in 1939. They are the heart of the AA program, the path that all of us with a drinking problem are expected to follow in order to find freedom. There are seemingly endless ways to interpret them, and women and men alike have written books to help us translate these unassailable steps in order to make this framework fit. A lot of people will insist there is nothing wrong with the steps, and if you think there is, it is probably you just misunderstanding them.

Here they are as first written:

Step 1. We admitted we were powerless over alcohol—that our lives had become unmanageable.
Step 2. Came to believe that a Power greater than ourselves could restore us to sanity.
Step 3. Made a decision to turn our will and our lives over to the care of God, as we understood Him.
Step 4. Made a searching and fearless moral inventory of ourselves.
Step 5. Admitted to God, to ourselves, and to another human being the exact nature of our wrongs.

Step 6. Were entirely ready to have God remove all these defects of character.

Step 7. Humbly asked Him to remove our shortcomings.

Step 8. Made a list of all persons we had harmed, and became willing to make amends to them all.

Step 9. Made direct amends to such people wherever possible, except when to do so would injure them or others.

Step 10. Continued to take personal inventory and when we were wrong promptly admitted it.

Step 11. Sought through prayer and meditation to improve our conscious contact with God as we understood Him, praying only for knowledge of His will for us and the power to carry that out.

Step 12. Having had a spiritual awakening as the result of these steps, we tried to carry this message to alcoholics, and to practice these principles in all our affairs.

In addition to the Twelve Steps are the Twelve Traditions, which provide guidelines for the relationship between the Twelve Step groups (local fellowships), members, other groups, the global fellowship, and society at large.

The Traditions are worth mentioning because they require anonymity of group members, for the sake of preserving not just other people's identity but the collective's. Tradition Eleven requires that no individual talk about their own experience of AA publicly: "We need always maintain personal anonymity at the level of press, radio, and films," and Tradition Twelve explicitly states, "Principles before personality." In other words, the organizational guidelines state the group is more important than you, and promote that favorite theme: the quieting, censoring, and dissolution of self. Again, not a radical concept for women, who are conditioned from birth to put everyone else's needs above their own and to not stand out.

The Traditions also do something else: they limit a central power and give individual groups control. This means: There is no central authority to step in when, say, a local fellowship is hostile or abusive to women or any other vulnerable group, or rejects those who use antidepressants or a medication-assisted treatment (MAT)—like methadone or naltrexone—because they don't qualify as sober. This also means: There is no updating *The Big Book,* the Twelve Steps, or the Twelve Traditions. They remain as originally written, like the Bible.

From the outset, AA felt like maybe a sword through my throat or an anvil on my chest or perhaps the most oppressive thing I could do to my already oppressed spirit. The flashing neon sign said this was not my path, and everyone else basically told me *that* was my problem, or rather, *I* was my problem. Having the audacity to believe I knew what I needed and could trust myself to pursue it was my issue, not this simple program that any idiot could do who had two cents and some humility. Because AA—the foundation of addiction recovery the world over—cannot be questioned, least of all by a woman addict. There was something wrong with me; there was nothing wrong with the program.

Which brings me back to my conversation with Cath on that walk: "I fucking hate the word *humble.*" It felt like a treasonous thing to say, or perhaps too revealing a thing to say. Like maybe I should have just told her I was a raging narcissist and that would have made more sense. The thing is, though, I love the *concept* of humility. I love the idea of selflessness and service. It was just that I couldn't stand the way humility—and its twin flame, ego—had been weaponized against women in the recovery community. The times I'd been told I wasn't humble enough usually wasn't out of love or to aid me in my recovery; it was typically done to silence me or shame me when I posted a selfie on Instagram, or wrote an article expressing any sort of opinion.

The word *ego* is the Latin form of the first-person singular pronoun; in English, it translates to "I." Sigmund Freud was responsible for bringing the word into popular use by theorizing that the human personality is made up of three parts: the *id* (the part of you that is present from birth), the *ego* (the part responsible for dealing with reality), and the *superego* (the part that judges and is responsible for morality). Using Freud's translation, which is the generally accepted one, the ego is not inherently bad—it's just *human*. It's also absolutely necessary—if we didn't have a part of us that was made to deal with reality, we wouldn't fare so well. The ego can take on as many forms as there are humans; literally, as of today, we are approaching nearly 8 billion flavors of ego in this world.

In recovery-speak, or according to the Twelve Steps and *The Big Book,* the ego is one very specific flavor. It is a monster of a fucker. It is overdeveloped, self-aggrandizing, narcissistic, and exploitative, a megalomaniacal power-hungry ghost. Or the ego, as described by AA, is Donald J. Trump.

Remember when I explained that AA was formed in 1930s America by upper-middle-class white men who were sick from believing they were God, sick from wielding too much power in this world? And that the foundational beliefs of AA came from white, evangelical Protestant organizations? Let's think about what that means for a second. Those who wrote the rules were those who sat (and still sit) at the top of society—a society made in their image and designed to protect them. They enjoyed unquestioned authority and unchecked power, and their ego—or way of dealing with reality—was developed through that experience. Their ego was formed to believe it was above the law, above reproach, that it was smarter than any set of rules. For an ego like this, the Twelve Steps and *The Big Book* make sense. To be reminded you are not God, to become right-sized, to refrain from questioning rules, to humble yourself, to admit your weakness, to chronicle what's wrong about you, to be vulnerable enough to admit your faults to another person, to shut up and listen: these are all behaviors associated with (and imposed on) women. They are in essence instructions on how to be a woman, and to those men, they were medicine. To act in this manner was a crazy, new way of being, and felt like freedom. But to a woman or any other oppressed group, being told to renounce power, voice, authority, and desire is just more of the same shit. It's what made us sick in the first place.

Prior to 2012, when I started to stop drinking, I had never been explicitly warned—or typically thought—that I needed to fear my ego. That was probably the one thing about myself I had failed to hate, and I don't think I could have defined ego properly if you'd asked me to. That all changed, and immediately, upon deciding that I needed to ditch alcohol. It wasn't because the second I decided on sobriety some welcome committee showed up at my door with some literature on me and my ego. It was more like this: The very fact that I wasn't calling myself an alcoholic and was "doing it on my own" opened a vault of doubt I hadn't known existed until that moment, and I was all the sudden very aware of our societal pact that says people who can't drink are inherently ego-inflated, prone to fooling themselves, and not to be trusted.

Because AA is the pervasive model, and because most people—with or without direct experience—understand AA is what you do when you have a problem with the drink, society expects you to participate in AA. To a degree, a drinking problem implies you are subject to its rules. It also implies you have lost the capacity, or even the right, to know what's best for you. Once I admitted to having a drinking problem, people had even less of a problem questioning my agency, self-awareness, and ability to tell the truth. If you are a woman, it follows that you can't be trusted with yourself, and if you are an alcoholic woman, this is exponentially true. People, both familiar and strangers, had no issue telling me what I should do to fix my alcoholism, and what would happen if I didn't.

As I continued on my journey, refusing to participate in the traditional means to wellness expected of one who struggles with alcohol, the voices got louder on the inside and audible on the outside. I was told time and again that my "ego was talking," my "ego was running the show," that I was fucked up and would always be fucked up, that I was fooling myself and those around me, that I would drink again if I didn't go to AA meetings, that I was in denial if I didn't submit to a program I saw as oppressive.

In other words, my personal rejection of the "normal way"—of attending AA meetings and working the Twelve Steps—and my hesitation and eventual refusal to call myself an alcoholic, were seen as a further indication of defects in my character. I was in denial, didn't truly want to stop drinking, or just not getting it. My refusal to submit was further proof of my sickness and that my ego was running the show. From the Twelve Traditions: "Over the years, every conceivable deviation from our Twelve Steps and Traditions has been tried. That was sure to be, since we are so largely a band of ego-driven individualists."

Nevertheless, I persisted down a path that felt sane to me, that made sense to me, that was, in fact, healing me—against all the shaming, gaslighting, and fear mongering. It was almost as if each time someone told me I was wrong or lying to myself, a little part of me got stronger—there was a tension there, a pull between a developing sense of self-trust and agency, and a thirty-something-year habit of abandoning myself for what other people thought. Here is the part of my life where doubt made me more, not less.

Still, I didn't have the words to explain why women needed a different approach, or the exact argument for why AA was so absolutely oppressive. I had ideas, and plenty of them; I just couldn't express why the existing paradigms for recovery were so splintered from what women—especially in the wake of the 2016 U.S. presidential election—needed to heal. Enter Carol Lee Flinders.

AT THE ROOT

At the Root of This Longing is a book written by the author, scholar, and educator Carol Lee Flinders. Flinders holds a doctorate from UC Berkeley in comparative literature, with a focus on medieval women's mysticism; she has lived for most of her life in a meditative co-op under the tutelage of Eknath Easwaran, an Indian-born spiritual teacher. Flinders is a feminist and a deeply committed meditation student and teacher, with a profound depth of knowledge about women mystics. Her life is devoted both to the telling of silenced women's stories and meditative discipline, and she set herself on a course to understand why her feminism felt so at odds with her spiritual practice. In doing so, she identified four key areas where feminism and spirituality contradict each other.

According to Flinders, all religious and spiritual traditions and specifically meditative practices—because they were built by men and for men—promote the following: self-silencing; self-naughting (destruction of the ego); resisting desire; and enclosure (turning inward, sealing off from the world). As a feminist, naming these four requirements of transcendence troubled her. "I realized that however ancient and universal these disciplines may be, they are not gender neutral at all. Formulated for the most part within monastic contexts, they cancel the basic freedoms—to say what one wants, go where one likes, enjoy whatever pleasures one can afford, and most of all, to *be* somebody— *that have normally defined male privilege*" (emphasis mine).

What she is saying is that the underlying precepts of a spiritual path—in every lineage from which there is a path—seek to define a degree of spiritual freedom through reversal of status. And who has had that status in societies all over the world for the last few thousand years? *Men.* "Women, on the other hand," she wrote, "have not been in a position to renounce these privileges voluntarily *because they have never had them in the first place.*" In fact, "they are terms of our subordination."

When I read those lines in her book after that conversation with Cath, every hair on my body stood at attention because finally, *finally,* someone had put into words the thing that had been screaming in me since I was first told that my failure to submit to AA was really my ego run amok. Finally, what I read was: It makes sense that a woman might entirely refuse a program that asked her to give up something she's not only never had, but was finally just grasping: a sense of self, a voice, a sense of her own desires, freedom in a world not made for her.

The opposite of these precepts, as argued by Flinders, is to (1) "find your voice; tell your story, make yourself heard"; (2) "know who you are. Establish your authentic identity or selfhood. Identify your needs and learn how to meet them"; (3) "reclaim your body, and its desires, from all who would objectify and demean it, whether it's the fashion industry, pornographers, or even the medical establishment. Recognize the hatred of the female body that pervades contemporary culture, and oppose it"; and (4) "move about freely and fearlessly. Take back the streets. Take back the night and the day."

THE MISSING LINK

Alcoholics Anonymous isn't a spiritual or religious tradition, but it was conceived from one. It was born of the framework that is foundational to every single dominant religion and spiritual practice, the framework meant to break down male privilege into spiritual purity. AA grew out of the most evangelical Protestant group in the country at the time (the Oxford Group was later renamed the "Moral Re-Armament," if that tells you anything), and though it downplayed religiosity (by refusing such words as *Jesus* and *salvation* and referring to a "Higher Power" instead of God), it was built on the same tenets of a moralistic, puritanical, and patriarchal religion.

You might think that as a woman you could simply reject AA as your preferred method of recovery, to *just not do AA if you're a woman.* But it's more complicated than that—it's not just about whether or not to use AA, it's navigating an entire system built on its tenets. Alcoholics Anonymous was truly revolutionary, the first organization that helped people stop drinking on a mass scale. It entirely changed the way addiction was thought of, talked about, and treated. AA quickly became, and remains, the default recovery mechanism. At least 73 percent of treatment facilities use the Twelve Step approach, our criminal justice system remands people to AA meetings and Twelve Step recovery centers, and medical doctors go to Twelve Step meetings as part of their training. It has remained for almost a hundred years *the* option. So even if we don't rely on it as our recovery program, its principles and practices and steps and traditions inform how society collectively thinks about and treats those who are suffering from addiction, and further, how society thinks about alcohol consumption in general.

Addicts aren't just egocentric selfish liars prone to fooling themselves who need to be broken down in the eyes of the AA fellowship—they are that to everyone because AA has informed us of how we think about problematic drinking. One of my closest people who told me I was deluding myself if I didn't work the program had never set foot in a meeting and knew nothing about addiction or recovery—she just knew what I was because I had a problem with alcohol, and knew I couldn't be trusted until I submitted to the program. We don't need to have first-person experience with AA to wield it as an axe above someone's head; it's just there.

When I read *At the Root of This Longing*, it was like finally that hand wasn't holding my head under water anymore because finally I had words: What healed me wasn't obliterating my sense of self, silencing myself, or denying my desires or body, or closing myself off more from the world—it was the opposite that saved me.

When I think of what the disaster of recovery for women really is, it's that most of us come into it without the things it's beating us to deny. Women aren't sick from an overdeveloped sense of ego or a pathological lack of humility because all we've ever done is chase our desires; we are sick because we *don't* have these things, haven't done these things. We drink not because we have too much power but because we have so little. And when we are told our problem can be solved by getting rid of and denying even more of ourselves, we are not given a way out, we are given the same death sentence of subordination.

7

Quitting Like a Woman

We know what the world wants from us. We know we must decide whether to stay small, quiet, and uncomplicated or allow ourselves to grow as big, loud, and complex as we were made to be. Every girl must decide whether to be true to herself or true to the world.

—GLENNON DOYLE

In that moment all those years ago, when I finally fell to my knees and begged for help, I had no idea who I was, or how powerful I was. I had learned at a very young age that I wasn't okay. By age five, I knew that my emotions were all wrong—I had temper tantrums, had to be held down during teeth brushings, and my parents often reminded me that I was just like the "little girl who had a little curl": when I was good I was very, very good, and when I was bad, I was horrid. By the time I was eleven, I had cellulite on my stomach and had accumulated such nicknames as "Big Butt" and "Cottage Cheese Stomach" (BB and CC for short). I was too energetic for most people, especially my family and teachers, and I was often tempered, reprimanded, and punished. I had a reputation for being a slut by the time I was sixteen; in college I picked up the nickname "Holly Drama"; and in my early career I was often told I was too aggressive, emotional, and unpredictable, and that I would not advance if I didn't get these parts of me under control. One performance review literally said "unlikeable." Most of my romantic relationships ended with a list of flaws inherent to my character that were seen as deal breakers; too much of this, not enough of that, close but no cigar.

I took people at their word. I took all of it as evidence.

With every single instance of being told I was not enough, too much, gross, fat, dumb, loud, and wrong, I shut a door within myself. This is not acceptable, that is not acceptable, all these things are not acceptable, so you must suppress them. I went around the house that is Holly and I closed off all the doors to the places in me that were wrong. Soon enough there were so many closed doors, so many places I couldn't go or let other people see, that there was nowhere to live. So I left. I went somewhere else. The home that was me was no longer habitable.

I didn't have a God-size hole, I just had a hole, and it was the size of everything I'd ever been told not to be. It was a hole with manicured nails and flat-ironed hair that wore good jeans, and it was a hole that I filled with as much food, booze, drugs, cigarettes, work, shopping, and men as I could, and constantly. By the time I fell to my knees, I couldn't meet my own gaze in a mirror because: holes.

Do you know what I did with that broken girl? The one who had been attempting to destroy every single defect of character for as long as she could remember, the one who was already in advanced talks with a God she didn't believe in to "just take it away," the one who had no idea of self beyond what was wrapped into the life she thought presented well, men who abused her, friends she didn't like, and a career that ate her? The one who couldn't look at herself in a mirror?

I started to love her.

I began telling her she was okay, that she was loved and that nothing was wrong with her. I told her she wasn't fucked up beyond repair. I let her know we had lost our way a little bit, that we'd shut some doors along the way, and that I was going to stand next to her while we went around the house and reclaimed those disowned parts. "Especially the ugly ones," I said.

I didn't tell her she was bad for putting herself first. I didn't tell her she was selfish or warn her that her "self-will had run riot." I didn't tell her not to trust herself, or that she was wrong or deluded. I didn't tell her those things because if I had, I would have just been doing what I'd been doing to her for the last thirty years. I told her to save her life at all costs, to put on her own oxygen mask, and to put it on first. And when other people told her she was wrong, that she couldn't trust herself, that she was selfish and deluded—I told her: *Fuck them.*

I took her to yoga and meditation and massage and therapy. I danced her precious body around her living room, and I wrote her a million affirmations that I taped around her apartment: "You are beautiful." "You are perfect as you are." "Nothing is wrong with you." "You have nothing to fear." "You are loved." I took her to beautiful places, on walks in the park, on runs along the water. I held her when she threw temper tantrums, and I reinforced her when she said no. I inflated her when she needed inflating; I lifted her up when she needed lifting up. I was patient.

I didn't tell her to flay herself *more.* I didn't tell her to surgically remove her parts, ask God to take away even more of her, pray that she would become someone different, or urge her to get smaller. I didn't humiliate her any more than she had already been. I didn't terrify her into thinking her ego had stolen the show, or that her growing self-importance, self-esteem, self-centeredness, self-regard, self-respect, selfishness, or pride were a sure sign she was on a bus to drinking hell.

I told her, "Thank God we finally have those things." I told her, "Thank God this house we live in finally feels like home instead of a war zone." This is what happens when we don't try to demolish what is already rubble. This is what rebuilding a woman's ego, or her sense of self, looks like.

The funny thing is that when I didn't force on myself the need to be less—when I allowed myself the freedom to be self-centered, flawed, and self-willed—I still ended up on my knees, in the ever-so-impressed-upon-the-alcoholic state of surrender: to what was, to what I didn't have control over, to what I did have control over. And while my first prayers might have echoed some of what Step Seven begs, *Please make me good,* the prayers quickly became about something far more than me: *Help me do good. Put me in service.*

With time and the development of a sense of self that I could live with—with the building of an ego—I didn't become a person who couldn't fit through the door because of her mammoth self-importance. I became a person who could walk through the door with her head held high. A woman who doesn't need to be reminded of her place, but who has claimed her place.

MASCULINE VERSUS FEMININE

Each of us, regardless of our gender or genderlessness, has both masculine and feminine aspects, or energies. Our masculine aspect tends toward achievement, accomplishment, doing, driving, forcing. It is a top-down energy that is focused and goal-oriented. It is our get-shit-done and power-through-it-at-all-costs energy, and it dominates almost every system that exists in the Western world. The masculine (via the patriarchy) governs our schools, medicine, businesses, government, criminal justice system and Prison Industrial Complex, churches, and religions, and for certain it dominates the mainstream, popular methods of addiction recovery.

The feminine aspect, or feminine energy, is receptive, relational, and flowing. Where masculine energy is destructive, the feminine is creative and the source of all creation. It's what allows us to bring forth new projects and ideas and ways of being and then nurture them into existence. Feminine energy is inclusive, and it's able to multitask and take multiple perspectives; it's multitracked and meandering and energized, and it dances circles around that single-tracked, focused masculine energy. The masculine desires to dominate, while the feminine is a bottom-up kind of energy: it wants to allow and support.

While we all have both masculine and feminine aspects, many of us have a dominant energy or aspect. I have my fair share of masculine energy. I'm all about doing and checklists and forcing and pushing through; I'm into goals and getting shit done and achieving. However, my dominant energy is still feminine; my natural predominant way of existing is to fit in, support, receive, understand, commune, create, relate, connect, and nurture. I'm also emotive, intuitive, and sensitive, and because I've existed as a woman in a masculine, patriarchal society, I'm also *conditioned* to be these things. My value, like most women's, is perceived through my feminine qualities. But at the same time, I've been conditioned to fit my feminine self into a masculine system that rewards achievement and productivity—even though this system typically rewards the male gender for these things more than the female or nonbinary genders.

The implicit and explicit messages to me and women like me are to act like a lady, know my place, serve, be feminine—*and also* to deny these things if I want to be successful. Our society rewards success based on, well, how much we can get done and how much we can force our flowy, cyclical selves into a twenty-four-seven machine. In other words, do things like a man would, but since you're a woman, be extra nice and accommodating about it.

We were never meant to take what we are and cram it into a to-do list; we were never meant to have it all in the way we have been sold having it all. My recovery was about moving from one system that sold me a sick idea that to be a successful human I had to deny my intuition and gut sense, to a system that allowed me to use those feminine qualities to flourish. My recovery was about moving from a top-down approach that forces, to a bottom-up approach that grows. My recovery wasn't about more denial of my nature and my needs as a complete human being; it was about finally relenting to that nature and letting it thrive and lead.

FINDING A NEW WAY

The message of traditional recovery is that you need to shut up and listen. It says you need to go to ninety meetings in ninety days, adopt this label, know your place, read this book, work this program, do this thing. It says you don't know and you can't be trusted—the program is smarter than you are, all you have to do is work it and it will work.

Early on in my recovery, I didn't have the words to paint my opposition to the system, but I did have a scream inside me. The scream said, *If I do this thing, if I go this way, if I deny more of myself and my needs, if I fit myself into one more box that tells me I don't know best, if I have to sit down and shut up and listen one more time, I will disintegrate, implode.* The scream didn't want me to bushwhack my way through a masculine-centric structure. The scream didn't want to hear how I was seeing it wrong or that my ego was out of control. The scream wanted to be heard and yielded to. It wanted nothing more than to be taken seriously and to see what it actually needed for once, instead of what the system told me it needed.

And so I listened to it, and set out on my path, without the words, without the ideas or understanding I can so easily artic- ulate today. I set out knowing only that everything I'd been told I needed to do to be successful was wrong. To finally heal, I didn't need to deny myself further, I needed to lift up the parts of me that had been forever repressed and denied. I also didn't need a map created by a man; I needed my own damn map.

From the story I've laid out so far, it might sound as if I found Allen Carr's *The Easy Way to Control Alcohol* and questioned my drinking and that was that. But it didn't go like that at all. What did happen was, I stopped running. I had absolutely no plan, no quick fix, no scheduled way to perfection. I had only the hope and openness that come with facing the music, instead of turning it up louder or running faster into oblivion. Finding Carr was part of it—my way in—but then I found a therapist, and soon after that Eckhart Tolle, and it snowballed from there. The more I went forward, the more I wanted to live. The more I wanted to live, the more things presented themselves to me. I just had to keep going, I just had to keep my eyes open.

The pieces that laid the foundation of my recovery showed up in the oddest of places. I found Gabby Bernstein, a spiritual teacher whose work helped save my life, in *Bloomberg Business- week,* and at one of her talks, I found Kundalini yoga—a blend of spiritual and physical practices that incorporates movement, breathing techniques, meditation, and chanting—a practice that transformed me. In a business meeting, a co-worker convinced me his therapist was wonderful, so I made an appointment, and that therapist saw me through to sobriety. In a Kundalini training, I was paired with a woman who would become my third therapist, the one I credit with saving me (though let's be clear, I saved myself, as we all do). One of my friends, a doctor, introduced me to functional medicine, which helped me finally overcome bulimia. Another friend gave me a book about shadow work, another profound practice in my healing. And on it went like that; the pieces fell into place, and I fell into place. My healing became the point, *freedom* became the point, and I was hooked not on any specific result but on the idea of liberation, and the taste of finally having it as I moved forward, building the pieces of my recovery as I went.

This isn't how the story is supposed to go when you have a drinking problem. I'd seen enough portrayals of addiction on TV, and knew about enough people's relatives, to understand that life without alcohol is a life of deprivation, of white-knuckling; a paler set of colors. The fact that my experience was the opposite of that felt like cheating, like I was doing something wrong and it would all come tumbling down because it wasn't sad enough, or forced on me, or because I didn't feel deprived, or because it didn't resemble how you're supposed to do it. On the contrary, it was thrilling, self-directed, rich, and of my own design.

To many, my story and my experience seemed like an anomaly. Some people even suggested that I found success because I wasn't really sick in the first place, that I hadn't really been addicted to alcohol because my recovery was too fast, or because I didn't still want to drink. Either way, people wanted to know how I did it, and I typically said something like *Allen Carr!* Or *Meditation!* Or *Gabby Bernstein!* But I knew there was something more, a method, a reason it worked the way it did. It never really felt like simple luck.

I left my job to start Tempest Sobriety School, a recovery program tailored to the unique needs of women and other historically underrepresented folks in recovery. I had no idea where to start, but I was hell-bent on figuring out what exactly it was that had freed me so I could help other people repurpose it for themselves. Only I couldn't codify my recovery—it just looked a lot like reading books, going to therapy, meditating, and maybe buying a trampoline. That all changed in early 2014, when I was turned on to John Dupuy's book *Integral Recovery.* John, a therapist who'd spent decades working in the field of recovery, had once had the same problem I'd had. He knew there had to be another way beyond AA—he knew what existed wasn't enough and that there had to be some kind of template for recovery that put the person instead of an institution at the center, a template that allowed for a personal evolution. What John found was Ken Wilber's Integral Theory and eventually Wilber's AQAL (All Quadrants, All Levels) map, or Integral Map.

In the simplest terms, the Integral Map is a comprehensive map of human potential. It breaks down the whole human into four quadrants—It, Its, I, We—and says that in order for humans both to *grow up* and to *wake up*—to evolve—they need to nurture four areas of themselves: the "I" or the internal processes (psychology, beliefs, spirituality, existential meaning, knowledge, meditative states, etc.); the "We" or shared meaning (belonging, community, relationships); the "It" or physical body (nutrition and lifestyle, like exercise, or taking vitamins, or balancing gut health); and the "Its" or environmental structures (home environment/housing, career, health insurance). The map says that in order to heal and evolve, humans need to address pathologies and nurture growth in their whole life, and their whole life can be broken up into these four buckets.

I brought the concept of the Integral Map to the curriculum of the eight-week program that became the foundation of our sobriety school at Tempest. In looking at the map of my own journey, the answer to why my recovery had been so radically successful revealed itself to me. It wasn't that I had done things in the right order, it was that I had addressed all four buckets simultaneously. In terms of my "I" or my internal world, I'd worked with a therapist (psychology), found connection to my spirit (spirituality), changed my core beliefs about alcohol with Allen Carr's work (beliefs), studied addiction (knowledge), and found meaning and purpose in my life (existentialism). For my "It" or my body, I'd become a devoted meditator, a yoga practitioner, and I exercised; I also worked with functional nutritionists to balance my neurochemicals and heal my gut. When it came to my "Its" or environment, I'd changed my home so that it felt more like a sanctuary, changed my role at work (and eventually left that job entirely), organized my life, and created new habits and rituals to support sober me. And lastly, for my "We" quadrant or shared meaning, I'd built up a support team, ditched toxic relationships, made sober friends, joined yoga trainings and other organizations where I felt I belonged, worked on some of my most complicated and dysfunctional relationships, and learned to be alone without feeling worthless (i.e., I developed "shared meaning" with myself). In other words, it wasn't about what I did exactly, it was that I'd accidentally built an approach to healing that raised up every single corner of my life. The Integral Map codified my experience and allowed me to repurpose my own map into something larger, something that anyone could use to create their own way out of hell—and not just folks looking to change their relationship with alcohol, but all folks who wished to grow and thrive.

THE SIX ELEMENTS OF A
FEMININE-CENTRIC RECOVERY

A paternalistic or patriarchal recovery paradigm will start off with the assumption that you are compromised and defective; broken and in need of fixing; cannot be trusted with your own life decisions; and must follow an exact template, and rules, of someone else's making. This is a top-down approach, like the thumb of God descending from above to push you down into a little box. A feminine-centric recovery paradigm assumes that you are already whole and perfect; it is not you who is broken but the system; you are the expert on your own life, and therefore you make the template, and you make the rules. It is a bottom-up approach, which means that whatever systems exist are there to support your healing, decision making, and process.

Another distinction: The goal of the feminine-centric work is not—as it is conceptualized in some other programs—to be sober. Me telling you that your only task is to stop drinking and that's the point is yet another masculine, goal-centric, brownie-points-earning trope that places the prize above the process. The goal here is to create a situation you no longer have to escape, or a life you don't have to numb. The achievement of sobriety is not the point; it's a by-product of the work. The *work* is the point. Addiction is the hook that gets you in the door, and quitting is the catalyst to heal deeper wounds.

Through my work at Tempest, I've developed a simplified feminine-centric approach to healing. It brings in the concept of the holistic Integral Map, so every facet of your existence counts in your healing. It takes into account that our belief system around alcohol and its general importance needs to be blown; that the binaries established by AA (alcoholics versus normies) need to be tossed; that we need to address addiction in two distinct parts (the root causes and the cycle of addiction); that other societal factors and what we'd call "identity politics" belong in recovery; and that women and marginalized folks need to be built up, not broken down. (As an aside here, I don't think *anyone* needs to be broken down.)

The six elements listed below are not a checklist; they are a holistic framework to guide our evolution and healing. Existing within a patriarchal system means we've constantly equated our processing with the masculine; we are *conditioned* to think in a goal-oriented, linear way and approach most things as projects, as tasks to be completed. That is *exactly* how the Twelve Steps and the program of AA are structured: the goal is sobriety, and we progress through a list of assignments in order to achieve and maintain that goal.

To live another way, we have to approach our recovery a different way, one that honors our feminine qualities. We have to account for our tendency to cycle, our fluidity, our ability to do multiple things at once, our need for rest and regeneration; we have to honor our nature, instead of forcing our nature into the machine in order to achieve an output.

The six elements need not be practiced in order, and they don't have to be "checked off" like a task on a to-do list. They exist as guideposts. This doesn't mean there isn't a process; it just means we approach recovery with the understanding that it is a messy, evolving practice that unfolds in a way that meets us where we are. This means we relax into *what is* as we move through change and meet different challenges, and use these elements to support us through that evolution.

The goal of most recovery paradigms is to get you sober.

That's not the goal here. This paradigm isn't solely about absti-nence; it's about finding the lives we've got buried within us, and living those lives out loud. This is about finding the truest ver-sion of ourselves and letting that lead the way. Remember: this isn't so much about what we do, but how we do it.

1. Work with Our Core Beliefs
Our beliefs about anything flavor our experience of it. If we think quitting alcohol is some sort of punishment, that a sober life is impossible or a boring and endless void, then we are set-ting ourselves up for an experience that will feel punitive and pointless and ceaseless and depressing. If, however, we shift those perceptions and beliefs, and start to embrace a different idea—that recovery could be life-changing and emancipating; that the best is yet to come; that sobriety offers us everything alcohol promised—we're setting up a very different narrative.

The core belief system about alcohol, addiction, and sobriety is one shaped by AA and other patriarchal structures; it is a world in which we are powerless and chronically diseased, one drink away from being a drunk. In order to heal, we must chal-lenge everything we believe, everything we think we know. While most of this book is dedicated to blowing up that core belief system that was handed to us, Chapter 8 specifically lays out guiding principles to aid you in working with your core be-liefs about things that are typically confusing in recovery, such as power, surrender, selfishness, and guilt.

2. Weaken and Break the Cycle of Addiction
Instead of quitting cold turkey (or hyperfocusing on absti-nence), we focus on understanding, weakening, and eventually breaking the cycle of addiction. This means we engage with and reevaluate our concepts of will, work with our willpower, man-

age our energy, and develop new habits, routines, and rituals. Breaking the cycle of addiction also means facing cravings head on and learning to ride them out and eventually burn through them. Some of the things we do to weaken the addiction will be the same as what we do to weaken the root causes (such as meditation), while other practices are specifically geared toward breaking up the addiction (developing new rituals and habits). There is some overlap here, but healing root causes and overcoming addiction are distinct concepts. Chapters 9 and 10 are dedicated to helping you understand what keeps you stuck, and providing you with sample pathways to getting unstuck or breaking the cycle of addiction.

3. Add Healthy Coping Mechanisms

Regardless of how much work we do to heal our root issues, we will always need to deal with life, people, our family, assholes, emotions, pain, disappointment, anxiety, depression, loss, grief, and stress. So we need to not only work on the root causes and break the cycle of addiction, but also to replace our crappy coping mechanisms with healthy and constructive ones. Some examples of healthy coping mechanisms are: breathing techniques, spiritual practices, essential oils, chants and sound therapies, supplements, meditations, positive affirmations, and so on. We need to learn *how* to incorporate these healthy substitutes—not just know what we "should do." We need to create an existence where we *naturally* and *impulsively* reach for something that builds us up or reinforces us or heals us (a poem or mantra, a meditation, a cup of hot water with lemon) instead of something that just takes us down further (a cigarette, a text to an abusive ex-lover, a bottle of wine, a new pair of shoes we can't afford). Maybe this sounds obvious or even simple, but if you've been turning to unhealthy and destructive coping mechanisms to get by for your *entire life,* you'll need to learn an entirely different way of moving through the world. In Chapter 10, we'll dive into some strategies for collecting and implementing healthy coping mechanisms.

4. Get at the Root Causes

While we're working to break the cycle of addiction and adding healthy coping mechanisms, we must go deeper, to figure out what drove us outside ourselves in the first place. In other words, we need to intentionally deal with the root causes of our addiction. For me, the answer was never to just stop drinking, or to just stop sticking my finger down my throat, or to just stop weighing myself, or to just stop buying shoes in order to temporarily plug up some bottomless hole. The answer was to heal all those things that made it so desperately uncomfortable to be in my skin, so that I wouldn't *want* to do those things to myself. The answer was to learn to love and respect myself so much, I didn't *want* or *need* to do the harmful things anymore.

The reason you are turning to a substance to cope is as complicated as you are, and the only way you can get at what is causing you to need to numb out and escape is to look at the things that are driving that discomfort and to start adding solutions there. This means dealing with your fears head on, adding in meditation to start balancing out your anxiety and stress, working with your physical health, renegotiating (or healing) your trauma, creating a connection to something bigger than yourself, creating connections with other humans, finding joy, finding meaning, and really, just tuning in to an extreme mode of healing. You don't do this all at once, but you do need to get at the underlying causes and start doing things to ultimately make your body and your life a safe place for you to exist.

5. Practice Sobriety

One of my biggest criticisms of the rehab industry and AA is that success in sobriety is defined only by total abstinence. An abstinence-based program measures success in one dimension, which is the amount of sobriety you have under your belt. It assumes you must stop drinking immediately, or else you aren't really serious about getting better. In many ways, this is like expecting to run a marathon before you even start training for it. There is so much bullshit rhetoric about how drinking while trying not to drink is some sort of failing or weakness or flaw, some sign of eternal fucked-upness, or even evidence that we aren't taking it seriously enough.

The biggest problem with equating abstinence with success is that it immediately excludes people from treatment who can't quite get there. People are kicked out of rehab for using while trying to quit, or they are alienated and shamed for not living up to this philosophy of perfectionism. It creates too high a bar and ends up being counterproductive and disincentivizing to most people. The last thing you need when you're trying to quit drinking is stress, and being told that your success on this path is measured by your (perfect, seamless) abstinence, or that you must go back to square one if you drink while trying to quit, only makes you feel more helpless, more defeated, and therefore more in need of a drink.

When an individual joins Tempest Sobriety School, we don't even talk about quitting or abstinence until they're weeks into the program—we tell them to practice sobriety, or do stints of abstinence. We remind them: *You are in training and learning a new skill, and you need to give yourself the space to try and fail and try again, the way you would with any other great endeavor you attempt.* Practicing sobriety is exactly as it sounds; it's like any other thing you need to learn. You start where you are, you try, and when you fail or miss the mark—instead of beating yourself up or telling yourself you're a weak-willed piece of crap and always will be—you remember that success is built on failure, and all that's happened is you've gotten that much closer to where you're going, not further away.

There are two ways we practice sobriety in a feminine-centric model. What I've just described covers the first way, which is the practice of abstaining from alcohol and learning how to live without it. The second practice is a much more complex endeavor, where we learn to live sober, to show up in the middle of a deep, transformative process as newly sober people in a drinking world. While the first practice is basically spelled out in the paragraphs above and is touched on in Chapters 9 and 10, the second—living as sober folk—is covered in the remaining chapters of the book.

6. *Create a Recovery That Evolves as You Do*

Just like the Universe, we are constantly and forever expanding. We are not meant to adopt one belief system or one set of practices and stay there forever; we are meant to develop new belief systems, new practices and routines and rhythms and ways of being, wear them for a while, and eventually blow them up so we can grow into the next one. This is what Ken Wilber calls "transcending and including": as we grow, we transcend paradigms that once worked for us and keep the pieces of them that still work as we enter into new ones. This explains why sometimes AA works for a while and then stops, or why I moved from Bikram yoga to Vinyasa yoga to Kundalini yoga, or why some of us stop aligning with the religions we grew up with. Certain paradigms and constructs work for us until they don't.

You will evolve, you will change your mind, you will fall in love with philosophies and then one day wonder how you could have ever bought into that crap or been so naïve. For the same reasons that believing in Santa Claus serves a purpose until it doesn't, so do different frameworks you'll encounter. Use what feels right at the time it feels right, leave things behind when they no longer serve you. Trust the evolution of the process.

So many of us are raised to strive for perfection, as if being perfect were a worthier calling than the quest to be whole. I tried so very hard *my entire life* to be a good girl, a perfect girl, and yet I never could quite get there. The person I was supposed to be was always lurking right around the corner from where I was, on the other side of fixing everything that was bad about me. A feminine-centric recovery is the end of this madness. It isn't about fixing, or doing something exactly right or getting rid of your horrible bits. It is a reclamation of everything you lost along the way; a practice of gentleness; a return to wholeness that requires you to embrace every terrible and wonderful thing about yourself; the radical notion that you are already worthy, simply because you exist.

8

Working with Our Core Beliefs

You are entirely up to you.

—TESSA FORREST

In Rome a few summers ago, I stood in line at a fountain in Piazza Venezia on a sweltering hot July day. Tourists were swarming about, and I was waiting to refill an empty 1.5-liter bottle of water. I watched two men in front of me fill their bottles up completely without incident. When it was my turn, and the water in my bottle slowly inched past the halfway mark, the man behind me in line started to agitate. Arms folded, he *tssssked* and clucked, moved into my space, and talked to his friends while gesturing toward me. I was struck by two opposing thoughts. The first: to be mindful of the long line and take only what I needed; to be in service, to be selfless, to be like Jesus. The second: to take up space, to not apologize for what I needed or for god sakes *wanted,* and perhaps take more than I needed; to not give in to male intimidation, to not give any fucks about what those other people thought of me. I filled it up three-quarters of the way and walked on.

This might sound small or insignificant, but it wasn't. For me it was the crux of everything—that tension between the path of spiritual evolution, renunciation, and service, and the right to exist equally and fully as a human.

I took that fountain story with me back to the United States, and one day, maybe weeks or even months later when I couldn't get it out of my mind, I texted my friend Steve—a ridiculously handsome white venture capitalist who is also sober—and asked what he would have done. "I probably would have filled it up halfway." Easy, I thought, because he had the privilege of deciding to do so, without cost. He hadn't lived a life being told he was second; he'd lived a life being told he was first, and he could make decisions like that without it taking something from him, like his self-worth. Steve had the birthright to *decide,* and either way he would have won; I, on the other hand, had to make a *choice,* and either way I lost.

That story informed everything I was trying to create for myself and other people in the recovery world, recognizing how impossible it is to give up things we never had in the first place, but also how desperately important it is to renounce such things if we hope to transcend the human condition.

Pema Chödrön, a Tibetan Buddhist nun, says we have to learn to be both big and small at the same time. Big, as in we are worthy because we exist. Small, as in we exist to serve humanity. Such is the tension we navigate when coming at recovery with a culturally inflicted deficit of self-worth. We must learn to be big in a way we've never been big—we must claim our right to take up space, to say our words, to claim our desires. We must also learn to be small in a way we've never been small—to be in service, led not by our egos or by our desire for material goods or by our fears and aversions, but by our desire to be liberated from these things. And we must do both at the same time.

I've thought about this tension almost constantly since I began my recovery. I have a larger-than-life devotion to what I'd call a quest for spiritual purity, and I have an equally grand devotion to claiming my place in this world. I am tugged as much to own my success and my greatness as I am to claim my meekness, my humility. I am caught between two worlds, and navigating them is both exhausting and thrilling.

An addendum to Pema's advice based on my experience: Perhaps before we can learn to be both big and small at the same time, we first have to learn to be big. I've had to cultivate a sense of a right to fully exist in this world—to develop a sense of ego—to practice the relinquishment of it. I've had to learn to get big, in order to practice being small.

The core beliefs of a feminine-centric recovery model are geared toward building a whole and balanced sense of self— they are meant to help navigate the tension of learning to be big and small. The core beliefs are grouped into three sections: Self-Advocacy, Self-Trust, and Self-Practice.

SELF-ADVOCACY

Many of us have spent much of our lives putting our own needs and desires second, conditioned to believe that upholding boundaries or asking for what we need is wrong, selfish, or narcissistic. To be a woman is to be in service and never to ourselves. The five core beliefs that we address in this Self-Advocacy section—mothering ourselves, growing our agency, choosing guilt over resentment, setting boundaries, and cultivating a sense of power—are all foundational to developing a right to exist fully, and equally, as humans.

Mother Yourself

I used to call this practice extreme self-care, like extreme sports, except the goal is to go to the edge of taking care of yourself and isn't sponsored by Red Bull. I now call it *mothering ourselves*.

It's not merely assumed a woman's "nature" is to mother; it's her assigned responsibility in this world, and it's often where much of her perceived value lies. While women have made progress in redefining our roles in the last century, on the whole not much has changed: a hundred years of middle-class white women working outside the home and women having the right to vote don't undo millennia of conditioning.

We are not only expected to *be* mothers, we are expected to *mother*. And not just children, *everyone*. Which is another way of saying: You are skilled at putting everyone else's needs first because our society subtly and unsubtly tells you to. As a result, you are probably not only unskilled at putting yourself first, you are probably sick from putting yourself last.

No more. Recovery is where you are the first charge in your life. *You* are the baby

Here is the part of your life where you take three baths a day if you need to. Here is the part where ice cream is a complete meal, TV is a perfect babysitter, and wearing crystals in your lavender-scented bra is normal. Here is the part where you don't host Christmas, you don't return calls you don't want to return, and you wear the same thing to work that you wore to bed. This is the part where you sleep as much as you need to, lie on the floor staring at the ceiling as much as you need to, and basically do whatever you need to do as much as you need to do it. Here is where you finally learn to say, *I can't tonight, I'm watching Netflix.*

A note to mothers and caretakers: This is one of the hardest concepts and practices to navigate. I asked one of my friends, Whitney Combs—a mother of four who works full time at Tempest and had to navigate caretaking with self-caretaking while she was getting sober—what advice she has for mothering yourself while you are responsible for mothering other people. In her words, "Mothering yourself is particularly challenging if you have little ones who depend on you for everything. It sounds wild to think about prioritizing your self-care over caring for your littles. It may even sound impossible. But the thing is, you still have to do it. My first piece of advice here is to ask for help. Lean on your partner, your friends, your family, or anyone who's willing to step in to help out. If you have the means, pay for help. Get babysitters and house cleaners and anything else you can afford to take some stuff off your plate.

"The second thing I'll say is to lower those sky-high expectations of yourself as a caregiver. If you hate getting dinner on the table, feed the kids fast food or frozen dinners more often than you think is okay. If folding laundry takes up half your day, get two laundry baskets, one for clean clothes and one for dirty clothes, and stop folding that shit. Let go of the expectations you have around how much screen time is too much, and pop the kids in front of a show so you can meditate or take a bath. Give them treats for every five minutes they go without interrupting your morning routine [as described in Chapter 10].

"Finally, get creative with your self-care. Bring your kids into your morning routine if you can. Teach them to meditate with you. Have them color a picture of their feelings while you journal. Create an evening routine [see Chapter 10], like drinking hot tea and eating dark chocolate in your favorite spot on the couch, that allows the chaos to swirl around you rather than suck you in. Ask older kids to take a little more responsibility for household chores. You have to be extraordinarily determined to make this work. But it's worth it. The more time and energy you spend taking care of yourself, the more you have to give away."

Recovery requires us to stop prioritizing everyone and everything else and listen to our own needs so that we are better equipped to handle the stress of modern-day multitasking. Act like a person who needs to heal—because *you are* and *you do*. Take care of yourself, put your oxygen mask on first, and to hell with anyone who tries to tell you you're selfish.

Grow Your Agency

In his book on renegotiating trauma, *The Body Keeps the Score*, Bessel van der Kolk defines agency as "the technical term for the feeling of being in charge of your life: knowing that you have a say in what happens to you, knowing that you have some ability to shape your circumstances."

In other words, having agency means we feel empowered to conduct our own affairs. In recovery, especially early recovery, we tend to have a deep disconnect with our agency, and our care providers, therapists, friends, family, and even other people in recovery often reinforce this disconnect. People think they know how we should heal, and they can feel threatened and then challenge us when we assert that *we* know what we need.

Example: You're in couples therapy, and your partner wants you to quit drinking. They and your therapist agree that if you were really serious about getting well, you'd go to rehab.

Example: Your sister writes you an email when you're ten months sober, telling you that you're kidding yourself and you need "real help" because you didn't do the Twelve Steps.

Example: You decide that AA isn't for you, and a woman you've been to coffee with once after a meeting tells you she'll save a seat for you at the meeting when your way of doing things ultimately fails.

While these scenarios are more common when the individual seeking treatment is severely addicted (where people are either coerced into treatments they don't agree with or are denied care when they oppose parts of the treatment or fail to abstain), not being trusted with our own decisions, or even having our capacity to make decisions questioned, is a double blow to women, who are generally not trusted with their bodies and life choices. Women of color or queer or trans women with addiction have it even worse—to be believed that we know what's best, and to make choices about how we will or won't recover, is a privilege, and one typically conferred upon white cis men of means.

None of this is to say that other people don't have insights to offer—they do. Other people's feelings (especially those who are closest to us and suffer as a result of our addiction and substance abuse) are valid, and we *will* need help and direction and advice from professionals, peers, friends, strangers, teachers, and those who have gone before us. But a fundamental principle I know to be true is that we have to be at the center of, and in control of, our recovery. The process of healing, especially for those of us who have been marginalized throughout our lives, requires us to exercise our personal power, perhaps for the first time. The act of reclaiming our power *is* the healing.

Choose Guilt

There's no way for me to explain this one without sounding like a complete asshole.

This one time my mom and I went to Dallas to go see the George W. Bush art exhibit on display at his library, as one does.

I'd driven from Los Angeles to Fresno to pick her up so we could fly out of LAX together, and we spent a glorious four days together in Dallas. We ate a lot of good food and laughed and shopped and did all the things. I was planning at the end of the trip to fly back to L.A. with her, then drive her to the train station in Bakersfield, a five-hour round-trip.

However, as these things go, I'd put off all my work and my life for that week in order to be fully present with my mom during the trip. I wasn't meditating or doing yoga, practices that are very much my medicine. That pile-up, along with the fact that I can be around a member of my family for only forty-eight hours at a time, culminated in what I can only describe as a nuclear meltdown; I'd given too much of myself without taking care of myself and I'd hit my breaking point.

My mom offered to take the bus to Bakersfield to save me the five hours, and oh my God, I put that woman on a bus so fast it would have made your head spin. I was the Flash.

Let me remind you that my mom has also had eight hip replacements and could barely walk, and the bus driver didn't really seem to understand that he'd have to help her get her bag in Bakersfield. The sight of the bus driving off and my mother's little body jerking helplessly in the front seat *will forever be singed into my memory.* I still have guilt. Massive, soul-crushing guilt.

But—and here is where it gets important—my only alternative to that guilt was doing something I didn't have the capacity to do, to the detriment of my mental health and recovery, that would inevitably make me resent my mom. Here is where I chose guilt over resentment.

A lot of times when we are holding a boundary—especially one important for our sobriety, mental health, and emotional well-being—it won't be as simple as not returning a call or declining to explain why we don't drink or aren't going to a party.

Sometimes we will need to send our kids away to a relative's while we get our shit together, or decide not to visit our abusive father at Christmas even though he's on his deathbed, or insert any moral dilemma here where we are confronted with choosing what we need to do to not drink, versus what we need to do to demonstrate we are really good humans.

Guilt is always preferable to the thing that might give you brownie points for being a good person but ruin your mental health. Choose guilt over resentment, because guilt is a natural part of life, a thing we can work with and absolve ourselves of, while resentment is something that we heap on other people who weren't asking for it anyway.

Set Clear Boundaries and Embrace the Word No

When I first started working full time on Tempest, I struggled to find a balance between self-care, recovery, and the demands of early entrepreneurship. I was burning through my savings, writing blogposts, reading books by internet-rich white men and life-coach-rich white women who'd figured it all out, living in my pajamas and out my best depressed life, working from the moment I got up until the moment I passed out on a business that seemed insane to most everyone I tried to explain it to. I was hell-bent on keeping up all the rituals and practices that had gotten me sober in the first place. I was also trying to appease every single human being who needed something from me. I'd been building boundaries in recovery, but I still didn't feel entitled to those boundaries nor use them consistently, especially when it came to work.

About a year into my sobriety, my therapist once asked me about someone in my life who demonstrated good boundaries. My mind checked to earlier that day, when my ex-boyfriend/ex-boss had run into our coffee meeting ten minutes late and left on the dot to make his next appointment. I'd always marveled at his ability to not give a fig about how that abruptness came off, or rather, how his boundaries just existed without apology. I explained the encounter to my therapist, who told me that I too could possess that power. I remember so clearly at the time thinking, *No way could I own that much of myself and my time—only men and bitches can really pull that off.*

Check to today, where that power is mine. I don't say yes to things I don't want to do, I don't reply to most text messages, and I leave when a meeting is over even if the conversation is half-finished. I don't eat my own discomfort to appease others, and I don't apologize for any of it. I live within my boundaries and my *no,* and I don't suffer people's negative reactions.

Saying no to people who want you to say yes, and upholding your boundaries with people who are used to you having none, will at first feel terrible, like death, and it is a death of sorts—the death of the part of you that thinks you have to violate yourself to make it in life or be valued. You will most likely be surrounded by people who are used to you being accommodating or passive, and at first they will feel threatened by you asserting your boundaries. This is okay. In time they'll get used to it, just like in time you'll get used to understanding that if other people act like assholes when you say no, that it isn't about you—it's about them. Protecting yourself from demands you can't or won't accede to is a practice, and one you'll get better at over time. But it's one you absolutely must engage in. Lastly and most important: If you want people to respect your boundaries, you have to respect theirs.

Cultivate a Sense of Power

Step One of the Twelve Steps is "We admitted we were powerless over alcohol—that our lives had become unmanageable." I agree that the only way to control alcohol is to remove it from the picture, and to stop trying to make it work for us in a way it never will. What I have a problem with is how much that word *powerless* has been appropriated and smeared all over the entire experience of recovery.

An example: I once tweeted the Yogi Bhajan quote "You are very powerful provided you know how powerful you are." To that, a very nice man from the fellowship replied something like I was going to die and burn in hell unless I admitted how powerless I was. It's a concept that has been carved out of its original context and used to beat everyone into a state of humility and right-sized-ness, and it's the opposite of helpful for many of us.

Again, those of us who are women and/or part of some historically marginalized group—those of us who are not straight white cis men—will not come to this affair feeling like we are particularly brimming with power. Often we turn to substances *because* we feel powerless, because existing in a world that we were told from birth is not ours to exist in in the way we need to feels terrifying and limiting and defeating. Which is to say that adopting an idea of powerlessness runs the very real risk of re-traumatizing us, since that was what made us sick in the first place. Countless articles, studies, and texts prove that acquiring a sense of power—not diminishing what little we have—is the foundation of a meaningful recovery.

Power is a tricky thing. In general, we as a society have come to believe that power is external: how much influence we have, how much money we make, how much prestige we have. We equate power with leaders, with the rich, with the famous. This isn't real power—it's reliance on something outside ourselves to make ourselves *feel* powerful. It's patriarchy's definition of power. And for that reason, it's not just a few people who are confused about it—the *world* is confused about it. All you have to do is flip through a business magazine or scroll through a Kardashian's Instagram account to remember what we worship. This grasping of something we *think* equals power is a hallucination that only ensures we are kept out of our true power. This illusion is what you are giving up or, at least, waking up to.

Real power doesn't come from having a million followers, good hair, a Louis Vuitton purse, a new car, a new home, a title, a partner, or anything that can be weighed, measured, or acquired. Real power is the thing you've always had inside you. Real power doesn't need to be demonstrated or boasted. Real power is the ability to be in your skin, to know who you are, to know you will always be okay. Real power comes from your gut and your heart and your courage and your bravery and your love. Real power can never be taken away from you and never lost once it's found. It's the kind of power that people like Nelson Mandela and Mahatma Gandhi and Martin Luther King, Jr., and Rosa Parks and the Dalai Lama all had or have—a quality within unaffected by outer circumstances, an eternal flame that cannot be touched. I repeat Yogi Bhajan's words here: *You are very powerful, provided you know how powerful you are.*

I imagine you're wondering where you even begin to acquire this kind of power. My answer is, by having enough self-awareness to question your relationship with alcohol; and by using that self-awareness to drive more self-discovery. In other words, you are already on your way to claiming your real power.

SELF-TRUST

In his book *Reinventing Organizations*, Frederic Laloux says, "Life is not asking us to become anything that isn't already seeded in us." We are born with all the truth; it's not out there, it's *in us*. But then we encounter a world that tells us we are wrong, and the voice from within that knows everything we actually need to know gets written over by a society that wants us to become something else—to fit in, follow the rules, conform. By the time most of us get to adulthood—especially those of us who come from a history of societal oppression—we have lost all capacity to listen to ourselves, to trust ourselves. We seek answers outside ourselves because we are told time and again that our innermost intelligence is wrong. The three core beliefs that follow—trust your gut, know what you can't fuck with, try everything and show up empty—are intended to lead you back to your all-knowing self.

Trust Your Gut

A month into sobriety, I stood before a piece of art in a tattoo shop in San Diego. It was a picture of a woman-tree; her human legs became roots that drove into the earth with an intricate, visible system; her arms turned into branches that supported the world. It was captivating, mostly because of the quote pasted below it: "We already know everything, we have only to remember."

Imagine that, we already know everything. We have all the answers buried inside us, and our issue isn't that we *just don't know,* it's that we *just don't know we know.* Yes, the process of recovery is about seeking and gaining knowledge from outside sources, but all that is just another route to finding a truth we already know. This is a process of "re-covery" or recapturing a part of ourselves that has been dislocated. It's unlearning all the shit we've been fed that's made us forget ourselves, and reclaiming who we really are. You are the wisest person of all in this process, so you have to learn to trust what your gut is saying to you.

So, what is gut sense?

We all have had—at some point in our lives—a sense of knowing something is wrong or right, not by thinking with our minds but by *feeling it*. When I was twenty-one, I was hired by the local Maaco to sell car paint. My job on paper was to drive around to different fleet owners and "estimate" paint jobs and sell the quote, but my real job was to be a twenty-one-year-old piece of ass with a clipboard.

Everything in my body said no to doing this, but my $300-a-day paycheck said yes! Gut sense is the part that made me vomit foam and quit three days later; mind sense is that I still remember how much money I would have made. Similarly, when I tried AA, my gut sense screamed, *This is not for you;* my mind sense had me believe that there was something wrong with me for feeling that way.

Gut sense is a deep *knowing;* it's physical and without explanation. Mind sense is just *thinking*. Gut sense will tell you to quit your job because you get hives on Monday mornings, and mind sense will remind you that you don't have another one lined up. Gut sense will tell you to GTFO of an Uber because something is off with the driver, and mind sense will tell you that would be rude.

You are already wise. Learn to trust yourself and *feel* what's right for you, and then stick up for what's right for you. What will work for you won't work for the next person because the next person doesn't have your life, experiences, beliefs, or feelings, or your emotional, energetic, or physical body.

Know What You Can't Fuck With

I was once involved with a man who had a real sweet habit of endlessly texting me about sleeping with me, and also a really sweet habit of (almost) never *actually* sleeping with me. For years we would cycle through the same thing: I'd text him, we'd talk about how horny we were for each other while trading naked pictures of ourselves, the texting would go on for days, I'd invite him to come over, he wouldn't want to, I'd get upset, he'd call me a psycho hose beast, I'd block him in my phone. Inevitably, two weeks later we'd repeat the entire scenario. We did this for *four years,* and we had sex maybe ten times. He was a horrible, terrible person, and yet there I was every few-ish weeks, *missing* him and thinking that maybe if I took another angle with him, we'd get it right. Eventually it became clear to me that the only way to change the situation was to stop messing with him, stop trying to manipulate the relationship, stop trying to fix it or make it work. Finally I understood: this man was not for me. This man was not mine.

If you think four years is a long time, consider that some of us spend decades trying to do the same thing with alcohol. We look for that third door of moderation or ease, and it calls us a psycho hose beast and so we chill and wait a few weeks; then we try again.

Hear me on this: There are some things you can fuck with. There are some things you can't. Know the difference.

Things I can't fuck with: alcohol; pot; cigarettes; sticking things down my throat to puke up my food; diets of any kind or restriction of food; starvation; counting calories; men named Francesco; some very specific tall, bearded, emotionally unavailable men who live in San Francisco; probably all tall, bearded, emotionally unavailable men who live in San Francisco; Swedish fish; cheese plates (gas!); "all you can" anything; Tinder, Bumble, Hinge, Match, OkCupid, and all yet-to-be-invented dating apps; sleep deprivation; casual sex; Vicodin (I get migraines); perfume (I get migraines); gossiping; meat.

Things I can fuck with: coffee; gluten; dairy; mayonnaise; credit cards; not having renter's insurance; a seven-hour Netflix binge; two hot yoga classes back to back; casual making out; traveling without an itinerary; social media; scary movies; drinking unfiltered water; basically all sugar but Swedish fish; Diet Coke; all men not named Francesco; so much fizzy water it hurts.

What I am saying is I know the difference between the things that take me down into a hole—the things that would destroy me—and the things that might not be great for me but I do anyway. Because there is a difference.

Know the difference between things that might not be great for you, and things that take you down and keep you stuck and bring out your worst and get in the way of your best life. Know them and stay the fuck away from them. The world is full of both terrible and good things that will make you just as happy and leave you less destroyed and consumed.

Try Everything and Show Up Empty

I'm a certified yoga instructor and a certified control freak. I'm also a judgmental bitch (with a heart of gold). Which is my way of telling you that when I take a yoga class from basically any-one but a chosen few, I judge, judge, judge. I also learned a long time ago that walking into a yoga class thinking you aren't going to learn anything is a great way to not learn anything in a yoga class. I have to remind myself constantly to empty out when I'm on my mat.

Check to: a time right after the 2016 election, when I went to a yoga class in order to *not* think about Donald Trump, which meant that the teacher immediately started to talk about Don-ald Trump. I groaned, audibly voicing my discontent, and as the teacher directed us to get into plank pose and then started talk-ing about her friend who wanted to move to Canada, I had to restrain myself from groaning again. I remember it vividly because I considered walking out and somehow caught myself and reminded myself to get over it, to empty out, to let myself learn something from her. Really, truly, this was what I told myself because most of the time in my head I am a sensible, diplomatic adult who wonders WWJD.

So there I am simultaneously hating this yoga teacher and trying to be like Jesus and sweating from the plank pose when she says, "So I said to my friend, 'Does this suck? Does this hurt? Do you want to run to Canada? Good, because this is when the real work begins.'" Then she pauses and asks us the same: "Does this plank pose suck? Does this hurt? Do you want to run? Good, because this is when the real work begins." I mean: Mind. Blown. From her I learned one of the most profound teachings that I employ in my work today—that when we taste discomfort and want to run is when the actual work starts.

Most of the time we show up like I do in a yoga class, full of our own ideas and judgments. Sometimes we are so full, we can't hear some of the more profound lessons and teachings. To find what works for you or to learn new things on a path of recovery, you have to empty yourself of the things you think you know. You have to be willing to try things you normally wouldn't try, and you also have to allow yourself to experience them and make decisions based on those experiences. You have to create the space for change to occur and allow yourself to be changed.

You don't have to like everything you try, or fill yourself up with shit that, upon investigation, is just totally not for you. Discernment should come from experience, not just judgment or what your friend Sally said about Kundalini awakenings or what your uncle Ken said about The Fellowship.

Another thing to note about trying new things and showing up empty: Sometimes doing something weird or outside your comfort zone will be terrible. But even those experiences are part of the path; they help you figure out what isn't for you, and they sometimes also challenge you in the places you need to be challenged. My experiences in AA were mostly horrible, but they gave me some of my deepest lessons on this path. Being told I would drink again if I didn't work the steps and choosing not to believe that gave me a certainty I wouldn't have had if I'd not met it head on.

Last but not least, remember you get to take parts of things you like and leave the rest. Be careful to not throw out an entire body of work or experience or program because you disagree with a facet of it or even a lot of it. Make your journey your own, built from all the experiences you've had along the way.

SELF-PRACTICE

The last set of core beliefs are all about Self-Practice, or the practices necessary to claim the self. They move through how to use willingness, surrender, commitment, and abundance thinking, as well as how to approach co-occurring (multiple) addictions, and navigate the overwhelm that can come from feeling like there is so much broken or so much to fix. They end with the ultimate point of all this work: how to treat it as your great adventure. These are some of the more active core beliefs, and taken with those related to self-advocacy and self-trust, they can set you up to build an empowered, constructive recovery.

Willingness Is Phase Two

Like all great teachings, this core belief starts with an episode of *South Park* called "Gnomes." In it, a roving band of Underpants Gnomes break into people's homes at night and steal underwear. At some point in the episode, the boys track the Gnomes down to their underground lair to recover their stolen underwear. Hilarity ensues, and the Gnomes explain they steal underwear in order to make a profit. The business plan consists of three stages.

Phase One. Steal underpants.
Phase Two. (?)
Phase Three. Make profit.

The punchline is there is no Phase Two, which is why the Gnomes aren't wildly rich.

So let's say that you've decided you want to quit drinking. That's Phase One. Phase Three is: Never drink again. Phase Two is missing, because even though you (or some part of you) *wants* to make this grand sweeping change, getting your cognitive, emotional, and survival brain in on it isn't so simple. Those parts of you have all kinds of arguments, objections, fears, attachments, and reasons why you shouldn't make this change.

Willingness is the thing that bridges the gap between where we are and where we want to go. It is the way through; it is what we use when we want to say, "I can't," or "It's impossible," or "I'm not ready." It allows for the "can't" and the "not ready" to exist at the same time as the desire for something more.

So how does it work? Let's say you know you have to change your drinking habits, but everything in you is saying no way. Fine. Let that be where you are—let that resistance exist—and use the statement "I am *willing* to be ready," or "I am *willing* to believe I can change," or "I am *willing* to trust that I can be happy without alcohol." Take out *willing to* and you have: I am ready; I believe I can change; I trust that I can be happy without alcohol. See the difference? Not only do the latter statements feel impossible, they also don't feel true, and then we feel defeated before we even begin. When you add "willing to" before any aspirational statement, you let yourself off the hook of having to be somewhere you aren't at the moment, all the while still keeping the north star of your intention.

Willingness is an energy, a vibration; it is a destination in itself. It says, "I don't know how to do this thing, but I am going to try." It says, "This right here is enough," and then it tells you that you can rest here, *be* here. It says, "I am open to something different while I honor where I am." Mostly it says, "I am going to allow parts of me to move slower while I take this leap forward."

Willingness is the word you turn to when you are stuck, when you are in the dark and you can't see a way out. Willingness is always the way forward, and by operating from this place, you are signaling that you are ready, that you are open. Willingness carries us through the hard parts, the fuckups, the letdowns, and the dips. When you simply remember that willingness will take you where you long to be, you can relax into the process and trust that it will all work out in your favor.

Surrender Is Not a Four-Letter Word

I come from a long line of proud, stubborn assholes. We are a people who don't give up, don't give in, don't ask for help, and for sure don't show our weakness. Which is why, I imagine, I'd always considered the word *surrender* to be blasphemous. Surrender was never a possibility to consider; it wasn't something self-respecting, self-reliant folk like me do—we scheme around and bulldoze through whatever stands in our way. That all changed, abruptly, on that day in 2012 when I finally ran out of options and did the thing I thought I could never do—concede.

In *A Return to Love,* Marianne Williamson says, "Until your knees finally hit the floor, you're just playing at life, and on some level you're scared because you know you're just playing. The moment of surrender is not when life is over. It's when life begins." It is entirely cliché, but this was exactly my experience. The moment I finally let my knees hit the floor was when I finally stopped playing at life, and every bit of good that's come to me since then stems from this reversal of opinion on surrender.

Surrender is the strongest, most subversive thing you can do in this world. It takes strength to admit you are weak, bravery to show you are vulnerable, courage to ask for help. It's also not a one-time gig; you don't just do it once and move on. It's a way of existing, a balancing act. For me, it looks like this: I pick up the baton and I run as far as I can, and I hand it over when I'm out of breath. Or actually, maybe it's like: I'm running with the baton, but the Universe is holding on to the other half of it, and we have an agreement that I'll figure out the parts I can and hand over the parts I can't.

In a practical sense, surrender just means that when something isn't working, I don't force it. When something is out of my control, I stop trying to control it. And when the shit comes pouring down, I know I'll survive it. It means: I know everything is happening exactly as it should at just the right time, and I no longer believe I'm responsible for everything in the world. Something bigger than I am has my back, and I'll always be okay. No matter what.

I cannot sing the praises of this practice enough. Life no longer feels precarious, or about to crumble—even when it is, in fact, crumbling. By surrendering to whatever is unfolding and by accepting what is, by giving up on the outcome and allowing life to flow the way it's meant to, by stepping out of your own way and letting the natural order take the lead, you not only get a break from the exhaustion of having to control everything, but you also get to experience life, instead of what you think life owes you. (Hint: What life wants to give us is infinitely better than what we think it owes us.)

This Is Not About Deprivation

I've heard a lot of smart people say again and again that they "lost their drinking privilege"—as if they'd lost their membership to a club on account of bad behavior. Let's get clear on this: It is not a privilege to "be able to" ingest a substance that's sabotaging your health and spirit and life in a hundred different ways. Being able to tolerate a poison and all its nasty effects is not something to envy. No one "gets" to drink; they're duped into it.

Having issues managing alcohol or not being able to tolerate it or suffering severe consequences from ingesting it—these are invitations to show up for your life. They are the opposite of deprivation: *They are opportunity presenting itself.*

This doesn't mean you're going to be walking around just thrilled and delighted that alcohol isn't part of your future. There is a real grieving period involved for some of us, and that grief is real. But hanging out on Deprivation Island is a total motherfucker, and after a while it will work against you, reinforcing the idea that life isn't fair, and that drinking is some sort of prize.

You get to decide whether you'll invest in the deprivation story—how much you tell yourself that no longer drinking is *the worst thing,* and how much suffering you endure from living that story in your head, how much you make it true—or invest in the bigger story: that this just might be the best thing that ever happened to you.

What you're doing here is not a diet, and it's not an extreme ascetic practice, any more than quitting cigarettes is either of those things. This is an invitation to stop doing something that *billions of people* have been conned into thinking they're supposed to do.

This is an invitation to a better everything.

Commitment, Not Discipline

Merriam-Webster defines the word *discipline* as "control gained by enforcing obedience or order; orderly prescribed conduct or pattern of behavior; self-control." Its secondary definition is one word: "punishment." Which makes sense, because often when we say we need more discipline, we mean we need to punish ourselves into pulling something off.

Most of us will draw a connection between our lack of discipline and our status at work, credit score, calorie intake, alcohol intake, lack of exercise regimen, and inability to stick to [everything you've not been able to stick to]. If we could only control our unruly, cyclical, temperamental selves—if we just had more *discipline*—we'd be so much better off. We wouldn't text him/her/them back or say things we don't mean or eat entire cakes or miss our workouts or quit our keto diets or eat carbs or eat gluten or run up our credit cards to buy those shoes. If we had more discipline we'd be good and perfect. Discipline is basically a witch's bridle—a tool that exists for the sole purpose of keeping us out of our power and in shame.

Commitment, however, is the complete opposite of discipline, in that it blossoms from one's own will; we commit to things we want to do, not things we're supposed to become. It is also more forgiving than discipline. If we are committed to quitting drinking and we drink a glass of wine, discipline will tell us that we must pay and atone and repent and go back to zero. Commitment, on the other hand, will tell us that we veered off track but can recommit now. Commitment calls us "sweetie" and beckons us forward; discipline calls us "lazy" and kicks us in the vagina. Commitment has intention and doesn't worry about the result so much as the action and the journey; discipline has one goal in mind and will achieve it no matter the cost. Commitment loves us and wants the best for us and cheers for us like we're friends; discipline basically says, "I will cut you, bitch, if you fuck this up."

Commit to showing up when you fail, commit to trying, commit to staying with yourself as you attempt something new. But please, for the love of God, do not try and discipline (punish) yourself into abstinence.

Throw the Kitchen Sink at It

There is no one thing that will help you move beyond the need to rely on alcohol—there is no silver bullet. There are only a lot of things we throw at the wall and see what sticks.

It is not a matter of disciplining yourself into doing everything exactly right. It is a process of leaning toward love, creating subtle shifts, and doing lots of little and big things that ultimately have a cumulative effect. You will not be successful because you meditate for a certain amount of time every day, read the right books, find the right therapist, go to a hundred meetings, write a thousand pages of gratitudes, or do a thousand sun salutations. You will be successful if you do whatever you can in your power to heal yourself. You will be successful if you consistently return to your intention, to your *commitment* to your own liberation.

Throw the kitchen sink at it, and do whatever you can do to quit drinking. Listen to beautiful music. Eat good food. Be around good people. Meditate five hundred different ways for as many minutes as you can. Try yoga. Get a psychic. Dance naked. Get massages. Drink water. Sing in the shower. Remember to smile (but only because smiling is healthy, not because some douchebag tells you to). Read good books. Read good quotes. Learn about neuroscience! Run through fields or city streets. Scream when you need to scream. Cry when you need to cry. Repeat New Agey mantras. Hug yourself. Hug someone else. Listen to podcasts. Find spiritual teachers. Find places you belong. Find other people who are going through what you are. Go to weird festivals. Go to church. Get your hair done. Pet your cat. Write yourself love letters. Get acupuncture. Watch Oprah. DO WHATEVER IT TAKES.

Most important: Be scrappy about it. Do not let your perfectionism tell you this needs to be a perfect, list-checking process.

One Thing at a Time

This is pretty simple. If you have myriad crap you'd like to change, start with the thing that is getting in your way the most. In 2012 I was bulimic; addicted to pot, cigarettes, sugar, coffee, and alcohol; nearly six figures in debt; a raging codependent; stuck in a job that ate me up; depressed and anxious; and lots of other things. For me, alcohol was the first thing that had to go, and it was the only thing I could realistically focus on. It was the thing that was costing me the most, and it fed a lot of the other behaviors: bingeing and purging, smoking, spending, and so on. There was no way I could work on anything else first, and no way I could work on giving up everything at once.

A lot of us will come into this thinking that we need to be all the *-frees*: alcohol-free, drug-free, tobacco-free, sugar-free, meat-free, dairy-free, caffeine-free, debt-free, drama-free, gluten-free. The problems with this are at least twofold. First, trying to be all the *-frees* is just a different address in hell. This shouldn't be about perfection or some unattainable bullshit we see on Instagram; this is about freedom from what makes us feel sick and powerless. The second and bigger issue with going for all of it at once is: Doing everything means doing nothing.

Start with what's killing you, with the intention of health, not perfection.

For me, the alcohol went first. Nine months later I stopped sticking my finger down my throat. A month after that, the pot and the cigarettes went away, and two months after that, I left my job. (It's important to note that my pace was relatively fast; your timeline should be *your* timeline.) The things I did to quit alcohol supported me in changing other habits and behaviors. It took many more years to get my taxes in order and my credit score up and my debt paid off. I still struggle with codependency, but the drama that came with it dropped off at some point. Being caffeine-free and sugar-free, things I once thought would be the pinnacle of success in sobriety, are ideas I've ditched along the way. All this has come in time, on the schedule that was sane for me. One step, next step, next step.

Start small. Do the first thing. Do the next thing. Remember the work you do on the first thing transfers to the next thing. Getting out of my seventeen-year relationship with bulimia was possible only because I learned a lot of things while I was getting out of my twenty-year relationship with booze.

Get Excited

There was a time in all our lives when we thoroughly enjoyed life without alcohol. For me, it was up until about age sixteen. I didn't need alcohol to be with my friends, watch a movie, go to a party, or do anything—because I didn't know I was supposed to need alcohol to do these things. Allen Carr was the first to suggest that I could go back to this pre-alcohol life in *The Easy Way to Control Alcohol,* and this is exactly what happened to me. I don't sit around thinking things would be better with wine or lamenting that I can't drink. Alcohol to me is the same as cigarettes are to people who've never smoked, something that exists but something I don't consider.

Imagine what this means for you. No more hangovers, no more forgotten conversations, no more mystery receipts. Your dinner bills are less than half of what they used to be, you get your Sundays back, you don't hook up with people you otherwise wouldn't. Your depression lessens, your anxiety lessens, and your self-worth and self-confidence finally have room to grow. Your skin is better, your liver is better, and you stop having to wonder if you're drinking slower or faster than everyone at the table. You are no longer stuck in the fraud that everyone around you is stuck in—you are free.

This is not a consequence. This is an upgrade.

It's a Life Practice, Not a Life Sentence
There's an idea that we are stuck forever in recovery when we stop drinking. This thought depressed me when I first started thinking I needed to quit. It felt like I was always going to be "sick," always an "addict," always in recovery from an incurable, relapsing "disease." I imagined a white-knuckled existence on the other side of fun, one day at a time, with a paler set of colors, with those other people who "can't anymore" either.

When you are breaking an addiction, you are actually fixing the things that were leading you to addiction. And because the things leading you to addiction are *life* things—relationships, trauma, stress, anxiety, depression, bad jobs, lack of purpose, poor health—you'll need to use tools that help you to fix your life problems: meditation and yoga, healthy coping mechanisms and therapy, nutritious food and learning your own boundaries and finding purpose. My friend John Dupuy, author of *Integral Recovery*, calls this Life Practice, and he notes that all humans can benefit from the work we do breaking our addictions. I agree with John. I think if everyone had to go through what my friends and I had to go through to quit drinking, the world wouldn't be such a fucked-up place.

Today I don't think of myself as being in recovery from illness. I think of myself as being on a mission to recover the truest version of myself, and as being in recovery from long exposure to a sick society that actively wants to destroy all that is good about me. Consequently, I get to do a bunch of rad things to manage life better, so I don't need to escape. The weirdest twist to my story is that I don't *want* the work to end, I don't *want* to stop this process. My friend Meggan Watterson said it perfectly on my podcast: "May I never reach the point where I think I am done." I love that I will never be done.

The last seven years have seen me evolving past needing alcohol to cope and then diving into realms of self-development I never thought were accessible to me. Quitting drinking is just the baseline of sobriety for me. What this Life Practice has meant for me is better relationships, a better sense of self, better sex, better boundaries, better skin, more money, more time, more joy, more love. It's given me purpose and fullness, and it means I have a lifetime ahead of me to evolve. I am ripe with possibility because I cracked open, and that is thrilling.

As you are going along, think of this not so much as things you are doing for sobriety, but rather the things you are doing to have a really big life—because that is exactly what you are doing.

Treat This as Your Great Adventure

In his book *Buddha Brain,* Rick Hanson suggests that humans, through evolution, developed three main strategies for survival: creating separations, maintaining stability, and approaching opportunities and avoiding threats. In other words, in order to survive, we create unique and distinguishable personas, cling to the known, and do what feels safe at least and opportunistic at best.

Most of us don't really think of it this way, but when we quit drinking, we explode this entire system; we trash every known strategy that defines our means of survival. Our curated ideas of self—*I'm a drinker* or *I'm a wine connoisseur* or *I work hard and play hard* or *I'm the one who closes down the bar* (there are lots when it comes to alcohol and identity)—go out the window, thereby throwing ourselves into the vortex of *Who am I?* The known systems in place that support us—the routine at the end of the day or the circle of friends we drink with or the partner we meet at a bar and match drinks with or the family where we are the perfect one or the messed-up one—are disrupted, changed, or abandoned. Our formed sense of self and our systems disappear as we plunge into the unknown.

Recently, I got a facial from one of my childhood best friends. It was November 2018, my mom was sick, and I was a mess. Because being sober means my coping mechanisms are mostly spas and yoga classes instead of whiskeys and spliffs, I made an appointment for someone, anyone, to touch my face for ninety minutes. I hadn't seen Julie in years, and we don't really talk unless we run into each other when I'm back home visiting, but we do follow each other on social media; running into her is always like accidentally running into 1991.

A lot has happened since I got sober. In many ways, my life is hardly recognizable from what it was, and I don't really stop to appreciate this. It's almost like there's so much to do, so much lost time to make up for, that I just don't pause to consider how vastly different it all is or how vastly different *I* am, or to think about what I've gained, or to notice what I've lost. Things change, and I adjust—I am preternaturally good at marching forward without looking back. It also, by this point, feels entirely normal to do what I do for a living: to share myself openly with the world, to be who I am, as I am, on display. But from the outside—especially to those who have known me my whole life—what's changed is very obvious.

At the end of the facial, Julie sat on the table with her arms around me and told me she was proud of me. She'd been following me closely from afar, she said, and was in awe of what I'd managed to do. It was like the Ghost of Christmas Past coming to hold me. Maybe because I was exhausted, or maybe because my mom was sick, or maybe because I was sitting in a dark lavender-scented room with the girl I used to go tee-peeing with—or maybe because of all these things together—my life finally caught up with me, and I couldn't stop the tears, or the vision of me burning everything I had ever been to the ground.

Michael Singer, in *The Untethered Soul,* says, "You end up loving your edges because they point your way to freedom." What he means is, we have this unbounded soul, this boundless energy and essence, that is the truth of who we are—we are limitless. But limitlessness doesn't do so well within the context of reality, so we create walls, or edges, or identities, and before we know it, we are boxed into a cage. The most insidious part about that cage is that we often don't even know it's there or that it's movable. We think it's fixed—*I'm this person, I'm this way; I'll always be this person, I'll always be this way*. And so we move about in that cage, living the same day over and over again, unless we are lucky enough to get knocked out of that cage. Maybe someone dies, or maybe we lose our home, or maybe our partner cheats on us, or maybe our plane crashes and we are the only one who survives. Or maybe drinking is murdering us and we can't ignore it anymore.

I'll tell you what I know for sure: I would have kept going, trying to grasp that shitty little life, that fixed identity, for as long as I could. I would have done anything to avoid the pain of transformation. I would have stayed in that dull, aching pain for as long as I could. But I was forced in another direction, the absolute last direction I would have ever chosen for myself, and all I can tell you is I will never get over how lucky I was to be so totally messed up, to be so sick and in so much pain that I had no choice but to confront it and challenge everything I thought I knew about myself.

Most people go through this world clinging to what they think is safe, having an idea of who they think they need to be in order to be liked, and passing through this society with the least amount of friction. *This is what we hope for;* this is what we think means success. But then some of us won't get that chance; some will be ejected right out of the normal way and into the fire, launched into the adventure of *becoming*. When this happens, we can cling to what we think is safe and try to construct a socially acceptable version of ourselves. Or we can jump into the void, risk everything we think we are for what we are being asked to become, swim far from the safety of the shore for the unknown horizon, answer the call of every wild, bleeding desire we have buried in us, and use this one life we've been given to blow every edge, limit, and wall we've ever constructed.

Addiction and recovery and sobriety are nothing more than your call to adventure, your ticket to everything you've ever told yourself you can't be, and every dream you've ever had. This is your great adventure.

9

How to Quit Alcohol
When You've Never Stuck to a Diet

*Where we think we need more discipline, we usually
need more self-love.*

—TARA MOHR

At some point in the middle of my second attempt to quit
drinking, I went with my friend Amy to see the movie
Flight with Denzel Washington. I had no idea what it was about
beyond flying, and zero clue that it was mostly about alcoholism
(superfun surprise when you're trying to not think about your
own potential alcoholism). Washington's character, a pilot,
lands an out-of-control, failing commercial airliner by flying it
upside down; it's a *wild* stunt, and he pulls it off—nearly everyone survives. The daring maneuver can't be replicated in
simulation without killing everyone on board, and he's a total
magician, a hero, a Sully Sullenberger. The only catch is he was
shitfaced the entire time, a fact that comes to light when his
blood is drawn at the scene of the crash. The rest of the movie is
dedicated to the investigation (of his alcoholism), the trial (of
his alcoholism), and his general alcoholism. Mostly though, it's
about his alcoholism. At least this is how I remember it.

There's a scene toward the end of the movie: It's the night

before his trial, and because his lawyer is desperate to keep him sober, he locks Denzel in a hotel room without booze. Denzel—whose character's name is Whitaker, FFS—is freaking the freak out about the possibility of a prison sentence. He (of course) needs booze to calm himself, and so he breaks in to the hotel room adjacent to get at the minibar. He goes back and forth, hemming and hawing over whether to drink, and we (or I) want so badly for this fucker to just go to bed, to not be the proto-typical Hollywood alcoholic who screws everything to hell by drinking when everything is on the line. Finally, just when we think he's made it, he caves in and grabs the little airline-size bottle of Ketel One off the counter. It's like a scene from *Jaws* where just when you think they're safe, all of a sudden one of them is up to their waist in shark teeth—except for me, it was worse than *Jaws* or any scene in any movie ever. It's one thing to be the victim, and it's another thing to be both the victim and the perp, to be terrified of yourself, of what you might do when left alone.

On the way out of the theater, I was visibly shaken, and my mind was somewhere else. My friend Amy asked me what was wrong, and before I could answer, she said, "Are you afraid because you think that's you?"

"Yes," I said.

Leading up to this moment, I had every bit of proof that I could not quit things, could not be trusted with myself. I'd been biting my nails for nearly twenty-five years and had never managed to stop—not even for a week. I began smoking cigarettes at fifteen, and by the time I was eighteen, I was up to a pack every few days. I'd tried quitting a dozen times before I even entered college; I'd tried patches, gums, and hypnosis without much luck. I once made it an entire year without smoking, but then I went right back to it. It was always *I'll quit when I'm twenty-one;*

definitely by twenty-five; no more after thirty. I was thirty-three, and I was definitely going to stop by the time I turned thirty-five. For sure.

When I quit eating meat at eighteen, I had a strong resolve, but then I'd get drunk and there I'd be, sucking taco meat out of a chalupa. My vegetarianism was an on-again, off-again affair, like most of my relationships with men, who typically quit me far sooner than I was able to quit them. When my anorexia— which I was exceptionally gifted at from seventeen to nineteen— became impossible to maintain, I resorted to bulimia; for almost twenty years I rotated between starvation, bingeing, and purging. When I got my first credit cards, I maxed them out within a month, and with every credit card that followed, I did the same. I could not understand people who lived within their means or showed restraint or control.

I was a woman who could not quit. I could not quit cigarettes, nail-biting, meat, food, men, or spending. I could not maintain discipline, or perfection, or diets, or workout regimens, or budgets. I could not keep promises to myself when it came to anything; I had a faulty brake system and had never quite developed any kind of willpower. Which was why, perhaps, alcoholism felt like such a death sentence.

I had only ideas of people who could not control themselves, people like Captain Whitaker. The alcoholic is always thinking about alcohol, or wanting alcohol, or drinking alcohol, or cleaning up, or falling off the wagon. They get some sober time under their belts, and we are *so relieved,* and then they show up at the party, or the wedding, or your doorstep, drunk. Alcoholism is a forever wanting of something you can't have; it's a white-knuckled existence where you are either trying not to drink, or are drinking and disappointing everyone, especially yourself.

If alcoholism was what I had, then I was so, so screwed.

Given all this, I should have failed fantastically at quitting drinking. Only I didn't. I succeeded, amazingly. To understand how, we need to dig through a few concepts that have been deeply misunderstood in addiction recovery: decision making, willpower, and habit formation.

CHOICE AND UNIFIED MINDS

Whenever there is fear, it is because you have not made up your mind. Your mind is therefore split, and your behavior inevitably becomes erratic. The strength to do comes from your undivided decision. —*A COURSE IN MIRACLES*

As I've described, the first time I quit drinking was with the help of Carr's *The Easy Way*—which I credit with much of my success in that early attempt. To understand the magic of that book, and why it made quitting so easy for me the first time (and supported my eventual sustained sobriety), we need to dig a bit deeper into two concepts Carr detailed, which helped me realize what makes quitting booze hard.

The first is *confirmation bias,* the tendency for us humans to search for, interpret, and recall information in a way that confirms our preexisting beliefs. It's our propensity to look for things that confirm something we are doing isn't wrong or that something we believe is right. When it comes to problematic drinking, we often use confirmation bias to delude ourselves. When my friend mentioned that she was going through an "alcoholic phase" and I was *relieved,* this was confirmation bias at work; she confirmed that it was normal to have little phases of "alcoholism." Similarly, if my boss was hungover at work, if everyone got a third round on a Tuesday night, if my friends on Instagram were posting memes that said wine is like duct tape (it fixes everything!)—my behavior was confirmed, nothing in particular was wrong with me, and I didn't really need to change or do anything about my drinking. Everyone else was doing it, it was normal, I was normal.

Confirmation bias works in the opposite direction, too. Let's say I believe that quitting alcohol is all but impossible, that people die trying to do it, or that people feel deprived without alcohol, or that their lives suck forever and ever amen—and I see this confirmed in the movies, or when Lindsay Lohan or Charlie Sheen ends up back in rehab, or when my friend's mom is still going to meetings more than twenty years after she quit—then my belief about quitting alcohol being terrible and impossible is right, and I should probably not try to do it. We see what we want to see, or what we've been trained to see, and our beliefs are constantly reinforced.

The second concept is *cognitive dissonance,* which is when we have two conflicting thoughts at the same time. It's the devil on one shoulder, angel on the other. We may not like hangovers, or saying stupid things, or forgetting portions of our evenings, or having beer guts or purple teeth, or fucking people we don't like. But we also love how booze helps us overcome our shyness and inhibitions, be the life of the party, connect intimately, be able to have sex, and relax. (Note: alcohol doesn't actually do any of these things, but we are conditioned to think it does.)

Suffice it to say, alcohol can polarize our thoughts from the beginning, and if we want to cut down or quit drinking altogether, cognitive dissonance really messes us up. Because we—and society—have attributed all this goodness to alcohol that it doesn't deserve. Because we see it as a necessary and joyous part of life—and then further, because we're simply hooked on it physiologically and psychologically—we really think we *want* the alcohol; we think we can't (or don't want to) live without it. Yet we also know it's ruining our self-esteem, freedom, lives, and looks, and maybe we absolutely hate it at the same time. I loved it because I was conditioned to believe in the magic of alcohol and that it was a necessary and persistent part of a good life, and I also absolutely loathed it. These competing narratives, this dissonance, keeps our mind split—as if we had two different wills inside us.

An example: Maybe you're trying to cut back on drinking, so you say, "I'm not going to drink during the weekdays." That's a vote against alcohol. But then you have a terrible day at work, and on your way home, where you intend to watch Netflix and not drink, your friends call you from the wine bar and say, "Just one." It doesn't matter how steely your resolve is or how much you don't want to drink or how much you want to control this thing and not feel miserable the next day—you listen to the voices in your head, and the one that's pro-drinking is a lot stronger than the one that's all about *The Great British Bake Off* and an early, sober night in. This is not because you're weak-willed or any of that nonsense we typically attribute to caving, but because to *not drink* when you haven't fully made up your mind about it requires willpower.

Carr totally blew my confirmation bias about alcohol because he endlessly repeats how pointless and poisonous alcohol really is: it ensnares us and keeps us stuck feeling like shit. He also blew some other beliefs of mine, saying it would be *easy* to quit, that I wouldn't feel deprived, that I would have more energy, and that I could fully enjoy my life without alcohol. He told me that there was no such thing as an alcoholic; there were just drinkers and nondrinkers. All this came together to dismantle my confirmation bias; drinking was no longer this precious wonderful thing, but a trap, and we were all in it. It was like learning that Santa Claus wasn't real; once we know, we can't go back.

Carr's book also smashed my cognitive dissonance into cognitive alignment. I was no longer of two minds: I desired to not drink, I believed not drinking could be fun and effortless, and I was excited for my nondrinking life to begin. When Carr instructed me to "never question the decision," he was giving me the golden ticket for success—a way out of cognitive dissonance and a way out of battling myself.

I decided not to drink, and I wouldn't question it or need to use my willpower. If a friend called me on my way home from work when I'd had a bad day and asked me out for a drink, I wouldn't need to think about whether I should or shouldn't; I'd made up my mind to not drink, and I would uphold the decision. Say you've made a decision to go to Mexico, and you're sitting on the plane, and your friend calls you and says, "Let's go to Ireland instead!" You're not going to get off the plane—you're going to go with the decision you made. Same thing when my friends called me during this period, or when I passed the liquor store. I didn't say "maybe tonight" or debate it at all. I didn't question whether I'd made the right decision; I fiercely honored the one I'd made. I had a unified mind, not a split one, so I didn't need to call on my willpower.

The unified mind thing worked for a few months, but I was smoking more pot and not really getting at the stuff that had made me drink in the first place. And then, as I've detailed, one night I did the thing Carr warned me not to do: I questioned the decision. As I was getting ready for a work party, the thought entered my mind that I *could* drink if I wanted to, and just like that, the whole thing crumbled. By the time my mascara had dried, I was committed to drinking. Once I crossed that line, it was hard to rein the drinking back in. I was back in the gray area of cognitive dissonance, and each opportunity to drink from then on presented itself as a new decision to be made: *Should I tonight? Why not?* When I was using Carr's method, I wasn't using willpower—you don't have to use willpower when you don't want to do something. You just don't do it. But as soon as I questioned my decision not to drink, I had to rely on willpower—a limited resource—to abstain. The next time I quit would require far more from me than just Carr's logic.

WILLPOWER AND BRAIN CAPACITY

Most of us are confused about what willpower really is; we tend to think some people have it in spades and that others— like those with chemical and behavioral addictions—are lacking in it. That's exactly how I saw myself, as a person with no self-control or willpower, which was not at all true. While *impulse control* was indeed a skill I had to hone (for instance, through meditation and mindfulness—staying present with feelings and reactions), willpower (as in repressing or inhibiting a desire) isn't a skill; it's a finite cognitive function known as *inhibition.*

To understand a little bit more how willpower or inhibition works, a few pieces of information will help. First, willpower is one of five functions delegated to the prefrontal cortex, or PFC. The other four functions are decision making, understanding, memorizing, and recalling. Second, it's important to know that the brain requires a crap-load of energy from the body; it accounts for about 2 percent of body mass and consumes about 20 percent of our energy. Most of our brain functions are automatic and don't require conscious processing, like the beating of your heart, or a habit like driving a car. These automatic processes don't burn up metabolic resources. The PFC, on the other hand, requires a massive amount of energy (or glucose) to work; the same way you need energy to run a mile, you need energy to make decisions or memorize facts, and this energy is not inexhaustible; we wake up every day with only so much gas in our tank to fuel our PFC, and we burn through it fairly quickly.

What this means for willpower is that (1) it's a finite resource, with only so much of it available to us each day; and (2) it's a resource shared with other functions. Every time you solve a problem, make a decision, memorize a fact, remember something, or try not to do something (like eat that second cookie or check your Instagram for the fourteenth time), you are draining your willpower reserves. Trying harder doesn't work when you've got nothing left in you to fuel the effort.

The thing about the PFC is that there's no way to give it more gas, so there's no way to increase your willpower, or decision making, understanding, memorizing, and recall. What you can do is approach those five functions as if they are precious resources (because they are) and plan your day in a way that uses them carefully, by creating more automation—or habits—so that you aren't using your decision making and willpower as often.

HABIT FORMATION

In *The Power of Habit,* author Charles Duhigg talks about the three components necessary to form a habit: a *cue,* or something that triggers us to perform a *routine,* so that we may receive a *reward.* For example: You smell cigarette smoke (the cue), you reach for a cigarette and light it up (the routine), and you get a nicotine buzz (the reward). Duhigg asserts that we don't really *break* habits; rather we change out the routine from existing habit loops. In other words, when we are trying to extinguish a habit, the cue remains and the reward remains, we just change out the middle part. In the case of cigarette smoking, you still have the same cues (stress, the smell of smoke, seeing people inhale). The difference is what you do with those cues. Maybe you go for a run, or make a pot of coffee, or do some breathing exercises instead. Whatever it is, the new, healthier routine needs to provide a similar reward so you are motivated to replicate it in the future. If it doesn't get you off, it won't work.

Creating new habits rests on this same exact framework; a cue, a routine, and a reward are all needed in order to make the whole thing work. But *repetition* is also a requirement—we have to do something enough times for it to become a habit (something we do without thinking, automatically). A good example of this principle in action was in early sobriety, when I got into the habit of brushing my teeth at night. I know it doesn't sound like the most heroic achievement—I mean you just brush your teeth—but I'd spent years drinking and smoking weed in order to fall asleep. My night routine wasn't me in a chemise at my vanity with some Pond's cream; my routine was "do whatever it takes to pass out." Brushing my teeth was something I sometimes did at night but usually didn't. One of my first goals in early sobriety was to change this.

At first I encountered walls and walls of resistance to this simple practice; I'd either forget or I'd be comfy in bed and about to fall asleep and not want to disturb that sweet moment, or I'd just not want to. But I was desperate to become someone who was responsible enough to have good oral hygiene, so I persisted. At first I had to use lots of brain resources (willpower) to get into the habit, but eventually it paid off. Now I don't even have to think about brushing my teeth at night: I shut everything down, wash my face, floss (yep, nailed that too), brush for two minutes, put my earplugs in, turn the light off, and fall asleep. None of it requires any PFC resources. I do it reflexively, and if I don't, that's when something feels off or amiss. My reward? The feeling of clean teeth (which I'm "addicted" to having now).

This exact same process can get us into a new workout routine, or a new evening ritual that doesn't include wine.

MANAGING OUR ENERGY

In *Awakening the Brain,* Charlotte Tomaino explains that most of the time, we are somewhere between two states: *hyperarousal* and *hypoarousal.* Hyperarousal is the state where our sympathetic nervous system has kicked in and our fight-or-flight response is stimulated—cognition and digestion slow down, adrenaline and cortisol are released, the heart pumps faster, our emotions are sharper, and we are reactive; all the things that help us when fighting or fleeing an attacker. Hypoarousal is a detached, dissociated state, where we are lethargic, unengaged, zoned out, and close to catatonia.

Tomaino explains that for us to thrive and be the most loving, open, and effective versions of ourselves, we need to constantly avoid hitting either the hyperarousal or the hypoarousal state by self-regulating (and not with coffee and alcohol). If we remain hyperaroused with no self-regulation, we will eventually hit a point of no return, where the only way out is to use something heavy (like wine) to drop us into hypoarousal, where we can recover. In other words, if we don't subtly manage our energy throughout the day, we have to manage it with a jackhammer at the end of the day.

WHY IT'S HARD TO QUIT BAD HABITS

We've now established three things. First, we don't need will-power when we don't desire to do something, and it isn't a thing some of us have in excess and some of us don't have at all. It's a cognitive function, like deciding what to eat or solving a math equation or remembering your dad's birthday. Willpower is also a limited resource; we have more of it at the beginning of the day and lose it throughout the day as we use it to write emails or not eat cookies. When you automate some decisions or processes (through forming habits), you free up more brain power.

Second, for us to make and change a habit, we need a cue, a routine, and a reward, and enough repetition must occur for the process to move from something we have to think about con-sciously ("I need to brush my teeth," "I don't want to drink wine") to something we do naturally, automatically.

Third, throughout the day, we must manage our energy so that we don't blow out and end up in the place of no return—a hyperaroused state where the only thing that can bring us down is a glass (or a bottle) of wine.

Maybe you've woken up hungover on a Monday morning and declared you're finished with alcohol and you'll never drink again. Maybe you even dump out every drop of alcohol in your house and make some declaration that you are finished forever. In this moment, you're committed to it, and that commitment is absolutely real; you aren't making it up or being dramatic. But then by five or six p.m., you can't even remember how you thought you'd ever not drink again. Maybe you have to make dinner for your family, or entertain clients, or you're hauling work home with you—whatever is ahead of you, even if it's just watching *The Real Housewives,* you can't imagine doing it without a drink, and you stop at the liquor store on the way home. You'll quit tomorrow.

This scenario feels impossible, like a vicious cycle you'll never get out of. I know because I've been in it, and it's why most of us—who are anything but lazy, incompetent, or weak-willed— feel like this is one thing we'll never be able to pull off. Let's think about it a little differently, though. If you decide you're going to run the New York City Marathon, do you go out the morning of, buy shoes, and run it? Or do you plan and train? Quitting drinking isn't rocket science, but it does take work, commitment, and planning. In order to see how one might plan and train to quit, let's look at two different scenarios.

In the first scenario, we start our day by waking up to our phone alarm. We haven't gotten enough sleep, we're hungover, and we take a moment to remind ourselves what huge pieces of shit we are for doing this to ourselves again. We go straight to the caffeine and our phones to motivate us out of bed, and we don't slide into the day, we slam into it, pumping ourselves full of stimulants (news, email, social media, caffeine, carbs). Most of us don't pirouette through a morning routine, we run through it against the clock, getting ourselves ready, making decisions about what to wear or whether to work out, getting our kids ready and off to school. By the time we get to our workplace, we've already used a substantial amount of that precious reserve of willpower to answer unnecessary emails, or deny ourselves that *pain au chocolat,* and we've kicked our sympathetic nervous system into gear before the day has even really started.

By ten a.m., we're hungry, and we mean to eat something with protein, but Barb has brought in doughnuts, and we try not to eat the damn doughnuts, but there's a maple bar, and we can't resist a maple bar. We start on a project, but our Slack goes off, our text messages stack up, emails come in, the phone rings.

We skip lunch, we forget to breathe, we're in a meeting and our dick of a boss speaks over us. We say yes to a thousand things we don't want to do or have time to do. We've still forgotten to breathe, and the loop in our heads is screaming that we are losers who can't keep it together.

It doesn't stop, and by five p.m., we are hyperaroused: We cannot think straight, we have nothing left that resembles willpower or any kind of power, we are amped, and we could run through a wall like the Kool-Aid man. But we're also tired and need energy, and the only thing that will make any of it better—the only thing that will turn off the stress and fuel our energy to make dinner or correct homework or finish the work we couldn't get done in the normal course of the day—is wine. But we said we wouldn't drink wine. But also, fuck anything we've ever said, because *we need wine.* And we find that the second we tell ourselves that it's okay, that we'll try again tomorrow, that tonight we can drink—we loosen up a bit, we feel like we got a second wind. By our second glass, or maybe second bottle, we are totally confused. How did this happen? Again?

Let's take it in the other direction and look at what someone who is training to not drink might do to prepare themselves for the five o'clock shitshow. In this scenario, we wake up to an alarm that isn't on our phone, because we've been keeping our phone out of the bedroom so we can have some mental space. We're hungover and we've not gotten a great night's sleep, but that's okay; we're in training and we're trying, and that's remarkable. We put on a pot of coffee, but we also make ourselves a cup of hot lemon water because it will do wonders for our digestion, and while the coffee is brewing, we take our lemon water to our meditation cushion, where we are in the habit of meditating for five minutes a day before we do anything else. We still haven't checked the phone—we haven't released a cascade of adrenaline and cortisol into our system by reading the news or agonizing over how we don't measure up on social media or checking our email. Instead, we pick up a book and read something positive that tells us we are badass motherfuckers who can do anything we want to do in this world. We laid out an outfit the night before and don't use any brain sauce to get dressed; we eat a breakfast rich in protein because we know we need protein to make new good brain chemicals and balance our blood sugar and manage our cravings. If we have kids, we get them ready for school and walk out the door and into the day. We still haven't checked the phone.

At work, we are careful to work in blocks of time, and we keep our distractions to a minimum. We set an hourly alarm to remind us to breathe; we make sure we eat protein and good fats every few hours to keep our blood sugar stable. When we are asked to do something, we weigh it against what we can and can't do; we hold boundaries because we know that there is only so much of us to go around. We don't treat everyone's ask as an emergency; we stop drinking caffeine by noon because we know it will rev us too high and mess with our sleep cycle. We go on a walk to clear our heads and shake off whatever came at us during the day; we keep our phone on airplane mode so we aren't consistently distracted. When Barb brings in those doughnuts, we have a freaking doughnut. When our boss is a dick to us or something unexpected happens and we kick into overdrive, we are better equipped to handle it.

By five p.m., when we are wrapping up, the thought of wine or booze crosses our mind, but we have some aces up our sleeve. We've got some reserve willpower left because we've been careful about how we use our brain juice by creating habits, cutting out unnecessary decision making, and limiting distractions. Because we've primed and activated our parasympathetic nervous system throughout the day—from how we wake up, to our morning routine, to breath reminders, to our walk—we have access to the expansive version of us that feels chill and has better cognition and digestion. We've kept our blood sugar stable, and we've given ourselves good brain food, and we've kept good boundaries so we don't feel shredded by the world because we've managed our energy.

And we've given ourselves a routine at the end of the day that doesn't include wine. On our way home, we don't question our decision to not drink; we aren't drinking right now. We get home, make a cup of tea, do some breathing work, and we get on with the second part of our day.

It's not easy to not drink, but it's also not impossible. We've been training for it.

10

Breaking the Cycle of Addiction:
Rituals and Healthy Coping Mechanisms

> *Anyone who thinks they can heal without doing the*
> *work is missing the point.*

—LOUISE HAY

During the four months between my first and final attempts to quit drinking, I started to give myself over to a new way of living. It began on January 2, 2013, when I woke up from a five-day bender at what I can only describe as the lowest point of my entire existence.

Quitting drinking for those first few months had given me a taste of what it meant to be a respectable lady who could be trusted with herself, and one night of drinking in late December had undone all that. Every shred of dignity I'd gained in those first sixty days of refusing alcohol was circling a drain somewhere; the shame of feeling like a failure, the terror of what was happening to me and where I might end up, made drinking a necessity. I could not stand to be consciously aware of who I was and where I had (yet again) landed.

The bender started after Christmas; being with my family for extended periods of time always turned me into a five-foot-six walking, throbbing, exposed nerve. I'd landed back in San Francisco a few days before New Year's with every intention of going to yoga and being a very good girl. But my first night back I managed to smoke and drink myself into oblivion, and the next day—unable to face life and the mess I'd made of it the night before—I drank and smoked more. On New Year's Eve, I canceled my plans so I could stay drunk and unaccounted for, and the relief at not having to be anywhere—of having an entire night to myself to sink into total numbing disintegration—was cause for celebration. I bought two bottles of Moët and ordered in my favorite food to binge: California Pizza Kitchen. I didn't make it to midnight, and when I woke up to my dumpster fire of a life the next morning, I decided to keep on drinking; I told myself *You can start tomorrow.*

I don't remember much of that first day of 2013, but I do remember an email from Gabby Bernstein, letting me know she'd just released a new book, a forty-day guide to help fuckups like me become happy people. Gabby was the only person I knew of who'd once been "full of insecurities, booze, and Subway sandwiches," so she'd won my trust immediately, because alluding to any form of an improprietous relationship with Subway sandwiches is basically the secret handshake of bulimics. Gabby was also no longer a fuckup, so I was 100 percent sure that following her forty-day program would turn me into Jesus.

The next morning I read the first passage of the miracle book (which is, in fact, called *May Cause Miracles*), wrote down the day's mantra, "I am willing to witness my fear," in a pink Moleskine journal, had some herbal tea, and dragged myself to a Bikram yoga class. I smelled like trash, like old bananas, and I sweated out as much pain, bloat, and booze as I could manage. Walking still felt impossible—everything felt impossible—but I somehow propelled myself from that yoga class to a massage I'd booked at the Kabuki Spa. I spent the rest of the day scrubbing my apartment, bleaching away all the evidence of my sloth, of my shame. I took a bath, read "Day 1: Evening Portion" of *May Cause Miracles,* and meditated. Gabby asked me to write down all my fears that night, and I could not stop writing because I was scared of absolutely everything.

The next day, January 3—my mother's birthday—I failed yet again at being a good daughter, but I did manage to read the morning passage of *May Cause Miracles* and did as instructed. Then I meditated (for the sixth time in my life), drank some hot lemon water, and danced around my apartment to shake some life into my spirit, or my body, or whatever was left of me. I went to work, I survived the day, I came home, and I did the same thing as the night before: bathed, read, meditated, journaled. This time I added a yoga class from the internet, in between or maybe while I drank Crane Lake Merlot from the bodega across the street.

The year crawled forward, the rituals became a lifeline. I built more of them. In the mornings, I meditated and danced to hip-hop and wrote myself kind and inspirational notes on Post-its that I stuck to my computer, my wall, my bathroom mirror, and my work notebook. I took pauses during the day to breathe, to read a sticky note that maybe said, "I believe in miracles." In the evenings, I came home to my apartment and did as many things as I could to stop myself from drinking. I often ended up drinking or getting high, though sometimes I didn't. The rituals and the meditations and the pauses became a drug in and of themselves, as did lavender essential oil and certain three-minute Kundalini meditations. I wasn't sober, but I also wasn't dying the way I had been. There was life, and there was death, and I was somewhere in between the two.

There was one morning that January I remember particularly well: I was on a business trip in Boston while still working for the health care start-up. I'd drunk the night before to the point of obliteration, or maybe just embarrassment, and woke up in my hotel room late for work. I was the boss and my staff was already at the office and I was tempted to scurry there as fast as possible, but skipping my morning ritual felt unthinkable—almost as unthinkable as skipping a drink. This was the moment the routine clicked—the moment I realized I could not face the world without doing a self-care ritual. I read my little book, wrote down my daily mantra, meditated, drank hot lemon water, and danced around my hotel room to Too Short blasting from my phone. By the time I made it to work, I found I could smile, and not the kind of smile that hides the pain of wanting to die, but the kind that is in and of itself a smile.

A few months later doing things that saved my life was almost all that mattered. *Life* was what I craved, *happiness* was what I craved, and for the first time ever, I could taste and feel them—they were *real*, and the alcohol and pot and cigarettes were preventing me from fully having them.

On April 14, 2013, a Sunday morning, I was on a company retreat in Austin with some co-workers, all of us fantastically hungover. One of them, a young woman—who'd just told us she was so sick she wanted to die—said something about how inspiring it was to watch a group of brilliant, together executives drink themselves stupid on the regular. She was twenty-four and seeing alcohol abuse and addiction in a whole new respectable light because of people like me who hid their damage and showcased their tolerance; everything about that sentiment crushed me. The others nodded and hear-hear'd, and all I could think was how hangovers weren't funny, how none of it was funny; it was tragic. All of it was tragic. I went back to my room, did my routine, and went to brunch where we laughed about our inability to sign our own names, and somewhere between there and the airport, I opened up an app on my phone and claimed my first day of sobriety for the third time. That was the last time I drank alcohol.

Part of me wants to tell you that sobriety was the point of all this; and it was. A life not dominated or even inclusive of alcohol was what I wanted, what I dreamed of. But the truth is, somewhere in this time period it became so much more; it became about being present for my life, *about having a life*. Maybe it started as not wanting to deal with hangovers or the threat of premature death or even escaping the hole that is addiction, but in these precious four months—where I started to prioritize what fed my soul over what destroyed it—my effort turned into what it still is today: the process of building a life I don't want, or need, to escape from.

Cravings

A craving can be defined as "an overwhelming desire to consume something," which is putting it a little lightly, because if you've ever tried to quit drinking and then had a craving for a drink, you're not likely to explain to someone, "I have an overwhelming desire to consume an alcoholic beverage, sir!" You're more likely to say or think, "I will cut a motherfucker if I don't get a fucking drink in my body this fucking second," then put your fist through a plate-glass window to demonstrate your seriousness. Or maybe it's not like that, because that just reinforces the out-of-control-junkie trope, but it definitely *feels* like that. A craving, especially one that can't be met while you're actively trying not to drink, can feel like your skin is being pulled from your body, layer by layer. Or maybe like: you finally understand those photos where people spontaneously combust and all that's left are two feet and a pair of reading glasses; you get how that might happen to a person.

A craving can come out of nowhere, for no good reason. Often enough it's because you're stressed and the booze is the only thing that can hit that hedonic set point, or because you've encountered some sort of sensory experience that is tied in with your drinking (like walking into a bar where you used to drink, or even hearing a song on the radio) and your body is anticipating the alcohol, and preparing to counteract it. Sometimes just the thought of drinking can prime your body to want it. Whatever the cause, cravings are real, and they feel impossible to conquer, especially if you've repeatedly had them and succumbed.

Here's where I tell you cravings are certainly not impossible to overcome, but they do require an understanding of how to work with them.

There are two ways to overcome the urge to drink. The first is to make intentional and specific changes to your routine to avoid succumbing to a craving (or to be better equipped when you do encounter one), and the second is to actively engage with the craving when it does arise.

Creating New Habits
Morning, Noon, and Night

We've already established that there are two very different ways to start your day, which yield significantly different results. If you wake up at different times with no plan, immediately expose yourself to social media and the news, pump yourself with sugary carbs and caffeine, and sprint forward into your day frantic, on alert, in survival mode, dumping cortisol and adrenaline into your system, you are setting the stage for how the rest of your day—and evening—will unfold.

To break the cycle of addiction, you don't just wait until you are in craving—you have to set yourself up so that you don't end up so fried and overstimulated by the end of the day that the only thing you can help but do is water yourself down with a firehose of Merlot. This means you start breaking the cycle of addiction not at five p.m. (when most of us feel it), but upon waking. The simplest thing you can do to change your entire day is put some intention into your morning, so that you set yourself up for the evening by preserving your cognitive function, or willpower. A morning ritual is how you do this.

The Morning Ritual: Planning for It

PLAN AHEAD

The first thing you can do is plan your morning the night before. This means making sure you have lemons for your hot lemon water, getting the coffee ready to brew, and setting your alarm to allow ten to fifteen minutes to center yourself. You can go a step further by making any decisions you might need to make the next morning, like choosing an outfit, looking at your calendar to mentally construct what lies ahead so you can adjust for it, or picking which guided meditation you are going to use.

COMMIT TO YOUR ROUTINE

Stick with the plan. Make a commitment for the next thirty to forty days that no matter how shitty you feel, you'll carry out your morning routine. When I set out to train myself to brush my teeth every night, it took some brain power. I had to make the decision to do it and debate myself almost every single time.

But without fail, I made myself brush my teeth until it became *automatic,* something I did without much fuss. You don't have to keep up this practice forever, and chances are it will fall off at some point, but right now you're in training to not drink.

DESIGNATE A PLACE TO MEDITATE

This might sound frivolous but it is terribly important: create a place where you will meditate every morning. You don't have to build an altar or buy a meditation cushion, although you can. It might even just be your bed (I meditate mostly in my bed, though I have a space set up in my basement). Remember you are investing in your healing, and understand that the more intention you put into something or the more special you make it, the more likely you are to do it. You can, if you want, go nuts and buy candles and a fancy silk pillow and some singing bowls or whatever, but you don't have to. Just decide where you will meditate, then meditate in that spot.

KEEP YOUR PHONE OFF

The second you open up your phone—a severely addictive device with even more severely addictive applications—you are no longer in the sweet cocoon of your early morning. You are in the news, in other people's lives, and in your email, which *never stops* and is full of things you can worry about later but typically elect to worry about sooner. Opening your phone invites all the chaos of the world into your precious moment of stillness. If you want to feel balanced, preserve your willpower, and keep your sanity and centeredness, don't check it until after you've done your morning routine. Bonus points for keeping your phone out of your bedroom altogether and using an actual alarm clock.

The Morning Ritual: Doing It

HOT LEMON WATER

I encourage you to drink a cup of hot lemon water to start—
before having coffee or tea. It sounds like a weird thing, but a
little cup of hot lemon water goes a long way. First, it creates a
healing sensory experience through taste and smell that locks in
the pleasure construct of the ritual (the same way the smell and
taste of a fine Pinot locks in the pleasure construct of you at
your favorite wine bar), which in turn makes you *crave* the
morning ritual. Second, it signals to your body that you're starting your day by loving it. Thirdly, hot lemon water is a great
liver flusher, and your liver needs some flushing. It does a lot
more, too, but let's leave it at that. You can add turmeric or cay-
enne pepper for some extra help combating inflammation and
balancing your blood sugar.

MEDITATION

We'll get into the benefits of a meditation practice in the next
chapter, but if you don't have a meditation practice already, I'll
be Richard Simmons–ing you to get one going. Almost every
single recovery program that exists has a meditation component because meditation is the superfood of recovery, and the
morning meditation is probably the most powerful time to
practice. Meditating for five minutes in the morning is like putting money in the bank; it centers you, primes your parasympathetic nervous system (the one we want primed), and gives that
brain of yours space to make decisions. You can do whatever
kind of meditation you want. If you don't have a practice already, I recommend starting with a guided meditation. The
Calm app, Insight timer, and glo.com are all incredible resources. I prefer Kundalini meditations, Transcendental Medi-

tation, and simple mindfulness meditations. This step might contradict the no-phone rule, so engage carefully: If you have to use your phone, don't check any other applications. Five minutes is good, ten minutes is better, and twenty minutes means you're Buddha.

MIND CANDY

After your meditation—or before, if you prefer—read something that will give you a bit of inspiration for the day. (Some of my favorite authors for this purpose are Pema Chödrön, Marianne Williamson, Tara Brach, Eckhart Tolle, Rebecca Campbell, Brené Brown, and Meggan Watterson. I also love the metaphysical text *A Course in Miracles*.) Almost every single message we've received since birth tells us we aren't enough, we need to be more beautiful or smarter or thinner or whatever to be loved, we need to buy this product to not be the hideous sasquatches we are. We are trained to believe that the way to make it through life is to beat ourselves into shape, and the feedback loops in our heads are horrifying. Healing means breaking this cycle of thought, and we don't change how we think about ourselves by wishing it different; we change by actively engaging with different words, phrases, and beliefs, and repeating these mantras to ourselves until they interrupt the old hateful story and make a new loving one.

You will probably be resistant or skeptical of this practice. I understand. The first time I told myself, "I am love," I felt ridiculous and thought it would never work on me—I'm far too smart to believe that crap. But I did it anyway, and in time telling myself that I was good, that I was worthy, that I was loved, became my normal way of thinking. We don't have to believe this stuff to say it to ourselves, and we probably won't at first. But our subconscious mind—which has absolutely no preference for what it consumes—eats that positive information up, regardless of whether we "believe" it.

To summarize, the morning ritual is as follows: (1) wake up at the same time, (2) don't check your phone, (3) boil some water and squeeze a quarter of a lemon into it, (4) meditate for five minutes, (5) read a positive affirmation that you've written on a Post-it note and repeat a few times throughout the day. Spending ten to fifteen minutes in the morning sets you up for an entirely different way of being and prevents cravings later in the day. Do the same thing every day for thirty to forty days to make this process automatic.

A few other things you can add to your morning routine to increase your chances of preventing (or lessening) the end-of-day crash are to eat a good breakfast and add some joy practices. Breakfast should include some sustainable, high-quality protein and healthy fats (coconut butter, almond butter, ghee, avocado); fats and protein are essential for balanced blood sugar and good brain health. A joy practice can be anything from shaking your body to dancing to singing; it's a small and powerful way to raise your vibration and remember that life is actually pretty spectacular. My joy practice was simple: I danced. I still do.

Managing Your Energy Throughout the Day

As discussed, we are mostly navigating between two states: hyperarousal, where we are overstimulated and living in our fight-or-flight response, and hypoarousal, where we are burned out and unable to do much of anything. Typically we move through our day by shooting immediately into the hyperarousal state and staying in that frequency, and we typically end the day overstimulated; we then drop into hypoarousal when we have the chance to, usually at the end of the day and usually with the aid of wine, drugs, food, or whatever is strong enough to numb us out and take the pressure off.

If you start with the morning ritual, you're managing that end-of-day process by keeping yourself out of the hyperaroused zone or minimizing overstimulation, but the morning ritual won't last you the entire day. You need to remain vigilant and keep yourself out of the red zone by doing a few simple things throughout your day.

BREATH BREAKS

A breath break is exactly what it sounds like: throughout the day, take a few minutes to consciously breathe. Breathing correctly is a technique you need to learn, so you'll need to do some research (search for Long Deep Breathing, Breath of Fire, Sitali Breathing, Alternate Nostril Breathing, or the Calm Heart Meditation, all available on YouTube), or go to a class and work with a breath instructor. Set a few reminders in your phone, or better yet, put it in your calendar at the top of each hour. Get into the habit of consciously breathing and priming your parasympathetic response throughout the day.

SNACKING

My friend Mary Vance, a nutritional consultant who works with people who are quitting drinking, regularly reminds me that over 95 percent of those with alcohol-use disorder have hypoglycemia or low levels of blood sugar. Alcohol disrupts the hormones that control and moderate blood sugar levels, and low blood sugar can trigger cravings for alcohol, so it's essential that you manage your blood sugar to avoid or lessen the intensity and frequency of cravings. An easy way is to snack regularly (every three to four hours), and choose foods that are low on the glycemic index or are mostly protein or good fats. Try an apple with a nut butter, or half an avocado—things like that. This doesn't mean that you need to cut out sugar entirely— sugar addiction in early recovery is certainly a thing, but right now you're trying to not drink, not quit sugar.

MIDDAY MANTRAS

The power of mantras is that they give us the reminders we need to change our thinking about ourselves and other people. They also change our behavior. I have mantras going off in my phone from morning until night (most of which come from Gabby Bernstein's Spirit Junkie app, mantras from Tempest Sobriety School, or from the workbook portion of *A Course in Miracles*), and I cannot stress how much this has helped me— these reminders go off sometimes in the middle of situations where I've lost my shit, and they offer me the opportunity to remember I can act differently. We manage our energy by managing our thoughts, and we manage our thoughts by managing what we intentionally choose to believe, and the best way to intentionally choose to believe something is to be reminded to believe it.

UPHOLD BOUNDARIES

Managing your energy means also managing your boundaries. Say no to things that deprioritize your healing or that make your life unmanageable—such as extra work assignments, favors, hosting events, or even going to events you don't want or can't go to. Think of yourself as being pregnant, or sick with cancer or the flu: your sickness is valid, your healing is valid, and you *must* put yourself and your healing first. Disappoint other people with your no; don't disappoint yourself with a yes you'll later resent.

USE YOUR CALENDAR

Use your calendar to work in blocks of time. Do harder tasks that require deep concentration and thinking in the morning, when you have more brain juice; check your email at designated times (and learn how to not respond to emails that aren't important, or respond in due time to nonurgent items); do easier rote tasks at the end of the day; and be supermindful about distractions like your phone, instant messaging, and social media. When you go home for the night, shut down and turn off—set clear boundaries with your colleagues to avoid the creep of work into your home life. Guard your time, try to use it as wisely as possible, and be sure to build chunks of time in which you are totally disconnected.

EMERGENCY BREATHING EXERCISES OR MEDITATIONS

Learn some breathing techniques, like Breath of Fire or Left Nostril Breathing, or even some quick Kundalini meditations like the Meditation to Prevent Freaking Out (all available on YouTube), so that when you get lit up by your boss, a co-worker, a deadline, or the dick in line at Starbucks, you can reset your energy in the moment.

MIND THE CAFFEINE

Coffee is your friend until it isn't, and it isn't after noon. Caffeine has a half-life, so you're still getting the rev from it up to ten hours after you consume it. If you want to come down easy in the evening, don't jack yourself up with caffeine in the afternoon. Try to have your last cup before twelve p.m.

The Evening Ritual

If you've done the morning ritual and engaged in some of the midday practices, you're set up for your evening, but there's still that five p.m. witching hour that you're used to greeting with a fat glass of wine. You'll need an evening ritual.

The evening ritual is a routine designed to invoke all your senses to create new pleasure constructs and rewards at the time of day hardest for most of us. You replace the routine of drinking your way out of discomfort with healthy practices that provide the same reward (you think) alcohol brings you, which is relief. As the habit for alcohol atrophies as you work toward quitting, these new healthy habits take root and eventually become second nature.

If you've been drinking at home to make it through your nights for the past umpteen years, something as simple as the click of keys in your door or the sound of the evening news will make you want a drink. Remember the formula to break habits: we are *cued* to perform a *routine* that will give us a *reward*. To break the habit, you need to switch out the old routine for a new one that will give you a similar reward. When you are trying to quit drinking, the cues (making dinner, driving home) will remain, the craving for the reward will remain (wanting to be relaxed), and it's the routine you have to switch out.

An intentional, healing evening ritual attempts to both replace the drinking routine, and create a new routine (or ritual) that combines as many healthful and sensory-driven components as possible. The goal of the ritual is to help you unwind—or bring yourself down from a hyperaroused state—without the sledgehammer of booze and with effective, constructive healing practices.

When I created my first evening ritual, I started with a simple practice: I took a bath, I read the evening passage from *May Cause Miracles*, did some journaling, and meditated. Something about this was medicine, and in no time I was adding to it, tricking out that small set of instructions. One night I added lavender essential oil to my bath, and then another night I wanted to read more than just the small passage from the miracle book, so I started reading all sorts of books in the evenings, especially inspirational ones. I got creative with my evening meditations and started using glo.com to explore more, which opened up a world of yoga practices I could do at home.

Before I knew it, I was putting on a curated Spotify playlist of chants and "spa music" as soon as I walked in the door (particular musical compositions have specific vibrations that lend themselves to a healing environment). I diffused essential oils with specific healing benefits: bergamot for relieving depression, cinnamon for brain function, clary sage for anxiety, Roman chamomile for insomnia. I made cup after cup of herbal tea—my favorites are holy basil, kava kava, mint, and bedtime mixes, which helped me overcome insomnia, calm myself, and raise my energy naturally. I took baths—a good hot bath lowers the heart rate and activates the parasympathetic nervous system, and adding Epsom salts aids detoxification. I read from inspirational texts—five minutes at night helped center me. I breathed to release the day and prepare for sleep. And I moved. Running, dancing, doing yoga, going on long walks, spinning— all things that helped me release my accumulated energy. By giving myself over to a different kind of absorption than the one I was used to, I slowly found myself feeling compelled to do the night routine—I craved it, and the alcohol and the pot became the sideshow.

What came of this evening routine was a new fullness, replacing what seemed like a forever habit of coming home to drink and get high. Other positive results came of it too, like how for the first time in my life I could be alone with myself at night without having to be drunk. I was evolving and growing from the work I was putting in in the evenings.

You need to put in some work to create a way to wind down at home instead of knocking off with a six-pack and some whiskey. The goal of the ritual is threefold: to help you wash off the day with something other than booze; to incorporate sensory components in a new pleasure construct that activates glutamate—the neurochemical responsible for creating pleasurable multisensory memories—making you want to repeat it (locking in dynamic reward); and to engage in activities that promote a different way of living.

This will all take time and effort, and at first—especially if you're still drinking—you'll feel like there's no way in hell you can find the time to make any of it happen. This is the part where I'm an impossible bitch and tell you that you found the time to drink, to think about drinking, and recover from drinking, and you did this because you prioritized drinking, and you prioritized drinking because it made you feel good (and then, of course, very, very bad)—all proof that you can find time to prioritize your healing. It will not only pay off in spades in how you feel, but it will also give you so much time on the back end. I've managed to accomplish more in the last seven years than I did in the first thirty-three because booze—not to mention the self-loathing, depression, anxiety, and other addictions—took up so much fucking time. Invest in your healing and it will pay off more than you can even begin to fathom.

Build a Toolbox

During those first few months of 2013, I met with a doctor friend, explaining that I was drinking again, and that this time I was consciously trying to employ other coping skills. I told him I had an alarm on my phone that went off every few hours to give me a positive affirmation mantra, I was carrying around various herbal teas, and I had a growing collection of guided meditations in my iTunes. He explained that I was creating a coping mechanism toolbox—a collection of actions and items that I could turn to instead of drinking—and suggested that I take it a step further and come up with a list of ten things that worked for me and stick the list in my wallet.

Me being me, I took it five steps further. I started a toolbox spreadsheet to serve as my database, replete with categories (cravings, stress, anger, exhaustion, PMS, depression, etc.). I printed out a list of my top ten tools and taped copies to my full-length mirror, my TV, above my kitchen sink, and my work bulletin board. I purchased physical items that would serve as tools (such as essential oils, tea bags, rosaries) and bought a special little leather pouch to hold them. I went toolbox wild! And made it my mission to become the MacGyver of my own impending dooms.

So what is a tool, and how does it work? Basically, a tool is anything that we use as a coping mechanism to shift or relieve our current state. Tools can be unhealthy (like alcohol, drugs, and sugar) or tools can be healthy (like breathing, meditation, and herbal tea).

Most of us are not raised learning how to manage our bodies, emotions, discomforts, and feelings, and we end up turning to whatever we have learned will achieve a desired release or relief. Before I embarked on sobriety, my tools were alcohol, food (overeating and purging), American Spirits, pot, coffee, sugar, explosive rage, codependent relationships, work, yoga, Netflix bingeing, online shopping, gossiping and talking trash, *Us* magazine, any Bravo show, hysterical crying, and long runs. I turned to these tools if I needed to find balance or couldn't deal, and however destructive some of them may have been, they got the job done.

I was long on unhealthy coping mechanisms and short on

healthy ones, so I started to switch out the mix. I didn't eliminate all the unhealthy coping mechanisms, but I began to binge on the good ones. When the alcohol was finally removed from the toolbox, there was plenty to fill the void—including some unhealthy tools I wasn't ready to leave behind (like pot). The idea was to add healthy tools as I removed the unhealthy ones, and over time, I came to rely on the healthy tools more than the unhealthy ones. Today my toolbox consists of breathing techniques, hot lemon water, herbal tea, hot baths, cold showers (this is called "hydrotherapy" and it's so, so good), coffee, essential oils, yoga, meditation, Kundalini music, autonomous sensory meridian response (ASMR), massage, French pastries, emotional freedom technique (EFT), and many other things.

I suggest that you—whether you are trying to quit some addiction or find a better way to live—make a toolbox. It's a pretty simple formula. First, find a handful of things that help you in moments of distress, be it a breath technique, a YouTube video of unlikely animal friendships, peppermint oil, or a mantra that reminds you of what you need to remember. Find about ten things, and make sure that some of them are actual physical objects—a tea bag, a GABA lozenge, or a bottle of lavender oil. Next make a list of these things, and carry that list and the physical items with you so that when you are in craving, in anger, or about to do something you don't want to do, you can go to the list and pick the thing you need. If this sounds like common sense, that's only because it is, which is why we tend to discount the power of being prepared.

ENGAGING DIRECTLY WITH CRAVINGS

So far in this chapter, we've left the *cue* in place and have been working with the *routine* in order to yield the same *reward*. In this section, we'll work directly with the cravings. This is generally known as urge surfing.

A story: In the spring of 2017 I ran away to Rome for a week. A few summers before, I vacationed there and fell madly in love with an Italian man. Because I'm the kind of person who thinks time stands still in other countries, when I returned a year later, I expected him to be single, waiting for me. I sent him a message as soon as I landed, and because WhatsApp is a cruel application, it told me he'd seen my message and decided not to respond. That was enough to send me spiraling, but then the next night, on my way back to my apartment from dinner, I found myself standing on a street corner staring directly at him and another woman; they'd just came out of a restaurant. They turned and walked down an alley, and I followed, hoping for some outcome I can't fathom. Confront him for moving on? I was stunned, heartbroken, consumed by a feeling I thought would swallow me whole.

This wasn't the first time I'd felt that specific bottomless pain one gets from rejection. Normally, in a situation such as this, I would manipulate it or find some other outlet—like maybe some other man. But this time I decided to try something else. I wanted to ride the edge of that pain and see what I could uncover. The next morning, I laced up my sneakers and set out to walk the streets, my only purpose to see what might happen if, instead of replaying the moment of seeing this man with another woman and riding the elevator down to the bottom of unworthiness, I focused on the actual physical sensation of being rejected. What would happen if I stayed at the trigger point, at its physical sensation, instead of covering it up or painting my story all over it?

On a bridge crossing the Tiber, I located the pain and named it: my throat felt closed and dry, my heart was tight, my stomach was fluttery, an acute and specific pain ran through my left arm. Then I asked myself if it was worse than a broken arm, a hangnail, a paper cut, and was surprised to find the pain registered somewhere below heartburn and slightly above a belly full of gas. For the rest of that day, every time I caught myself imagining him fucking her, him not responding to my text, him not loving me, I'd bring myself back to the actual physical sensation, which was at least a million times less painful than the story in my head.

I once heard Pema Chödrön explain that no emotion lasts longer than ninety seconds. You heard that right: no emotion we feel lasts longer than a minute and a half—if we let it run its course without interference. Emotions, the result of a chemical response to a thought, appear, intensify, de-intensify, and subside: and they do this in less time than it takes to microwave a frozen burrito. What prolongs them isn't emotional wiring gone awry but the stories we lay on top of them that keep our brains dumping more of those chemicals into our system. A prolonged emotional experience is the result of the stories we keep alive in our heads.

I came up with a method specific to the practice of disarming cravings. It's similar to what Judson Brewer outlines in *The Craving Mind*, but I modified it based on my own experience. I call it RASINS, or Recognize, Allow, set aside the Story, Investigate what is happening in your body, Name the sensations, and Surf. The goal is to learn to relax into the craving rather than distract ourselves from it; using the practice, we learn to stay in discomfort and *witness* our suffering, instead of creating more suffering.

So let's say you get home, and maybe you do your evening ritual, but out of nowhere the desire to drink smacks you across your face, possibly due to stress, or emptiness, or boredom, or even happiness. Maybe you think, *I can start quitting again tomorrow,* or some other allowing thought, even though you don't want to drink.

Here's how it works: First, you *recognize* what is happening—you are experiencing a craving to drink alcohol. Say it to yourself: *I am experiencing a craving for alcohol.* The next step might seem counterintuitive, but it's not: *Allow* the sensations to build, *allow* yourself to crave a drink. This allows you to conserve energy by giving space to the craving; instead of expending energy trying to resist the feeling by telling yourself it's wrong or terrifying or shouldn't be happening, you let nature take its course. In the third step, you set aside the *story,* which means you don't tell yourself that you are miserable, that the craving is a sign of some eternal and endless struggle, or something more powerful than you. Instead, you spend that energy doing the fourth step, which is *investigating* the sensations in your body. What does it feel like? Is your throat closing up? Are your fists clenching? Are your legs full of energy? Is your heart tight? The fifth step is to *name* those sensations out loud, or better yet, write them down. And the final step is to ride or *surf* the physical sensations as they intensify, peak, and then dissipate.

The thing about cravings is that while they present as almost entirely physical, what makes them so torturous is the stories we build around them. The RASINS practice allows you to remove the narrative in your head from what's actually happening in your body. A meditation practice will aid this process greatly. Mindfulness allows there to be space between you and your thoughts, so that you may direct the experience instead of being the victim of it.

Engaging with cravings directly has a whole host of benefits. For starters, it allows you to confront your suffering head on, instead of tempering it or running from it, which has implications far beyond just trying to not drink. Because of my practice of sitting in my cravings for pot or booze or whatever, I can also sit in my cravings to do other destructive things, like engaging with men who are terrible for me. And when we do this—stay in that space when we'd rather run—we learn to stay with ourselves, period. Staying with ourselves is a skill most of us severely lack, because we've learned through others and ourselves that our own bodies are the least safe place to be. This practice gives you the chance to stay with the parts of yourself that are hurting, the parts that need you not to go somewhere else, like down the neck of a bottle or the rabbit hole of social media.

RASINS also gives you something else, access to a practice known as deep learning. People learn better when they are challenging themselves just outside their ability (where things are not too hard and not too easy). In this state of deep learning, when we are trying to accomplish something difficult, we lay thicker neural networks, meaning that—with practice—our skill at *not* drinking becomes more potent than our skill *of* drinking. Lastly, it breaks the cycle of cause and effect: not reacting means not feeding the habit.

While there are distinct differences and benefits between building routines and using tools to overcome cravings, and engaging with them directly, there is no superior alternative; they are all helpful, all complementary, and each deserve a place in your toolbox. But learning to break the cycle of addiction is only half the story; to make lasting change, we need to work directly with the root causes of our suffering.

11

Get at the Root:
Learning to Mother Yourself

*When I realized I had to change my life—and that such a deep
change would happen only through gentleness, and not the discipline
I used on myself—I had no idea how to love myself. But I did know
how to mother. Caring for others has always felt instinctive; from the
moment I held them, my daughters have always been nurtured with
compassion, tolerance, and generosity. I just couldn't seem to do it for
myself. But I had to.* —KATIE BICKELL

Three years before I got sober, sometime after my One and I
split and before I started sleeping with my boss, I spent a
week with my family back home in Fresno, and then came
crawling back to San Francisco. I don't remember what exactly
had happened over that week, but I do remember my dad showing up in a motor home at my mom's house and that I'd done
something wrong, like maybe not asked him a question I was
supposed to ask, or maybe I just didn't show enough interest in
him being there. After I graduated from college, some window
had closed between my father and me. Any chance he had at
being my dad had now passed, because I had no more growing
up to do, or at least not the way one does under the tutelage and
care of their parents. When he popped back into my life like
this—randomly, unexpectedly, and with an aloofness that be-
trayed he was still living off the merits of the fathering he'd done
through 1994—showing even indifference to him felt generous.

Whatever I did to hurt my father's feelings that holiday, I was in trouble for it, or rather my sister was, because she was the one who cared. When Heather called to tell me Dad was upset, that *I* had done something wrong—not he who had abandoned us but me, the abandonee—something snapped, the way it always snapped when my father's feelings mattered more than mine. Suddenly I wasn't a thirty-one-year-old in her bed talking on the phone, I was a wild animal, mad with resentment and untended wounds. My sister, the only person apart from my mother who was privy to such breaks, cooed and soothed, and when I finally broke through the fury into the sobs, she gently said that perhaps I should see a therapist.

I'd gone that route before, in the throes of anorexia my senior year of high school, a session that ended when the *mental health professional* asked me if I knew what the Bible said about homosexuality, and told me that because my dad was gay, he was going to hell. So for that reason alone I wasn't keen on trying it again, but there was more to my unwillingness. I was a grownup, a professional, an adult by all measures, and women like me weren't supposed to get help for doing something we weren't supposed to be doing, which was regressing to our five-year-old tantrum-throwing selves. Help wasn't the answer; denying I needed it was.

I did what I always did after one of those breaks, which was pretend it hadn't happened. I shoved it down, and then I shoved myself into the four p.m. Bikram class, and then after that I shoved a cake, a bottle of wine, a Christmas ham, a prized cow down my throat until I ached, until I threw it up, until I had imitated some process of cleansing that might kill the little girl inside me who refused to get over it and grow the fuck up.

———

We have this idea that once we reach some arbitrary age or landmark in our growth, we are supposed to reach a pinnacle of maturity, as if we only have so much time to be the most damaged and stunted version of ourselves, and then *poof,* it becomes unacceptable. We tell each other to grow up and act more mature, and we think the worse thing we could be found out to be is a child parading in an adult's body. It was so absolutely unacceptable to me to be that arrested five-year-old with daddy issues, it somehow made more sense to eat ten thousand calories and vomit them up and drink myself into oblivion, than it did to say I was in pain and needed help. There is no room in our society for weakness, suffering, or grief, so we seldom allow ourselves to be the wounded children that we *all* are inside, and we certainly don't allow ourselves, or each other, the grace to continue growing up at our own pace for the rest of our lives.

In *Gift of Change,* Marianne Williamson says, "When children are young we know they're growing, and we take this into account in our dealings with them. We don't expect a twelve-year-old to have the maturity she or he will have at eighteen. And as adults we're still growing too, whether or not we can always see that in each other. We're not finished once we reach a certain age; rather, we continue to grow and develop as long as we're alive." The truth is we never really grow up—like, ever—but we've all agreed on an idea that we are supposed to age out of certain behaviors. So we learn to mask our insecurities and immaturities, and we get really good at maintaining a facade that says "I have my shit together." We are a culture of aching, maladjusted humans doing everything in our power to show the world we are not. We beat ourselves up, belittle ourselves, measure ourselves against some impossible standard that doesn't allow us to keep growing. What would we be if we gave ourselves allowances for being human, showed ourselves tenderness and sweetness in the face of shame or fear?

Quitting drinking was a reckoning, an excuse to claim the ways in which I was wounded and not functioning. It gave me a reason to go to a therapist, to do past-life regressions, and to get massages from people who encouraged me to cry, to release, to howl in an audible and external way that matched the howling that had been going on inside me for decades. It allowed me to accept how I'd been hurt and the ways I'd stopped growing in a manner that wasn't shameful. It allowed me to see the various points along my life where I'd stopped metabolizing emotions and instead numbed them. It gave me the space to make sense of an existence that had been mostly pointless and insufferable, and from there, to build.

Quitting drinking was also where the jig of treating myself like shit was up. I had no choice but to accept that I alone was responsible for taking care of this precious person whose life I was charged with. I could no longer allow for me, or anyone else, to treat this innocent, kind, hurting woman named Holly absolutely horribly. I finally saw that I was a life worth saving and protecting; I finally understood that my number-one job was to nurture this human who had been doing the best she could with what she had. This meant changing the way I spoke to her in my head, deconstructing the impossible perfectionism I'd always told her she had to have in order to be worthy, ending the abusive ways I'd let people treat her, and allowing her the space to finally do the work she needed to do to heal.

In her book *A Mind of Your Own*, Kelly Brogan quotes a Kundalini teacher who once explained, "As a mother you are supposed to sacrifice, tolerate, be very patient, be very thoughtful of others, and understand all the pros and cons of any situation. As a woman, you must give nothing, you have to protect yourself first, and you need not tolerate any nonsense. Woman must be able to ascertain which is the correct relationship—woman or mother, sword or shield." In many ways, when I quit drinking, I became mother to myself and woman to most everyone else.

GETTING TO THE ROOT OF OUR ADDICTIONS

When I came to recovery, so much was wrong with my life, I didn't really know where to start. Everything had in some way come apart—from my home to my finances to my relationships to my health—and all that was left was one big mess. We've already talked at length about breaking the cycle of addiction and changing our core beliefs, but the most essential part of recovery is working directly with the root causes of our suffering and getting at the things that make existing in our skin unmanageable. Unhealed traumas, an inability to be with ourselves, destructive patterns of behavior, abuse and self-abuse, defects in self-regulation, lack of purpose or existential meaning, nutritional imbalances, and neglected physical bodies all need to be addressed so that we don't simply move from one crappy coping mechanism (like wine) to another (like shopping). How we build a life we want to live in is the focus of the rest of this chapter.

Trauma

Trauma is a heavy-duty word loaded with baggage, yet we understand little about it. Trauma is also something that we can be sure we've encountered in life and are in some ways still carrying around with us.

The body is one of the most magnificent and complicated organisms—it has its own intelligence and its own innate way of operating. It seeks wholeness and completion of actions, and trauma interrupts this process of completion. People often mistake trauma for the harrowing event that occurred—the rape, the car accident, the horrific crime—but trauma isn't the disturbing experience itself. It's what occurs in our bodies when we aren't able to process the experience fully.

One frequently cited example of this "completing process" is that of a bunny being chased by a tiger. In this scenario, the fleeing bunny's fight-or-flight response is in high gear—its sympathetic nervous system is pumping all the survival chemicals into its system. If the bunny manages to outrun the tiger, it will shake to metabolize all the stuff that was released into its little bunny body so it could survive. Then the bunny will move on. In the real world, when we encounter something that triggers our fight, flight, or freeze response, we don't go behind a tree and shake it out. We just keep moving, and unlike the bunny, our process never completes. That trauma lives on in us, and then when we encounter something that reminds us of the traumatic event, we get transported right back into it, and experience it exactly as if it were happening in the present—there is absolutely no difference between a body that is running for its life, and a body that thinks it's still running for its life ten years later; only the environment has changed.

To understand a bit how trauma works, it's important to understand how it gets stored in memory. As we discussed in Chapter 5, the human brain has three distinct regions: the survival brain (reptilian), the limbic-emotional brain (mammalian), and the neocortex (human, cognitive). When we encounter something we perceive as dangerous—let's say a man with a gun—we go through each of these layers in an attempt to survive the threat. The first layer, the neocortex, is our rational, thinking brain, and its survival instinct is to socially engage—we try to talk to the man with the gun and reason our way out of the threat. The second layer, the limbic brain, relies on emotion to respond—it will either fight the man with the gun, or attempt to flee him. The last layer, the reptilian brain, kicks in our freeze response—if we can't reason, fight, or flee, we end up immobilized, helpless, and basically preparing for death. If the first layer deescalates the threat successfully, there is no resultant trauma— we've processed the event to completion. However, if the second and third layers are called upon—if we fight, flee, or freeze— and then don't complete the action (the bunny equivalent of shaking it off), the life force that was called upon to either mobilize or immobilize us is not discharged and remains in the body. Until that trauma is "released" or "renegotiated," it is as if this past event were still happening in the present.

People tend to think trauma is a remembering, something that gets stuck in our brain that we can't think ourselves out of, which means most people think that trauma is something that can get resolved through talk therapy. But trauma is stored in the body as unprocessed, stuck energy, and because traumatic memories are coded in the brain nonlinearly and through our implicit memory (the subconscious part of our memory we don't have direct access to), talk therapy doesn't get us very far in resolving trauma.

Addictive patterns are often misdirected attempts to manage symptoms of PTSD. We drink to self-medicate and to numb our feelings of fear or powerlessness; we drink as a surrogate to connection, when we feel totally disconnected from ourselves; we drink to dampen guilt or rage, to feel alive, to manage depression or anxiety, and so forth. As a result, if we remove the substance we've been using to manage symptoms of PTSD, we're without our medicine, so in addiction recovery, we have to start the work of renegotiating trauma.

"Fixing trauma" feels next to impossible for a lot of people.

We think it means some grand gesture, or some type of acute prolonged therapy; it doesn't. We also often think our experience really doesn't qualify as a trauma—it took me years to finally understand that my relationship with my father and the acute events that happened between us were traumatic. All of us have something to gain from working to release trauma, and none of this work has to be extreme.

RENEGOTIATING "BIG T" AND "LITTLE T" TRAUMA

There are two different types of trauma. "Big T" trauma is the kind related to an acute, severe event (a sexual assault, being held at gunpoint, a car accident, being physically or mentally abused as a child)."Little t" trauma is the kind that we pick up through the course of our lives (an argument, *almost* being in a car accident, getting yelled at in the workplace).

To renegotiate a "Big T" trauma—which can't be "talked through" because it lives in our tissues, not in our heads—we need to engage in a *somatic* or bodily therapy. As Bessel van der Kolk describes in *The Body Keeps the Score,* there are four main therapies that help renegotiate trauma, all of which must be accessed through a therapeutic relationship.

The first and most widely used is eye movement desensitization and reprocessing, or EMDR. In this type of therapy, a person typically follows a therapist's finger or moving object while being asked to recall the traumatic event; the eye movement, which is rapid, allows for repressed internal associations to arise, and for the "trapped" event to be processed, integrated, and released.

In the second therapy, emotional freedom technique, or EFT, a person typically is led by a therapist or certified practitioner to repeat a script related to the traumatic event while tapping on different meridian points (or energy centers) on the body. This process allows for stuck energy related to the traumatic event to be released and flow through the body to completion—it's not unlike unkinking a garden hose to let water flow through. You can also practice EFT on yourself—I've worked with practitioners in a clinical setting and regularly practice it on myself using scripts from the internet. (Nick Ortner's *The Tapping Solution* is a rich resource.)

The third therapy is somatic experiencing or SE, a method created by Peter Levine. It is a body-oriented approach that works directly with bodily sensations in order to release traumatic shock. Like EMDR and EFT, therapists are trained in the SE method, and it is available only through these practitioners.

Lastly, neurofeedback uses real-time displays of brain activity to provide the brain with a mirror of its own function. It can create new patterns in the brain that "enhance its natural complexity and bias toward self-regulation," and it has been shown effective in treating trauma.

All four therapies have proven to be effective in managing trauma, but they are all costly and require working with a therapist. If you can't afford or don't have access to any of these treatments, a good way to start renegotiating trauma is through taking smaller actions that are highly accessible and mostly affordable. We'll talk about them next.

"Little t" trauma, on the other hand, is not something that we release once and for all; it's not an acute trauma; it's the stuff we pick up throughout our lives. We consistently collect "Little t" trauma, so we have to develop practices to constantly discharge it. The practices discussed below help us to do that, and they can all help us recover from addiction. Many are coping mechanisms, some aid in self-regulation, and all are healing. If you incorporate a few of these practices into your life, you will get the double advantage of renegotiating trauma (they work on "Big T" trauma, too), and healing from substance abuse.

MEDITATION

Meditation is the lifeblood of recovery. If addiction is total lack of awareness (and it is), meditation is the opposite: it is the cultivation of total awareness. It allows us to develop the space to witness our lives, instead of being caught up in the drama of it all. It rewires and strengthens the prefrontal cortex of our brains that addiction compromises. Meditation practice is like strength training for the mind, the equivalent of working out your biceps with weights. If there is one thing that has saved my life in recovery, it is my daily meditation practice—it has entirely changed me as a human.

The benefits of a meditation practice are almost too many to list. Meditation cultivates a sense of peace and well-being, reduces stress, creates agency and personal power, strengthens the mind-body-spirit connection, alleviates depression and anxiety, gives us control over our emotions, and develops patience and compassion. It promotes clarity of mind and gives us an ability to be present with whatever is happening, and teaches us to ride out our suffering and discomfort. Almost every single recovery modality that exists incorporates meditation (or mindfulness practice), and that's because it works.

There are many ways to start a meditation practice. We've already gone over some of them in Chapter 10. My preferred methods are Kundalini meditation by Yogi Bhajan, vipassana meditation, and guided meditations. There are a number of apps that make adopting a practice easier, such as Calm, Insight Timer, Glo, and Headspace. My favorite books on the subject are *Awakening Joy* by James Baraz, *Meditation as Medicine* by

Dharma Singh Khalsa, and *Eight Step Recovery* by Vimalasara (Valerie) Mason-John. I'm also fond of Gabby Bernstein's guided meditations (they are supereasy), and Pema Chödrön's.

YOGA

It's almost silly to define yoga as separate from meditation, because meditation *is* yoga; here in this section, I'm talking primarily of the physical practice of yoga, or asana. In terms of renegotiating trauma, very few practices are as mind-body focused as yoga. It teaches us to connect the breath, movement of the body, and mind—and truly *inhabit* our bodies—as we move through a series of asanas. *Yoga* translates to "yolk" or "union" and is an ancient practice that, in essence, sews us up.

I began practicing yoga regularly in 2003, after I suffered a series of panic attacks and developed agoraphobia. It was the only thing that helped me manage my anxiety, and the practice stuck. What started as a purely physical act, with absolutely no understanding or respect for the lineage of yoga, has since become my spiritual practice with a physical benefit—something I mention because yoga in the United States is often a skeletonized, culturally appropriated form that focuses on body shape, competition, and Lululemon sports bras. That's not what yoga is; it's a reverence, a practice made available to us not through commercialization but through the passing of knowledge over generations, and something I believe can only truly be of benefit if we are mindful of this distinction. Susanna Barkataki, a sober yoga speaker and teacher, is an incredible resource for learning how to practice yoga without cultural appropriation.

Like meditation, yoga has so many benefits, they're difficult to summarize. In the context of recovery from substance abuse and trauma, yoga can teach us to stay in the fire, or discomfort: if we learn to ride out discomfort on our yoga mats, we can learn to ride out severe cravings when we're out in the world. It teaches us to develop control of the mind (again, rebuilding that prefrontal cortex that gets compromised in addiction); it repairs the nervous system; and serves as a healthy coping mechanism (my recovery was choosing the mat over the bar).

What it did for me went far beyond just these things. Yoga was not just my coping mechanism, it was (and is) my high—it's how I feel the way I wanted drugs to make me feel. It was also how I eliminated reactiveness and cultivated a fierceness I'd never known before in my life. Yoga was how I made friends and found teachers and community and connection, and it's what gave me control over my energy; yoga also helped me do things I couldn't have otherwise, like fall asleep without drugs and alcohol.

The mainstay of my practice is Kundalini yoga (as taught by Yogi Bhajan) and Vinyasa, a form of hatha yoga that's quite physical. I alternate between the two depending on what I need, and as part of my recovery, I got certified to teach both. I prefer Kundalini for the specific purpose of breaking addiction—it's highly accessible for all body types and abilities, and it's dynamic. A number of different styles of yoga—from bhakti to dharma to karma to raj—incorporate service, chanting, prayer, meditation, and devotion. I suggest you start with Kundalini. Kia Miller on glo.com is an excellent resource, or just search YouTube for "Kundalini meditations." If you're interested in learning Vinyasa, Stephanie Snyder teaches classes for recovery on glo.com.

BREATH

Breath (pranayama) work is another powerful practice that can help you in recovery. The breath is the ultimate unit of nutrition—we can survive for months without food, and days without water, but only about a minute without breath. And yet so few of us know how to properly breathe, or use our breath as a tool. Working with our breath means working directly with our minds: by breathing properly, we can directly control our emotional states. Try it for yourself and see. Inhale to a count of five, hold for one, then exhale for a count of five. If you pay close attention, you'll notice an immediate shift in your energy. Like meditation, breathwork has almost too many benefits to list. It carries our life force (prana), activates our parasympathetic nervous system (the rest-and-digest response), allows us to manipulate our energy at will (different practices can give us energy, relaxation, clarity, or even help us control a panic attack or snap out of cold fear), helps us enter meditative states and connects us to the present moment, directly cleanses the lungs and removes waste (detoxes), and helps us manage pain (think Lamaze breathing during childbirth).

My meditation and yoga practice incorporates breathwork, and Kundalini features many different targeted breath exercises. I prefer using specific techniques such as Breath of Fire, Sitali Breathing, Alternative Nostril Breathing, and Long Deep Breathing (all of which can be found in a YouTube search or any Kundalini yoga manual). A simple trick we talked about in Chapter 9 is to set an alarm throughout the day to do a minute of breathing to center ourselves.

OTHER TECHNIQUES TO RENEGOTIATE TRAUMA

We can incorporate many other practices to help us reconnect to our bodies and heal from trauma and addiction. Massage is an incredible way to stimulate the lymphatic system, detox, and start to re-inhabit our bodies. Learning EFT and practicing it regularly can help us to shake off high emotions on the spot, or release little traumas as they accumulate. A support network, as

discussed in Chapter 14, is another antidote to trauma. Acupuncture, reiki, and sound therapy all support this kind of healing. Whatever you choose, my recommendation is to use a
meditation practice as your cornerstone and build from there.

The Therapeutic Relationship

Because I'd had a terrible experience with psychotherapy in my
teens, I wasn't keen on working with a therapist again. But when
I (mis)diagnosed myself with Borderline Personality Disorder—
and came out to my family about it—it didn't feel like I had
much choice in the matter. I found the first therapist through
my company's insurance directory, a woman, not far from my
office in downtown San Francisco, who during our first appointment appeared to be genuinely terrified of me. When she
wouldn't tell me what neighborhood she lived in, I decided she
wasn't my person, and I did what any responsible, self-loathing,
nonconfrontational people-pleaser would do and emailed her
within the requisite twenty-four-hour period of our next appointment to cancel.

My next therapist was a man whose name I can't remember;
he too came from the aforementioned insurance directory, and
while I passed on asking him for the coordinates of his home
location, after a few months of sessions where I felt like we
weren't really getting anywhere, I broke up with him over email,
too. I told him it wasn't him, it was me, and he told me I was
difficult. My third therapist (in as many months) was Leah, a
woman who'd "agreed to take me on," and one who'd come recommended by a friend. Leah wasn't fucking around; she charged
$250 a session, didn't scrap with insurance, and spent the first
five minutes of our session staring at me in a way I could only
account for as her reading my thoughts. She was magical, and
just being in her presence made me a saner, kinder version of

myself. Leah was the one who helped me get sober, and I will never for the rest of my life forget her.

There are few things more depressing than finding a therapist in recovery. For starters, there's the process of just shopping for a therapist, an activity I can say with confidence is at least ten thousand times more depressing than shopping Tinder for a date. Then there's the process of meeting this person—sitting down across from a stranger who is quite possibly more fucked up than you are; who is allowed to ask you questions, who you're not even allowed to ask where they live. And then when you find someone tolerable, or even better than tolerable, the worst part is: you have to keep going back. There was really no act that revealed where I was—and wasn't—in my early recovery as much as the trip to the therapist. Which is all to say, finding a therapist and then going to therapy is a crap-ton of depressing and terrifying work. It's also extremely important in addiction recovery.

There are so many reasons to extol the virtues of therapy in recovery. For starters, if you find a good therapist, they provide a grounding relationship that tethers you, cares for you, and holds the fort down while you build a new life. Second, recovery is like a fireworks show where everything's blowing up all at once: your emotions have emotions, you're doing CBT and DBT while you're researching CBD and learning EFT, looking at the sky is a thing, you're worried about kombucha, you want to drink, you don't want to drink, you want to drink—and this is like a Tuesday. While a therapist isn't going to manage all that for you, they *can* help you sort through it, put it in order, make sense of it—or even just listen to you talk about how hard it is. Finally, a good therapist can help you to excavate the truth. This was exactly what Leah, and what Ann and Azita, who came after her, did for me—I could count on them to hold me up in the moments I simply could not hold myself up.

———

Finding a therapist can be a tricky affair, especially when it comes to finding one as a woman or other marginalized human in recovery. Many believe Twelve Step programs are the only valid method of recovery, and I've heard enough stories of people being pressured by their therapist to attend AA, or gaslit for their choice to not. I've also heard from a number of people whose therapists said they didn't have a drinking problem, or argued for moderation, or dismissed their concerns about drinking outright. Then there's the part where you have to find someone you actually like (and you do; you cannot develop a therapeutic relationship with someone you don't feel good about, or don't trust), and then, of course, there's the whole issue of having to find the means to pay them—it is a privilege to afford therapy, and many of us don't have it.

In Tempest Sobriety School, we've developed a protocol to help students find a therapist, and it's anchored in our core value of developing agency. Many of us have a tendency to elevate a therapist above ourselves as some authority figure, so we act as "takers" when we're shopping for a therapist, rather than buyers with power and choice. So the first thing I stress to students who are looking for a therapist is to try them out—any therapist worth their salt will be open to an introductory phone call or even a trial session at no cost.

FINDING A THERAPIST

There are a number of ways to source a therapist. If you have insurance, you can do it through your mental health benefit directory. You can use *Psychology Today*'s website, or try organizations like Alma (helloalma.com) or Two Chairs (twochairs .com), which are brick-and-mortar establishments that house various therapists. If you are looking for a therapist who specializes in EMDR, EFT, or any other specialized therapy, you can search the internet for their organizations or guilds. For example, Traumahealing.org is home to a directory of SE therapists. BIPOC femme-identified individuals can find a therapist through therapyforblackgirls.com. If you are looking for a cost-effective way to get therapy, talkspace.com is an option. If you live near a university with a psychology program, you can sometimes find therapists in training at sliding-scale rates.

INTERVIEWING THE THERAPIST

I can't stress it enough—you must interview the therapist, spend time with them, and ensure that you are aligned with them and that they are someone you want to tell your innermost secrets to. Once you've pulled together a list of therapists you want to work with, call them to set up times for a trial session or a phone interview. My friend Kim Kokoska, an LMFT trained in SE who currently works at Tempest, suggests asking the following: Are you licensed? Do you have experience dealing with addiction? How do you conceptualize addiction? How do you view AA and the Twelve Steps? Do you think they are necessary for recovery? Do you work with clients in active addiction or clients who are using harm reduction methods? Do you have specialized training in trauma, and have you been on the receiving end of this training? What are your rates? Do you offer a sliding scale or accept insurance? Are you willing to share your home address? (I kid.)

MAKING AND KEEPING THE APPOINTMENTS

Now comes the hard part: you have to actually go. Therapy isn't a quick fix. It's a relationship you build with another person that allows you to excavate your depths, to reveal yourself *to* yourself. It takes time to find a therapist, time to go to the appointments, and patience to see it through to results. Therapy isn't a panacea; it's not going to do the heavy lifting of recovery. But it does provide a dimension that's necessary for it.

MOVING ON

I've had six therapists in six years. With some, our relationship naturally came to an end when I stopped growing, and with others, a move precipitated the separation. As in all relationships, you may stay for a while with one therapist, or move on as you evolve past what's possible in the relationship. My current therapist is my longest-running. We've been together for nearly three years simply because we've been able to evolve together.

Nutrition and Lifestyle

Early sobriety was marked by many things: my understanding of how addiction works, my incorporation of meditation and yoga practices, therapy, trauma renegotiation, energy work, body work, relationship work. Nutrition was mostly an afterthought—something I addressed for a short period of time when I developed a severe sugar addiction after quitting alcohol (there weren't enough pastries in the world). I overcame sugar addiction by rebalancing my neurochemicals and gut health with something called amino acid therapy (under a doctor's supervision), which stopped the sugar cravings and eventually my bulimia. But other than that, I largely ignored nutrition.

The reasons why are valid. First, I have a history of eating disorders, so I can't diet without being thrown right back into the disorder. Second, I always considered myself "nutritious enough"—I didn't drink soda, I ate whole foods, I read labels, I drank three liters of water a day, I guzzled green juice, I ate mostly vegetarian. Third, just by not drinking, smoking, or drugging, I thought of myself as about five thousand times healthier than most. Fourth, I had a firm belief that recovery and thriving in life were built more on spirituality, purpose, creativity, healthy relationships, and yoga, and that nutrition was just a bonus.

However, in my second year of sobriety, I was sick and exhausted, plagued with a number of health issues that cropped up right around the time I quit my job. I got acne for the first time in my life, I had this unrelenting body odor that would not go away no matter how much I scrubbed at it, my PMS and periods got markedly worse, and I slept for anywhere from eight to twelve hours a night and couldn't get out of bed most days. My moods were all over the place, I couldn't eat enough food, I couldn't drink enough coffee, I couldn't really function. It was like walking through mud for a year.

All this seemed to happen at once. One minute I was working fifteen-hour days and sleeping five hours a night and popping out of bed with the boundless energy I'd found when I quit drinking. And then one day, just like that, I didn't wake up at five a.m., I woke up at noon, and I never really got over it, no matter how much yoga I did, or B_{12} I took.

At first I assumed it was part of my recovery. I'd worked myself to death, I drank coffee to make it through the day, and all those toxins were leaving my system. I told myself I needed to do more yoga and meditation and my body would right itself. Except I couldn't find the energy to do the yoga, or if I did, I was drinking coffee on my way to yoga and grabbing more afterward.

I was using coffee to self-regulate the way I had with alcohol and pot. So I quit coffee the way I had quit everything else. Only this time because I was so depleted, I went nuclear. I added vegetables and green juice and water and B_{12} and yoga and breathing. I meditated more than I ever had. I bought one of those fancy lights that mimic the sun. For a while removing coffee seemed to improve my energy and body chemistry and sleep, but then it got worse. The BO returned with a vengeance. The back acne spread to my chest and made a guest appearance above my right eyebrow. Some days I was so tired I couldn't shower. Even more frustrating, I turned to food to self-regulate and gained weight. So I ran more. I SoulCycled more. I juice-cleansed for three days. I popped more B_{12}. In other words, I did the opposite of what I would recommend any of you do: I beat the crap out of myself to "be better," and I berated myself when my efforts failed.

I consulted my friend Mary Vance, an expert in the diet and nutrition issues specific to those recovering from addiction, and learned how important a role nutrition plays in successful recovery. Specifically:

- We often have preexisting conditions when we start drinking, like imbalanced brain chemistry, blood sugar issues, or hormone problems, and turning to alcohol is often an attempt to regulate these imbalances.

- We exacerbate these preexisting issues with our drinking.

- When we stop drinking, we have the imbalances we started off with, *plus* the imbalances that we developed from choosing wine over food, plus depleted minerals and a whole host of other effects from the toxic nature of alcohol.

- In order to fully recover from addictive patterns (and not just shift from one to the next), we often have to address these imbalances and bring ourselves back to a state of health through nutrition. It's not just eating better, it's repairing the systems of our body in a targeted, individualized way (and doing the necessary intellectual, psychological, existential, environmental, societal, and other physical practices).

- If we *don't* address this piece, recovery can be much more difficult. We can plateau, and we are susceptible to addiction transference or drinking again. If we *do* address this piece, it makes all our other efforts that much more effective and the process much less painful.

I got off the phone with Mary, and mulling over the conversation, sipping my shame coffee, I had a breakthrough: I'd never fixed my body on this level. And I was running around with neurophysiology issues (brain chemical depletion), blood sugar issues, hormone issues (adrenal fatigue, nuclear period, mood swings), and most definitely mineral depletion. Green juice, meditation, and SoulCycle weren't going to fix what needed to be fixed. And until I fixed them, I'd just keep running to other addictive substances and behaviors in an attempt to balance the imbalances (like compulsively texting my fuckbuddy when I felt empty, drinking too much caffeine when I felt tired, or binge-eating when I was overstimulated and needed to escape). I didn't want that existence, because I hadn't come that far to only go that far. So I made changes that have, over time, resulted in more vitality.

You can make it through recovery from alcohol dependency on cigarettes and coffee and doughnuts. *Many* people have. I did. If it works, it works. But to have sustained growth, to support the spiritual and cognitive and ethical and environmental and relational practices that are part of any healthy recovery, you've got to take care of your body in a *much* different way. Green juice is great, kale is great. But it's not enough and you will, like I have, just move the addiction somewhere else until you fix ALL the things that caused you to reach for it in the first place. From the childhood trauma to the anxiety to the hormone imbalances and on.

There's a tendency to believe in order to "fix" our physical selves we have to go all in on it; do some cleanse or go keto or take fistfuls of costly supplements or work with a naturopath. We live in a society that impresses on us the need to be pinnacles of health in order to function, and often that drive to perfection ends up making us sicker. The thing I want to stress to you the most is that you *will* struggle with your vitality and health in recovery—we can't do what we've done to ourselves with alcohol and drugs and whatever else and not feel the effects. Once the body isn't being assaulted by alcohol anymore, it will have to go through a rebalancing, and that rebalancing will often show up as exhaustion, acne, painful periods, insomnia (or the opposite, an inability to do anything but sleep), body odor, and weight gain. This isn't abnormal, this is normal, a sign that your body finally has a chance to heal itself.

It can feel like a huge middle finger if you've done something as miraculous and healthful as quitting drinking, and then your body feels worse. This is part of the process—part of the healing—and you can't beat it away. Like everything else, you have to move through it, patiently and attentively. There are six simple things that you can do to start feeling better now. In our school, we stress that recovery is hard enough without the pressure of having to do a number of health protocols. Start with these six basic changes and build from there.

GET SEVEN TO EIGHT HOURS OF SLEEP A NIGHT

Remember if you've been drinking for a number of years, your body has been in an almost constant state of sleep deprivation. For that reason alone, sleep is important. But sleep is also essential for restoring hormone imbalance, mood regulation, brain health, blood sugar balance, and detoxification. If you do one thing, get sleep, and if you have trouble falling asleep without the aid of booze or drugs, don't worry. I had this issue at first, but with all the other changes I was making, along with some targeted work (good sleep hygiene, my evening ritual as discussed in Chapter 10), I was able to get to sleep at night with no fuss. There are a ton of resources on sleep on Mary Vance's website, maryvancenc.com.

EAT AT REGULAR INTERVALS

When you first quit drinking, you're going to have to work hard to stabilize your blood sugar so as to avoid unnecessary cravings for alcohol—nearly 97 percent of folks recovering from Alcohol Use Disorder are hypoglycemic. One way you can manage your blood sugar is by eating at regular intervals, at least every four hours. Make sure to include some protein, and avoid foods high on the glycemic index (empty carbs). Avoid caffeine and sugar first thing in the morning, as this spikes your blood sugar and sets you up for a crash. Eating at regular intervals is essential for keeping blood sugar levels stable, maintaining consistent energy, preventing cravings, and regulating mood.

EAT PROTEIN AND FAT

Try to eat a good amount of healthy proteins and fats. Healthy proteins include poultry, organic meats, eggs, and wild fish. If you're vegetarian, choose quinoa, brown rice, amaranth, legumes, and vegan proteins. Healthy fats include nut butters, avocado, coconut butter and oil, butter, ghee, and olive oil. These foods are essential for keeping you full and satisfied, providing your body with the building blocks for hormones and neurochemicals, keeping your blood sugar regulated, and improving your mood. Fats are especially important for brain health—remember, alcohol is a neurotoxin, and addiction decreases the volume of gray matter (cortex); the brain is made of fat, and you can aid in the rebuilding of brain health by consuming healthy fats.

HYDRATE

As Mary Vance says, "The solution to pollution is dilution." In other words, to detox we need to drink a lot of water. A good rule of thumb for how much to consume: take your body weight (measured in pounds), halve it, convert to ounces, and drink that much water. If you weigh 200 pounds, that means you should be drinking 100 ounces of water a day. Go for spring water, or filtered water that doesn't come from plastic bottles or plastic filtration systems. Hydration is essential for detoxification, emotional balance, and staving off cravings.

MOVE YOUR BODY

Moving your body (exercising) aids in a number of things. It helps you reembody yourself—addiction is a dysfunction in our first chakra, or the survival chakra (meaning when it's out of balance, you feel unsafe in the world, ungrounded), and moving your body helps you to feel grounded, at home in yourself and your environment. Exercise is also essential for detoxification, mood balance (raising dopamine and serotonin), hormone balance, stress regulation, and vitamin D production. Get fifteen to thirty minutes of exercise a day, preferably outside, in the sun.

EAT WHOLE FOODS

"Eat whole foods" simply means "eat foods as close to their unadulterated state as possible." In recovery, you need to provide your body with as many vital nutrients as possible. While some supplementing might be necessary in recovery, food can provide you with a good base for healing, and it affects all systems, promoting liver detox, blood sugar balance, brain health, hormone balance, and gut health (whole30.com is a great resource. Melissa Hartwig, its founder, is a champion of increasing access to whole foods for those who don't have the means).

A point worth repeating: You do not have to do everything I've discussed. Pick one thing, maybe water or sleep, and start there, and know that you are building. This is how you can make sustainable, lasting changes; slowly, over time, piece by piece. I am not some poster child of health because of the work I've done on my physical body; I am not dominated by it or consumed by it. I am mindful of my physical health, and I'm also mindful that I'm forever in process.

Finances, Spirituality, and Other Broken Stuff

A number of other things were core to my recovery, including getting out of debt and getting my finances in order, changing my career, finding purpose, and finding spiritual connection. Chances are, a lot of areas in your life need addressing, some of which are or aren't covered in these pages. Here's what I did: I focused first on the thing that was killing me (alcohol), then on the next thing that was killing me (bulimia), and from there, the other things fell into place. As I became more in touch with my gut sense, I understood the next steps I needed to take. When I was ready to start working on my finances—two years after I quit drinking—I was guided to the right resources and people, as I was ready to receive them. Tend to your most broken parts first, then add the things that feel right, and trust this *unfolding path*.

I follow a set of practices I call "nonnegotiables." They're yoga, hydration, therapy, meditation, sleep, and spiritual investigation. These are my priorities, and if I'm checking these boxes, then I'm okay. Find a few things that are absolutely meaningful to you, that you can stick with, and keep them close. Learn to use your discrimination and to counter the belief that you have to be everything to be anything; you don't. This isn't about being perfect, or doing everything. This is about finding the things that work for you, being brave enough to prioritize those things, and letting that be enough.

12

Navigating the Sober Illuminati

Simply because we have convictions that work well for us, it becomes easy to assume that we have all the truth.

—BILL WILSON, CO-FOUNDER OF ALCOHOLICS ANONYMOUS

Once upon a time, I went to an AA meeting against my will. I was about ten months sober, and I'd sworn off meetings ever since I'd been told one too many times that if I didn't keep coming back I'd become a toothless whore. But I'd made some new sober friends and they thought it would be fun if we went to a meeting together, so I conceded.

I told my new buddies that I had a certain stink about me that book-thumping fundamentalists could smell, but they promised that this meeting was different. Younger. Hipper. So when an hour into the meeting I found myself cornered in the bathroom by a yogini in a trucker hat asking me if I "wanted to drink again" because I wasn't working "the program," I couldn't help but feel a deep sense of *I told you so, bitches.*

That moment in the bathroom, when a woman who didn't even know me—who had no idea what I'd been through, what my life looked like, what the shape of my heart was—stood there telling me I was screwed for life because I did yoga instead of AA, was life changing. It turns out that being dragged against my better instincts to an AA meeting finally put me in the position where I had to confront my biggest fears: Did I really know what was right for me? Could I trust my own gut sense? Or was I kidding myself? In other words, I finally had to face the question I'd been running from: *Was my (oversized) ego running the show?* I was terrified of this question because from the moment I decided not to drink, people had warned me about this deeply ingrained notion: that the alcoholic is a liar, can't be trusted, can't trust herself. Her ego and pride and self-centered thoughts will be her end.

The meeting was held in the rec room of a church, and afterward I ran to the chapel adjacent. It was empty, and I walked to the front pew, dropped to my knees, and begged God for the truth.

Please tell me I'm not kidding myself.

Please tell me I'm okay, that it's okay to trust what feels wrong and what feels right.

Please tell me I don't have this all wrong.

I prayed so hard I shook, and then I opened my eyes, half expecting Jesus to be there. He wasn't, but right in front of my face was a huge wooden eagle, which felt like a sign from God. The eagle, my power animal, the bird inked across my chest, the sign that had repeatedly shown up when I asked God for signs.

I got the message. I didn't need to be afraid of whether or not my ego was fooling me; it was safe to trust myself and what I knew to be right for me, which was not AA.

Maybe this doesn't sound like a big deal to you, but I was the only person I knew in the whole wide world who had gotten sober without the Twelve Steps and AA. For the past fifteen months, I'd been telling people how I got sober, which sounded a lot like just doing a lot of yoga and repeating positive affirmations, and often I'd get that side-eye look that basically says, *She's so fucked.*

I realized in the church that night that my freedom wasn't about breaking up with alcohol alone. It was also about breaking up with other people's truths that didn't work for me. As I left the chapel, I skipped down the street, passing that yogini and a bunch of other people who had found what felt right for them, knowing in my heart I had found what was right for me, too.

I wish I could tell you that deciding for or against AA as part of your path is the only thing that's confusing about sobriety. But holy hell, it's not. There's a whole host of confusing stuff to navigate. Like, are we really powerless? Do we have to call ourselves alcoholics, and if we refuse to, are we in denial? Is relapse a sign that we are eternally screwed? What about atheists who don't have a higher power? Does taking psychopharmaceuticals or using ayahuasca or still smoking pot count one out of sobriety?

I could go on. And on. And on.

There are so many rules to getting sober and being sober. Rules and coded language developed from the patriarchal framework that shapes and polices our society, bent on keeping us out of power and subject to a system of control. What follows is not intended to be more rules, or my better, worthier version of the truth. It's a collection of stories of how I navigated the often oppressive language and culture of recovery, and it's an attempt not to give you the answers, but the courage to make your own way, as you see fit. Go forth and do whatever the fuck you want, so long as it's *aligned* with what you want and allows you to be right with yourself. There is no single version of the truth. There are versions. Make your own.

ARE YOU SOBER IF YOU STILL SMOKE DANK?

I stopped smoking pot about a year after I stopped drinking alcohol, and sometimes, now that I've quit, I feel like my parents talking about the Marijuana Cigarette (they called it that). Like, I used to know the cool words that actual pot smokers use, but time moved forward without me, and now I say "dank" the way people in 1980 said "grass." I digress. The question at hand is: Are you really sober if you still smoke pot? What if you take antidepressants? Are you sober if you use Antabuse or Naltrexone? What if you used Nyquil last month for three days in a row? If you drink kombucha or caffeine, smoke cigarettes, get your forehead pumped up with Botox, or use laughing gas at the dentist—are you sober? What if you get in a car accident and take Vicodin or Percocet? Does that mean you're half-sober? Temporarily not?

Sobriety was the last place I wanted to end up, until it wasn't. When I first came to sobriety, I wanted it and I wanted it bad— Allen Carr had sold me on an idea of a better life, and I was after it. I *liked* those first few months of sobriety; I *liked* proving I could do things I never thought I could, like going to bars and getting high off Red Bull or making it through Thanksgiving or staying out until four a.m. drinking chamomile out of my teacup while my friends filled theirs with whiskey. I liked making it through dinners and waking up not hungover, and I liked the freshness that was life. In the strangest turn of events, I got high off being sober. When I started drinking again after those first two abstinent months, I missed being able to say that word and all the things it afforded me, and when I stopped drinking for good, I welcomed it back with open arms.

I. Am. Sober.

The word *sober* comes from the Latin word *sobrius,* from *se-,* "without," and -*ebrius*, "drunk" or "intoxicated." In other words, it means "not drunk" or even "not toxic." It never occurred to me back when I first stopped drinking, but still smoked pot and cigarettes, used molly and cocaine, binged and purged, consumed coffee and green tea, and used people, Netflix, and my iPhone compulsively, that I was not officially sober. One time on Instagram, when I was no longer using drugs but was using men and social media and coffee in deep excess, I read a post from a man I was following. It said, "Don't call yourself sober if you're still using drugs: You are not sober." I wondered about him and that post, about what would make someone say such a thing. I wrote back to him that I had used drugs to help me stop using drugs. I used pot, Chipotle, nicotine, cocaine, a very unfortunate man named Justin, and half the coffee Starbucks produced in 2013 to stop drinking. But that shouldn't matter to him, should it? Unless he owned the word *sober* and I was missing something.

I used the word *sober* while by all accounts I really wasn't, because it was *my* word. Because it made sense to me, it instilled a sense of pride, and an intention: *Here is where I am headed.* It made sense when my last few addictions were down to social media and coffee, as much as it did when I was smoking pot all day every day. And fuck anyone who told me something different.

Recently, a woman commented on a post about sobriety on the Tempest Facebook page that she hadn't had a drink for some time, maybe a few months, but was still smoking pot: "Does that mean I'm not sober?" She asked this of no one in particular; she was simply addressing the random people of the comments section, who I am guessing she presumed to be the Sober Committee. I was surprised by most of the responses; they said, in summary, *No, girl, you are not.* They might as well have said,

Sorry to inform you, but you don't get that certificate just yet. Come back when you're more perfect.

Some of the more fundamentalist circles of AA consider the use of antidepressants a disqualifier—you can't be on Prozac and be sober. In 2018 a *New Republic* article titled "Rejected by AA" profiled people recovering from opiate addiction who were on life-saving medication-assisted treatment (MAT), like Suboxone or methadone, who were withheld chips, or otherwise rejected by the only support group available to them—their local AA or NA (Narcotics Anonymous) fellowship. Which, of course, is not only complete and utter bullshit but an outright death sentence for some. It is essentially refusal of treatment based on what amounts to a moral imperative.

On the other hand, when I was freshly clean from all drugs and cigarettes, I remember meeting a woman who told me she'd had a bout of addiction to pills in her twenties and was sober now . . . she only drank alcohol. Guess how much I wanted to slap (what I then thought to be) her not-really-sober face? So I get it. All of it.

The point is, I don't remember going into this with the belief that I'd stop doing all the things, as in all drugs and the cigarettes and the people and the coffee and whatever else becomes addictive, which is basically everything. I wanted to escape from the hell that was drinking, so I decided to stop drinking. I wanted something to make that not drinking thing real, and one of the things that made it real was calling myself sober. Calling myself sober, and not ingesting ethanol on the regular, led to greater clarity, and also a mad desire to break through all the limitations I had accepted for my life. Sobriety from alcohol led me to want more sobriety. Or rather, freedom led me to want more freedom.

As my smart friend Mel says, "Arguing about what constitutes sobriety is a little like arguing about whether a finger pointing at the sky is pointing correctly—regardless of critique, the finger is still bringing your attention to something vast and beautiful and important." When I think about whether someone should use that word, or who gets to decide what sobriety is, my eyes roll back in my head because it's *such* a *boring* conversation. Seriously, let's talk for hours about how my use of coffee, sugar, and Juvéderm somehow means I'm not really sober. Or how that chick over there does ayahuasca, so she isn't. Or how people who use antidepressants aren't. That sounds like a great use of time and not the same bullshit patriarchal shame-cycle that drives us to need to numb our fucking faces off in the first place, right?

Or.

You can decide what you are and what you will and won't be called, because you have to live with yourself, and I'll do the same, and we can tell anyone who wants to argue with us about it to go eat a fig.

RELAPSE FAILURE

The first time I talked to a venture capitalist in order to get funding for Tempest was in 2014; it was a chance encounter, and he offered to let me pitch my idea to him. I spent four days working on a pitch deck that amounted to about twelve slides in Lobster font, and at the end of my presentation, he gave me a little pat on the shoulder: "Keep trying, kid." Two sleepless years later, after running a few sobriety schools and losing whatever shreds of a sex life, a social life, a romantic life, a *life* life, I went out to raise funds from investors again, this time with a pitch deck that reflected a few years of accumulated experience. That attempt also failed, miserably, and I wasn't just defeated, I was devastated, out of money, out of whatever things people who succeed have in them; I spent two weeks in bed before I snapped out of it and went back to work.

A year later, after dedicating what felt like every precious minute of my life and youth to building and running Tempest and figuring out how to get capital to grow it, I spent a month in my childhood bedroom at my mom's home, working fourteen hours a day on a new pitch deck, and one without Lobster font. This time—because of those previous failures and accumulated experience—I had swagger and know-how, and when I started pitching my business to investors, I didn't fail. I raised a couple million dollars—a feat considering at the time only 2 percent of venture capital went to female founders. That success wasn't some anomaly, and it wasn't despite all those early failures—it was *because* of them. I succeeded in raising capital only because I failed multiple times. Those failures weren't some setback; they were rungs on a ladder—precious, painful, and defeating experiences I had to endure in order to learn the things I needed in order to succeed.

If you are Steve Jobs and you get fired from Apple, your failure sets you up for your comeback; it's part of your legend, or your canonization. If you're Elon Musk and you blow up the first few rockets you launch and lose millions upon millions of dollars—and years—in the process, you're just working out the kinks. If you're Elizabeth Gilbert and you write the wildly unsuccessful *Committed* after publishing the epochal *Eat, Pray, Love,* nothing bad has happened—you're just practicing for your TED Talk, your Oprah tour, your next *New York Times* best seller. For them, failure never equaled going back to square one; failure was a leap forward. None of their careers are seen as a zero-sum game where the only things that count are the wins, and their failures aren't measured as stumbling blocks; they are measured as legacy.

We live in a society where failure isn't just part of the story—sometimes it's the entire story. Companies encourage it through initiatives such as Failure Walls and Failure Meetings, where employees showcase their biggest fuckups; there are Failure Festivals, books on failure, and almost every successful person in the spotlight loves to regale us with their biggest humiliations. Failure is prestigious; it says *Look how far I've come, look where I used to be, look what I did to get here.* Every modern-day guru with an ear-mic on a stage will evangelize the power of the fail as the way to lead, innovate, develop, conquer, and grow. We are steeped in failure porn, and if you didn't fall flat on your face in some fantastically degrading fashion on your way to the top, maybe you weren't going big enough.

There's really only one exception to the failing phenomenon, which is when you're trying not to drink, to get sober, to not use. Because here in Soberland, we don't build on failure, we don't have comebacks, we aren't just working out the kinks: we relapse, which is a different word, and not an additive one that advances you—it's subtractive and it plunges you back to day one. In recovery, failure isn't part of your legacy; it's the writing on the wall, or the signature on your death certificate.

Quitting drinking, like anything else on this earth we attempt, is an undertaking, a practice, an endeavor, and if it were an easy thing to even *try*—let alone succeed at—there wouldn't be an entire rehab industry devoted to it. It is hard, and not in the way that it's impossible, but in the way that makes it worth doing. It takes guts and risk and trial and error, and we don't just sprint out of the gates abstinent in all our sober glory. We have to learn how to not drink; we have to fail at it—sometimes again and again and again and again—until we stop failing.

When you mess up, and you will, here are some helpful things to consider. First, your failure is not proof of your inability to pull off sobriety; it is proof of your courage. Second, your mistake doesn't equal losing something, and it doesn't mean you go back to the place from which you came—sobriety isn't a zero-sum game, it is a sum of its parts, and failure is one of its parts. Third, the failure point isn't the moment to get out the whip and tell yourself what a piece of crap you are; if you hope to learn from it and use it, the failure point is the moment you bring in severe compassion for the person who is trying, which is you. Last, the only way to get to success is by navigating the shitty sea of failure and mediocrity. To get where you are going, there is no other way but through, and failure is the way through.

ODAAT

When I first started posting on Instagram about sobriety, I found myself in a clique of "sober personalities" from around the globe. Some of them would hashtag ODAAT, which I would sound out phonetically in my mind as *Ohhh dat*. As in *Ohhhh look at dat sobriety,* or *How about dat sober life tho.* Every time I read ODAAT, I would secretly judge the person for using it because I didn't want to be associated with culturally appropriated pithy sayings about that #soberlyfe. Then one day I decided there had to be more to it, and I finally used the internet and discovered it means *One day at a time.*

I get the quality of this sentiment and what's behind it. I think of my friend Kristi Coulter confronting her drinking problem, making it through one night without drinking by dropping to her knees in her kitchen and just staying there, or the moments in my own life where I want to text him *just one more time* and I literally have to fall to the ground and press my head against the floor until the urge passes. It's not lost on me that things happen in moments, and that we string these moments together into points on a graph that eventually become lines. But if someone had come to me at the beginning of my journey toward sobriety and told me to take it just one day at a time, I would have forked their eye out. Or mine.

I am an extremist, a *let's get to the point* kind of woman. I don't dabble in gray areas for long or suffer through things pixel by pixel. I drink the ocean. What worked for me at the beginning was not deciding day by day that I wouldn't drink *that day*. What worked for me was obliterating the idea that I would ever drink again, striking the possibility completely, making a decision, and never questioning it. *Never question the decision—* NQTD—four letters now inked on my arm. A decision, made once, that you never have to question again. This doesn't mean the decision has always stuck; it just means I don't want to be deciding *every single day* that I won't drink that day.

There is the part of me that understands the beauty in how things develop over time, and how I've built my business is a testament to this. I started with a laptop on a friend's couch and made my way to writing a book for Random House and built a company that as of this writing employs *twenty-eight persons*. I built my business minute by minute—one Instagram post at a time, one client at a time—with increasing patience and tolerance for the monotony of what it is to do something worth doing over time. And every time I wanted to quit, I greeted myself with basically the same sentiment that ODAAT promises: *Just make it through today. That's all you have to do, little bunny.* But applying that same idea to quitting drinking would have made it an endless ordeal for me. I wanted drinking to be out of my mind completely—it had taken up enough time and space already.

I've worked with a lot of people who feel they can't imagine a year without alcohol, let alone a month, or even a weekend. So we start with a weekend, then a week, then a month. And we count all those moments, all those wins and pivots and changes that create dots on a graph that eventually become lines. For these people, ODAAT makes sense, and it feels like freedom. I've also worked with people who feel like I do, who prefer to rip the Band-Aid off in one fell swoop and sign their names in blood on the sober registry and that is that. And then, of course, there is everyone in between.

What I'm saying is: If you're having a bad day, and you're (trying to be) sober, at some point someone will look at you, nod their knowing head in a knowing way with a knowing smile, and say *One day at a time,* like they are the Illuminati and now you don't have to hurt because it all makes sense. Just know that's a thing. I'm also saying that ODAAT could be your thing, or not—that's something only you decide.

BREAKING GOOD

In 2016, Cat Marnell, a former beauty editor for *Glamour* magazine and xoJane—more infamous for her editorializing of her drug addiction than famous for her actual work—released a book, *How to Murder Your Life.* In it, Marnell chronicled how the prescriptions given to her by her psychiatrist father to help her manage her ADHD in boarding school ended up addicting her, and detailed her subsequent struggles with drug addiction and eating disorders. While she was at xoJane, Cat also wrote—in real time—about what her drug-addicted life was like. She didn't pull any punches or sweep anything under the rug. By the end of her book, she was still trying to recover from drug addiction—still taking pills, still drinking booze—and didn't present it as some kind of happy-ever-after story; she was in process, in *progress.*

I was in love with her book and astounded by her bravery. Who of us actually talks about our active addiction and what it looks like? None of us, that's who. We go from blissful ignorance of any problem at all to awareness of the problem, and somewhere, immediately thereafter, we are expected to work a recovery program and have a severe intention to be ascetics. When Cat caught flack for her book by one of my contemporaries—who herself had spent the better part of three years drinking and not drinking in the public eye before fully choosing sobriety—I was pissed. In fact, almost every review of the book I came across was critical that Cat was still using drugs and wasn't the polished, pretty, clean "after" picture we are accustomed to finding at the end of a story. A lot of people wanted to love it, but felt that loving it—and loving Cat where she was in her battle with addiction—was somehow dangerous, as if accepting her process were cosigning her death certificate. It reminded me of the opening sentence from Roxane Gay's *Hunger:* "The story of my body is not a story of triumph. This is not a weight-loss memoir. There will be no picture of a thin version of me, my slender body emblazoned across this book's cover, with me standing in one leg of my fatter self's jeans."

When I read Gay's opening line—as a woman who has struggled with eating disorders ever since I can remember, since well before my first period and long before any girl should know the word *cellulite*—I rejected it at first, automatically. I wanted the fat-jean-skinny-person scenario. We *all* want this scenario, with everything. We love a good "before" story, we love a good "after" story. Don't show us incremental or barely visible change. Don't show us the part where we can't really tell the difference between who you were then and where you are now.

———

Not long ago, at a WeWork in Brooklyn, I walked up to the counter to meet the community team. A woman behind the front desk asked me what I did, and I explained that I ran a company that helps people stop drinking. I was waiting for the typical response, which is usually something like *Oh, I thought something like that already existed and it was free,* or a really intense conversation about the inquiring party's Uncle Fred and his liver, but hers was different. She mentioned the "sobriety movement" and Instagram accounts like the Sober Glow and the Numinous, both run by women I know, both relatively unknown in the larger context of the world. I said something to the effect of *Oh my heavens you know about this?* And she went from excited to ashamed in about five seconds as she "admitted" she still drank—although consciously, less than before, and with an eye on sobriety. I was struck by what this woman was doing, by her process and her honest examination. It was something few people venture to do, and something to be proud of. And yet because she wasn't in the "after" scenario—nor even sure she wanted the "after" scenario—she was apologetic.

Three positions are typically recognized in recovery. The first is ignorance: *I don't know how bad alcohol is,* or *I haven't acknowledged I have a problem with it,* or *I haven't recognized that it's causing problems.* The second is acceptance: *I do know alcohol is bad, I do know I have a problem, I do know it's causing problems, and I'm actively trying to quit it forever.* The third is sobriety: *I have quit alcohol forever.* I propose that we also include a fourth position, nestled right in there between one and two or maybe after two or even three: *I am aware of how bad alcohol is, I am aware it's causing me a problem, and my awareness is all I can, want, or need to handle right now.* Or the fourth position is: *I am human, and being human is a messy affair with lots of twists, turns, and in-betweens.*

Breaking good means perfection isn't the goal. Recovery is not about "doing it right" or trying hard to please everyone by approaching sobriety in a way that makes sense to them. It's about remembering that the path is long and winding and messy, and that our reward isn't paid out in absolute terms, like thirty days of sobriety, or "before" and "after" photos. Our reward is the pride we begin to accumulate for just showing up and trying, perhaps with our bottles of wine still uncorking in the background.

How You Recover Is Nobody's Business

When I was ten months sober, Philip Seymour Hoffman died. I'd been keeping a secret blog called littlemisssurrendered.com, which was really just a collection of five essays I'd written about sobriety. The night Hoffman died, something snapped in me. I'd been up since before four a.m. for yoga teacher training, had absolutely nothing left in my body, and upon seeing his death notice, I was overcome by an otherworldly need to pen a post on my experience with addiction. The piece was (compared to the stuff I'd been writing for the past year) good; it felt less like I wrote it than like my body had been used to write.

I'd just quit my job at the health care start-up, so I thought, *Why not share my most shameful secrets on the internet while I'm looking for gainful employment?* Which is to say that I outed myself and the depths of my sickness on the internet because of Philip Seymour Hoffman.

Sharing that blogpost publicly meant outing those five secret essays, many of which were stories about my dysfunctional relationships with my mom and my sister. After reading those essays, a friend of mine—a daughter of a man who'd recovered through AA—wrote me a note. It said in effect: *You seem to be in pain, your family seems to be in pain, maybe you should work the Twelve Steps, my father did that, it helped my family.*

At this point, I'd been working on myself and toward sobriety for sixteen months, and it was going, by all accounts, pretty well. Further, throughout my recovery, this woman hadn't once asked me how it was going, what was happening in my world, how I was saving my life, or how she could help. She was a spectator; one who read a few blogposts, interpreted them through her lens (which I get—if you're the kid of someone who drinks, that's not nothing and you have severe opinions for a reason), and decided she understood the missing course of action in my fucked-up life, which led to her unsolicited advice about my recovery.

If this were the only time some well-meaning friend or acquaintance chose to explain to me that I didn't know what was best for me and that perhaps I should try what worked for them or their father/aunt/cousin/best-friend's-mother's-sister's-boyfriend, then that would be one thing. But it wasn't the only time. Unsolicited advice was my new normal, and almost every time I let the depth of my humanness show, someone was standing at the ready, Twelve Steps in hand, saying, *Have you thought about trying this? You should try this.*

I found it all so interesting. At the precise moment I took my shitshow of a life by the vagina was the precise moment people lined up to tell me I was doing it wrong.

Of my own volition, I decided I needed to stop drinking and took steps to quit. I spent thousands of dollars on therapy and programs and acupuncture and health care and vitamins and gurus. I spent hundreds of hours reading books and going to therapy and meditating and journaling and chanting and acupuncturing and praying and doing whatever the hell I could to save my life, forgoing nights out and girls' trips and happy hours and dating and sex and everything else normal thirty-four-year-olds do. And in a little over a year of this work, I managed to stop not only drinking but doing all drugs and smoking cigarettes, and I overcame an eating disorder I'd suffered from since high school.

And yet, some of those around me—acquaintances, strangers, family, friends—were skeptical. They felt the need to express concern that I wasn't getting *real* help and to tell me that perhaps I wasn't truly on my way because I hadn't done the things they would have me do.

For millennia, women have been told how to think, act, speak, be; they have been told not to trust their bodies, their intuition, their knowledge, their guiding force, their gut. No woman is more bereft of her sense of trust in herself than a woman confronting herself for the first time. For her whole damn life the world has told her that her worth is wrapped up in her looks, service, and submissiveness; that her power comes not from within but from without. For her entire existence, she has trusted the advice of others who surely know better about her than she does. How well did that work out for her? How well has suppressing our own knowledge in favor of what other people think worked out for any of us?

And yet still you arrived, against all odds, knowing something had to change. That thing that got you to this point is inside you and it is smarter than all the men in the world combined. It is truth, and it is guiding you. When you begin to listen to *It*—the all-knowing all-powerful *It* buried deep within—people will become scared for you, think you are making mistakes. They will think they know better than you, tell you what you are doing is wrong, and give you so much unsolicited advice. You will get confused and be pulled apart, because you are still learning to trust yourself. That's okay, because what is really happening is you are being tested, being given the opportunity to learn to hear yourself and trust yourself over all those other voices. When you find yourself in that place where someone else's truth makes you fearful of trusting your own, remember this: Only you got yourself here, and it is safe to trust that you can take yourself the rest of the way.

This is not to say that there aren't teachers on this path; I am where I am only because I found people I trusted and could learn from—yoga teachers and therapists and sober folk and doctors and kinfolk and people who wrote very important and smart books and people from the internet who I will never meet but who somehow knew my soul. This is not even to say that those who think they know better than us aren't our teachers, because every single person who impressed their opinions on me helped me to turn further into myself. This is not the path of giving more of ourselves to the world at the cost of our deepest knowing self; this is the path of finally, *finally* learning to trust that we already know everything; we just have to learn to re-member.

IT WORKS IF YOU WORK IT

"It works if you work it" is a slogan born, again, of AA. It's a simplified version of the opening lines to a chapter in *The Big Book*: "Rarely have we seen a person fail who has thoroughly followed our path. Those who do not recover are people who cannot or will not completely give themselves to this simple program, usually men and women who are constitutionally incapable of being honest with themselves. There are such unfortunates." It's a convenient idea, one that has ensured AA's dominance in the recovery space for nearly a century: *There is nothing wrong with the program, there is only something wrong with you—if it doesn't work, it's because you're not trying hard enough.*

The idea that there's something wrong with the person—instead of the society that made them sick or the program that was possibly ineffective or oppressive—is inherent to the patriarchy, a sweet little tool to keep people in their place, and by that I mean second place. It's the same as saying it's not the alcohol's fault, it's *yours* because you can't drink it right; or there's nothing wrong with rape culture—or the rapist—it's you and what you were wearing, how much you drank, that you led him on perhaps. You were asking for it. It's the same as blaming the homeless man for his lack of home, the single mom on welfare for her lack of ambition, the battered wife for staying. Victim-blaming tactics like these protect the system—and those who benefit from it—and fault those who are oppressed by it.

During Brett Kavanaugh's Senate Judiciary Committee hearing on his nomination to the Supreme Court—in which a series of privileged, entitled, and misogynistic prep school stories were woven into an innocent boys-will-be-boys narrative, while the victim, Dr. Christine Blasey Ford, was portrayed as a revenge-seeking opportunist—alcohol had a starring role. Dr. Ford, who was the real one on trial, was asked if she'd been drinking at the time of her alleged assault. (She hadn't been.) In the end, it was Kavanaugh—who *had* been drinking—who was believed, and Kavanaugh, the attempted rapist, was rewarded with an appointment to our country's highest court. Because it is always *his* reputation, career, family, and rights we are wont to protect over *her* body, pain, trauma, voice, and rights. In a meme that circulated on Instagram, women asked, "Why does alcohol excuse his actions but condemn mine?" The answer, of course, is: Because of the patriarchy. As Rebecca Solnit wrote in *Men Explain Things to Me*, "The story of Cassandra, the woman who told the truth but was not believed, is not nearly as embedded in our culture as that of the Boy Who Cried Wolf—that is, the boy who was believed the first few times he told the same lie. Perhaps it should be."

When we tell a hurting human that it's their fault they are hurting, their fault that a treatment doesn't work, their fault that they became addicted in the first place, their fault that the alcohol doesn't work for them like it's supposed to, we are upholding the same system that says it is their fault they were raped, assaulted, can't find work, can't pay their bills, can't find housing, can't afford childcare. It implies that the most vulnerable among us are the ones to blame rather than the system that has failed them over and over again. In this way, we uphold the impunity of the system and of those who benefit from it. Having the right to choose in recovery is no different. If we don't have power to choose our treatment, the power to say, *This simple program doesn't work for me,* how can we expect to have power in any other dimension of our life?

Most people hear the word *recovery* and think of it in a one-dimensional sense when it comes to addiction: an addict trying to not drink, to not use, to not masturbate ten times a day to Xtube. *I'm in recovery* can be synonymous with *I am sick, I was sick, I am still sick, I am mindful of my sickness.* Because of this some people have argued for variations of the word—*uncovery, discovery*—in order to promote a more noble pursuit that implies evolution. But I like the word *recovery* because it reminds me that we aren't unworthy people fumbling toward worth, bad people trying to be good, or people looking for something we never had. We are a people who know everything already, who are worthy simply because we exist, and we are on a path to remember the truth of us, the core of us.

It's diminishing and dangerous to say it's a person's fault that the system didn't work for them. We need to remember that the system is set up on behalf of the system. It is never about it working if you work it. It is about finding what works to free you, and working that.

13

Hell Is Other People

For a seed to achieve its greatest expression, it must come completely undone. The shell cracks, its insides come out and everything changes. To someone who doesn't understand growth, it would look like complete destruction. —CYNTHIA OCCELLI

When I was a little over a year sober, some of my closer friendships had shape-shifted. One in particular became distant and tense, and to try to mend it, my friend M invited me to her home for brunch, where everyone was at least a few drinks in by the time I arrived. This in itself was sketchy—I'm not sure what goes through your mind when you decide to invite your sober friend over to a midday drinking party in order to *make things good with them,* but whatever. You get used to a world that drinks, and you eventually notice it less, and then at some point, not really at all. And you also stop hanging out with people like this, or people you don't really like in general.

Because these were Wine People, everyone there was really into the wine and talking about it constantly. I did that thing I used to do in early sobriety when I couldn't figure out if I was supposed to be cool or enthusiastic or indifferent or maybe repulsed when someone talked about the life-giving magic of booze; when someone remarked that the Cab was really tannic, I nodded in the same way I might nod in agreement if someone had said it was hot outside. *Yes, I agree.*

At some point M's aunt—who I'd known for years and drunk many a glass of Central Coast Chards with—looked at me, as if noticing I was there for the first time. She stared for a minute and cocked her head to the side, like my cat does when she's trying to decide if she should eat me. "Holly"—she said, moving toward me slowly, deliberately, holding the kind of eye contact someone might if they were about to flick a tarantula off your shoulder—"Holly . . . have you *seen* this *wine*?" Which is when she pulled an open bottle of wine (out of thin air), pushed it to my nose, and said, "Here, smell it," and then: "You can still smell it, can't you?" The worst part was, *I fucking smelled it!* And then appreciated the minimalist art on the label, as she instructed. I agreed it was indeed a fine bottle of wine, and that she had made a great investment.

That was five years ago, and I still remember it like it was yesterday, because you don't forget when—in perhaps the loneliest, most confusing, and broken time in your life—someone not only doesn't ask you how that whole saving-your-life thing is going, but also shoves the drug that almost killed you into your face and asks you to smell it. Or what it feels like to find out you weren't invited to someone you thought was one of your closest friend's bridal shower from Instagram, where they are posing in front of a winery in Napa with eight or nine other people and you *know* they don't like Todd and *fucking Todd is there.*

You don't forget seeing your social life move forward without you, and your friends cutting you out of it— either because you don't want to go to events centered on drinking anymore or because they don't know what to say to you or maybe they don't want to have to think about their own drinking; you don't forget what it feels like when someone asks you if you are "still not drinking," instead of asking if you need help, if you need support, if you need a hug; you don't forget how your heart hurts when your best friend tells you he wants you to come to Italy only if you're drinking, or what happens to your soul when someone you care about, are madly in love with, tells you that they don't want a partner who can't drink at their wedding.

You don't forget any of these things and how they made you feel, and not because you're some bitter human with a list of resentments, but because these things shape you into who you become, how you treat other people, and how you let other people treat you.

On my first day of third grade, I showed up at a new school wearing brand-new white Keds. A girl in my class, a fantastic bitch named Melissa Brown, came up to me, introduced herself, and then stepped on those perfect white Keds, smearing dirt across them as she said, "We aren't allowed to wear white shoes here." I don't know why I believed her, or had to ask my mom later if she'd heard of such a rule. I also don't understand why this made me so hungry to be her friend, but it did. Later that year, when she lined us up in the outer field on recess and stuck her hands down our pants, one by one, I remember being confused or maybe disgusted; I stuffed my confusion down because to question such things was to bring into question my loyalty. My desire to be liked and included, even back then, trumped my standards, my voice, my worth. And when one day Melissa got all the other girls to call me a Yellow Dodo Bird, to kick me and chase me into a stall in the girls' bathroom, I refused to tell my teacher or my parents. This was the price of popularity. This was the price of being friends with the Melissa Browns of the world. It didn't matter what I wanted; it mattered that I belonged, because belonging was how I mattered. When you live in a society that encourages you to hate yourself, and you build relationships on this principle, this is the result.

That story stands out in my memory because in many ways, until I got sober, I was still that little girl. Maybe I graduated to friends who presented themselves more civilly, but I learned from a young age that safety comes through conforming, from putting up with, from settling, from denying and swallowing the terrible ways people treat you. I also learned a number of other things, like to not have boundaries, to say yes to things I didn't want to do, to please, to gossip, to exclude, to manipulate.

To enumerate all the ways my relationships fell short, or the ways I acted like a terrible person, would be beside the point. The point is, I was mostly a taker, a clinger, a joiner, a settler, a chameleon. I never demanded integrity in my relationships; nor did I have standards, because I didn't have those things myself. *Dysfunction* is a catchall adjective that seems to fit; so does *inauthentic*. And those two words seem like a fine way to describe the nature of how I related, because they were the absolute nature of myself: dysfunctional, inauthentic.

Not long after that brunch at M's, on a Megabus traveling from San Francisco to Los Angeles, a group text circulated, a "who's in" for the next girls' weekend among our circle of friends. There was a moment where I considered hanging out with M again, and then there was clarity: *I don't like being around this person anymore.* Somewhere on the 101 it dawned on me that I no longer had to hang out with people I really didn't like, even if I'd been in their wedding, had known them for years, had loved them, still loved them. So instead of replying, I deleted the thread and her number, without offering any explanation. In this moment I became: A woman creating room for things that mattered, a human telling the truth, a thirty-five-year-old—a person in recovery—with a wine bottle pushed to her nose who walks away. An eight-year-old in a courtyard telling Melissa Brown to fuck off.

The thing about sobriety is that once you stop and face the three-headed monster that is your terrible relationship with alcohol, you can't help but look at all the other things you've been running from or that you've been forcing. When I realized I didn't have to drink anymore—that I could be this version of myself I'd never been before—I also realized I no longer had to put up with people who made me feel less than, or react to people who provoked me. I didn't have to be the mean one or the intolerant one or the nice one or the one who settles or the one no one respects. I didn't have to hang around with people I couldn't be myself with, or people who didn't like me, or people I didn't like, or people who cratered parts of me. I didn't have to compete for love, or earn love, or manipulate for love. If sobriety taught me anything, it was that I could be anything, or anyone, as long as I was myself.

John O'Donohue, in his essay "The Question Holds the Lantern," writes, "When your soul awakens, you begin to truly inherit your life. You leave the kingdom of fake surfaces, repetitive talk, and weary roles and slip deeper into the true adventure of who you are and who you are called to become." Sobriety, for me, was exactly as he wrote—I truly inherited my life. I slipped deeper into the adventure of who I felt called to become, and the tired roles I had played forever became obsolete as I moved forward into a world where I was finally naming the terms of who I would be, and who I wouldn't be.

Which is exactly where relationships come in.

Because here's the thing: People are going to be dicks about you not drinking. You'll lose some (potentially all) of your friendships; people will say awkward and awful things about your choice not to drink; being around your family will make you regress back to your most maniacal, infantile self no matter how much you work on yourself; friends and strangers alike will assume you owe them an explanation for why you stopped imbibing, or try to pressure you into drinking. And not only does no one in your life show up with a casserole, *no one even really talks to you about it.*

I share this with you not to scare you off of sobriety (really, it's great!) but because I wish I had known about the fantastic and terrible other-people things I would encounter in response to my choice to stop drinking *before* they happened, so at least I could know what I do now: that all these other-people-things are not there as some huge middle finger to punish us for choosing to stop consuming ethanol—they are there to burn away everything we no longer need in order to grow us into the humans we were always meant to become. You signal to the Universe that you are ready to grow up, that you are ready to do the work by choosing sobriety, and the Universe responds, *Oh, yeah? Let's see if you're being serious. There are some folks I'd like you to meet.*

"The work" of sobriety is achieved through all the things we've talked about—through meditating or changing your beliefs or making it through your first wedding sober. But the most vital work—the core of this path—is the work you do with other people. Reclaiming your whole self doesn't only happen on your meditation pillow, in a hot yoga class, or during *Super Soul Sunday.* It happens in the real world, among real people, in every single encounter you have. How you show up with other people is how you show up for yourself, and if you want to show up for yourself in a way you never have before—if you want liberation and transcendence and to own yourself fully—you have to engage with people in ways you never have before.

SEVEN THINGS I WISH I'D KNOWN ABOUT RELATIONSHIPS BEFORE I GOT SOBER

1. Amends and Self-forgiveness

> *The people who most need to say they are sorry—those highest in the hierarchy—are seldom aware of it, and the ones who don't need to continuously apologize are all too willing to take the rap for everything.* —CHARLOTTE KASL

Step Eight of the Twelve Steps instructs us to make a list of all the people we've wronged, and where possible to go forth and make amends, which means "to compensate or make up for." Like all things born of AA, making amends has become an expected step of a person in recovery: our healing depends on our ability to apologize and right our wrongs. I don't think there's anything wrong with making amends, or with admitting wrong and making right. But I do think there's something wrong with focusing *first* on the idea that we're sick because of what we have done to other people, instead of focusing on naming how other people—and the system—have wronged us or how we have wronged ourselves.

Many years ago on my podcast, my cohost Laura McKowen asked me if I had gone through an amends process. I hadn't premeditated a response and blurted out that I needed to have amends made *to* me, *by* me. If there was one person I had been the worst to it was myself, and in order to heal, I was the first person I needed to make things right with. I don't remember how Laura received it, but I do remember feeling like my narcissism was showing. There was something so wrong with stating that self-apologies come first, and in retrospect, what felt wrong about it was what makes it so right. Women don't need to be groomed to apologize further. They need to be groomed to be worthy of their own apologies to themselves.

Often people ask me how I was able to move on, to forgive myself in such a way that I wasn't carrying around every dirty secret, humiliation, and terrible thing I'd done in the life I'd lived up until sobriety. And every time they ask, I stammer, because I don't know exactly how I did it. I can't pinpoint what led me to be able to shed the guilt and shame I'd been carrying around for a lifetime. What I do know for sure is that it came from the idea that I was already worthy, that I was already redeemed, no matter what I did or didn't do, and that everything— every terrible and great thing—I ever did only served to make me into the person I am today. It also came from a concept I got from *A Course in Miracles,* that everything any of us have ever done is already forgiven, and that the release comes not from repenting but from atoning—or remembering that we're guiltless. In other words, the problem isn't that we've done bad things, the problem is that we can't let ourselves get over that we've done bad things.

Until I understood that I was guiltless and worthy already, and until I did the work required to forgive myself, any attempt to apologize to someone else wouldn't have been "corrective" or healing or even come from a place of love. Seeking amends would have only reinforced that old idea that I needed something from someone else, or that someone else's forgiveness would make me whole. It would have come from the same cratered space that looked for other people to save me, or the same corrupt system that told me my worth was measured through the esteem—and forgiveness—of others.

As Charlotte Kasl writes in *Many Roads, One Journey*, the first step for women and other historically oppressed individuals isn't the same as the first step for those who have held power or benefited from being at the top of the hierarchy. For many of us, the first step is naming the people, the institutions, and the systematic ways *we've* been hurt; naming the sexual assault, the domestic abuse, the racism, the homophobia, the poverty. The next step is to look at the ways we've hurt ourselves, or held ourselves in contempt; we have to make the home that is us habitable. Only then—when we become whole humans who understand their worth and who can forgive themselves—will the practice of making amends to others be possible.

2. Every Relationship Is an Assignment

> Life will give you whatever experience is most helpful for the
> evolution of your consciousness. How do you know this is the
> experience you need? Because this is the experience you are having at
> the moment.   —ECKHART TOLLE

Every person you meet—be it for a minute or a lifetime—is placed there by design, part of the universal plan to give you exactly what you need, exactly when you need it, in order to grow into your potential; to show you the parts of yourself that you have forgotten to see or have refused to see; to build you into the most beautiful, kind, forgiving, loving version of yourself, one encounter at a time.

We call the people who love us—those who build us up and

affirm us, those who make us feel safe and seen and special and important—*our people*. And we call those who nail us and bring out our worst—*our enemies*. Pema Chödrön defines a good spiritual teacher as someone who can see through us straight to all the places we so desperately try to hide from the world. She says we seek out these teachers in order to work with people who will challenge us to fulfill our highest potential. In this way, Pema says, our enemies—or those difficult people we encounter—are exactly like our spiritual teachers. They bust us in the places where we need to be busted, so that we may grow in the places where we need to grow.

The people who see through me or don't like me, and the people I judge as idiots or monsters, now represent delicious opportunities to file away another piece of me that holds me back from my potential. If my anger is roused, I examine that anger. If my intolerance is inflamed, I dig deep within for compassion. If I feel unworthy or disregarded or invisible in someone's presence, I claim my inherent worth. If I am made to feel like a fraud, I discover the parts of me that aren't true. If I find myself judging people, I look inward to find out what judgments I hold against myself. And if I'm judged as something I'm not, I practice not giving a shit about what other people think, returning to only what I think, which is all that matters anyway.

This doesn't mean I love this process; anytime I encounter someone who challenges me in this way I typically hate the experience. But it does mean on some very basic level that I'm grateful for the difficulty, for the challenge, because my deepest lessons and growth haven't come from the easiest situations and relationships, they've come from the hardest ones. When you start to think of it this way—as every person existing for the sole purpose of furthering your growth—it no longer feels like the world is out to get you, but rather that it's trying its best to help you realize your full potential.

3. You Are Allowed to Change

> *The important thing is to be able at any moment to sacrifice what you are for what you could become.* —CHARLES DUBOIS

My most vivid memories of those early days of sobriety are the ones that involve breaking the news to the people in my life who were most invested in my drinking. I remember almost every significant outing of myself as a nondrinker like it was yesterday, and that's because it was the first time in my life that I made a sweeping break of a social pact. I was looking for permission to be different, and I made every effort to make my change palatable for everyone else. I made promises: *Nothing will change. I'm still me.*

But then something else started happening, which was that all the work I was doing on myself wasn't just making me a nondrinker, it was making me a happier, more fortified version of myself. I was no longer into gossip, I believed in miracles and *Jesus* of all things, I started reading Tarot and buying crystals and meditating on sheepskins and all sorts of crap my friends weren't doing. I was falling in love with myself, and it felt like a complete and total affront to the bigger social contracts I'd drawn up along the way. We aren't supposed to be madly in love with ourselves, or shine, or be happy with our lives. Coming out as happy, or even spiritual, was at least ten times as hard as coming out sober.

We think that if we change, if we tear up our social contracts, if we become a person who others stop recognizing or having things in common with—that if we alter the thing that people are attached to us being, "they'll" come after us, "they'll" try to stop us. The system benefits from our belief that it actually has that much control over us. Hear me on this: You are allowed to change. You are allowed to be whatever you want to be, at any moment you want to be it. There are no social pacts. There are no rules. Nothing is set in stone, ever. You get to be exactly who you want and need to be. No matter what. And the right people will always be on board with it.

4. You Teach People How to Treat You

The only people who get upset when you set boundaries are the ones who benefited from you having none. —UNKNOWN

I used to believe that every piece of correspondence that landed in my SMS, inbox, voicemail, and DM was my immediate responsibility. I was the queen of the timely response, and I carried that behavior over to Tempest when I started. I replied to every single request, and the result was that I was always on and always connected. When my story and my work started gaining traction, and I began reaching more people, the emails started to pile up, as did the comments on Instagram and Facebook, the letters, the texts. I was overcome with an anxiety and resentment toward those messages; it was no longer about the privilege of knowing someone's story, or celebrating a stranger's success, or holding someone's grief—it was about failing them, not doing what I thought I was supposed to be doing.

The time came when I had to choose. I could either build my company, support my students, write my words, do my research, and serve a very large population; or I could respond to every single note I got. Or as Glennon Doyle put it to me: I could either do my job, or do the things that made me want to quit my job (but made me look like a very generous, selfless person). I chose the former.

This meant that I went from being the person who responded to everyone all the time, to being a person who doesn't respond to hardly anyone, at all. At first, it was hard. My text inbox went from typically ten unread messages to over four hundred. I would read letters from readers, and instead of responding with a novel-length letter, I began saving them to a folder and sending out energetic blessings instead. If an email landed in my inbox, I would let it sit sometimes for up to seven days before even opening it. I got to things when I got to things. At first, some people were super annoyed, but after a few years of this practice, people came to understand I don't respond to things immediately, and sometimes I don't respond at all. To me, this is the only sane way to live. I'm not chained to my phone or to other people's expectations of responsiveness. I don't prove my love by texting back in two minutes.

This change also thinned the herd, because not everyone wants to deal with a person who isn't always available, always on, or who replies to one in every ten texts. In the end, I created a very clear boundary—which I needed so I could breathe and continue my work in the world and not burn out. I set a standard for myself, I upheld that standard without apologizing for it, and over time the people who remained in my life learned to honor that standard.

We think we have so little control over how people treat us, and to a degree, that's true. We can't make others do our bidding or like us or accept us, and we for certain can't change other people. But we underestimate our power to create and uphold boundaries. When I first stopped drinking, boundaries were an entirely foreign concept. I was a contortionist, someone who fit into whatever situation she had to, without asking for what she herself needed—like support, or space, or respect for her decisions. But quitting drinking changed all that: bringing tea bags to the bar, scheduling meditation during girls' trips, not drinking when people pressured me to, bringing LaCroix to family gatherings—all this required me to lay down some ground rules and stick with them. From there, it just became the way I operated. I realized I had the right to prioritize my needs because sobriety forced me to realize this right. I learned early in sobriety that people will act terribly when you don't do things that make them feel good; that they will punish you for sticking to your values and claiming your needs, or just leave altogether because this version of you isn't what they bargained for. I also learned that people either move with you and adjust to this new boundaried, self-loving version of you, or they leave, and that both situations are perfect.

5. The Other Person Is You

There's something about that guy I don't like about myself.

—UNKNOWN

When I was fifteen months sober, I left my big corporate job, went on a two-month trip to Italy, and came back wearing feather earrings and tie-dyed yoga pants most days of the week. I considered myself a free-spirited-world-traveling yogini; I was very Zen. I knew things. And I was certain that people—merely by being in my presence—would know that I was very Zen and that I knew things.

The first week of June, my Zen all-knowing ass walked into a Peet's Coffee to meet up with a group of people from my neighborhood—we were carpooling to what would be my second yoga teacher training. And that's when I met Bob. He was in my carpool. We had mutual friends—we didn't know each other, but we knew of each other—and after a few seconds I knew the thing that us sensitive types tend to know immediately: *Bob did not like me.*

I spent the first few weeks of that yoga training consumed in a Bob-flavored hell. If I spoke, he looked away. If I told a story, he interrupted. If he told a story, he addressed everyone but me. He moved his yoga mat away from me in class if we ended up next to each other; he brought food and would skip me when offering it to the other carpoolers; he took an interest in everyone else's affairs, and he couldn't even bring himself to make eye contact with me. By the time I got to the studio in the mornings, I would inevitably have a hate-filled lump in my throat. I'd sit in meditation and think only of Bob, searching for the answer to the deeply confounding question: *Why doesn't Bob like me?* Throughout the day, I would watch him in our classes, noting his interactions with other people, looking for evidence that he didn't like all humans and that it wasn't personal. But I couldn't make the case—it was, in fact, just me.

I couldn't fathom what I'd done to him or how the rest of the students couldn't see through his crap. I was consumed with trying to fix it and win him over. More than once I asked him why he didn't like me. The second time I asked, he called me a drama queen, told me I cried too much, and confirmed that he didn't like me, which inevitably made me cry. He made me feel like the most invisible, pathetic version of myself. Like a fraud. I fell into my first true period of depression in sobriety: Bob was the pin that popped my precious pink cloud.

The thing I couldn't get over was that I'd been so wrong about myself. I'd walked into that second yoga training sure of who I was and my place in this world. I was a good person, a *spiritual person,* an evolved person. Yet here I was, weeks into it—a jealous, hateful, insecure version of myself. All because some asshat in yoga shorts didn't like me.

I tried to be the bigger person, I tried to be unbothered, to not be jealous or insecure or diminished because at fifteen months sober (and an almost-twice-certified yoga teacher), I was sure I should be pretty close to being like Jesus. I didn't realize it at the time, but I was denying what I actually felt—what was actually happening—and therefore I was denying my humanity. The depression broke only when I talked to my friend Sally about it, who flipped it around and asked me if I liked Bob. When I told her "Hell no," she explained that it probably wasn't about Bob at all; he was a mirror of the parts of me I couldn't stand. In other words, he was my shadow, embodied.

The shadow—a concept in Jungian psychology—represents the things present in ourselves that we disassociate from because we deem them bad, ugly, dark, or inadequate. The shadow is all the things we suppress, reject, or deny in ourselves—the things we would rather not be. And while it is not easy to see our own shadow clearly, we can see it very, *very* well in other people. In fact, the more we judge others, the more likely we are judging our own shadow (even though we usually don't know it).

When I reflected on the things I hated about Bob and wrote them down, I realized I'd written a list of the things I hated about myself—behaviors I had ditched in my evolution and behaviors still active within me. I saw Bob as a catty, gossipy, insecure, dramatic bitch. So was I. I saw him as a spiritually disingenuous fool. So was I (see: feather earrings, tie-dyed yoga pants, eagle tattoo). The problem wasn't Bob. The problem was, *I was Bob,* and I hated the things about him that I hated in myself.

In this situation, the answer wasn't to manipulate Bob into liking me, or to force myself into liking him. The answer was to use the things I saw in him as unlovable and intolerable as a blueprint for how to love and forgive myself. If I could accept his bitchiness, pettiness, meanness, and insecurity as parts of him that were also parts of me, *and as parts that were lovable and acceptable,* then we could both be whole humans. Not just the socially acceptable version of worthy, but wholly worthy.

Like most things that feel terrible as they're happening, my experience with Bob turned into a profound turning point in my quest to evolve. It helped me to see that the things I can't stand about other people are little nuggets of treasure in plain sight. Now, if I'm judging some woman for being full of herself, I dig into whether it's because I'm too full of myself or—more likely—because I'm feeling like I'm not allowed to be that self-assured and proud. If I judge someone for being too loud, again, it's because I'm judging myself for that same thing, or I'm feeling resentful because I think I'm not allowed to take up that much space. If someone's pettiness is getting under my skin, I use it as a perfect opportunity to check in with the ways my own pettiness is running the show.

When we talk about this shadow concept in my sobriety school, people often ask whether there are exceptions: Aren't some people really just terrible? The answer is always twofold. Yes, some people are really terrible, and running around constantly trying to turn everything that rubs us wrong into a spiritual quest is exhausting and not beneficial. We are all capable of being murderers and saints—we all have that potential—because we are human. When we condemn a behavior in someone else—and recognize that it is simply a reflection of us—we empower ourselves to make peace with what we find unacceptable in ourselves; to remember we are not made only of good parts, that we are all of it, and therefore we must try to love all of it—in ourselves and each other. As Martin Luther King, Jr., said, "You come to the point that you love the individual who does the evil deed, while hating the deed that the person does. This is what Jesus means when he says, 'Love your enemy.'" In other words, when we recognize ourselves in others, we discover our capacity to *truly* love and be loved.

6. Act Like a Log

> *Defense is the first act of war.*
>
> — BYRON KATIE

There's one person on this earth who knows how to push every single button I have, and that's my sister, Heather. For my entire life, she's known exactly how to take me from feeling on top of the world to throwing a tantrum on the floor in a matter of seconds. Up until a few years ago, I consistently gave into it—and gave it right back to her. (Her husband calls us expert knife fighters.) Whenever I gave in to any sort of provocation from her—an eye roll, her *Are you really wearing that?* face, some snide comment about my singing voice—I was basically provoking her to act that way by giving it an energetic response. She would swing, and I would let her strike a blow, so she'd swing again, and the knife fight was on. At some point it occurred to me that I could actually sidestep the blow and not let it land—not react to the eye roll or the comment or whatever random, lame shit she said—and the situation would be defused. There's no place for the comment to land, and with no reaction it's no longer a two-party problem. It's her problem. In the past few years, she's also gotten keen to this practice; when I'm out of line, or just fishing for a reaction or a fight, she's learned she too can sidestep it and not feed the beast.

The term "act like a log" comes from the *Bodhisattvacaryāvatāra*, or *The Way of the Bodhisattva*, an eighth-century Mahayana Buddhist text, written by the Buddhist monk Shantideva. The verse: "When the urge arises in your mind / To feelings of desire or angry hate / Do not act! Be silent, do not speak! / And like a log of wood be sure to stay." I've heard Pema Chödrön explain it like this: a log of wood is an inanimate object; you can call it every name in the book—tell the log its singing voice is terrible or that it shouldn't wear that top because it makes the log's boobs look saggy—and the log remains unchanged. None of these things affect the log because the log's true nature can't be affected. This is the same with me now: neither my sister nor anyone else can touch my truest nature. No one is powerful enough to take from me what is eternally, untouchably mine. Only my defense mechanisms can be shaken, which means I always have a choice. I can take the bait and waste my precious, limited energy on defending something that doesn't need defending, engaging in a tiring fight that no one will ever win, or I can meet these things with indifference; I can remain like a log, in my center, in my power.

7. Love Is How the Story Ends

> Nothing real can be threatened. Nothing unreal exists. Herein lies the
> peace of God.   —A COURSE IN MIRACLES

One of the most captivating videos I've ever seen is an *Oprah* clip in which she recounts the story of a woman whose son was dying: "She said she crawled into bed with him, and his last words were '*Ohhh*. It was all so simple.'" Meaning that what we're supposed to be doing here is so simple—we're here to learn to love one another. That's it.

My friend, the beautiful, kind, and fierce Meggan Watterson, once said that she knows how the story ends, and *love is how the story ends,* because love is all that remains when everything else falls away. Love is what's *always* left standing. Love is our natural state—it's what's buried underneath the layers of shame, and hate, and resentment, and anger, and torture, and abuse, and war, and every other terrible thing we encounter on this planet. Love is the only thing we have to remember, and love is the only thing we continually forget.

If you think people are terrible, or just some people are terrible, or that hate is valid, or that humans are inherently evil, or any insane idea that keeps us separate from one another and separate from ourselves, here is where I tell you: *Of course you do.* The delusion that we are all separate, unlovable, scheming, completive, selfish dicks keeps hate alive. There is no hell, there is no punitive God. There is only us, making hell on earth through our beliefs about ourselves and especially about each other. The world teaches us to hate, even though our inheritance is love, and the only way to undo this oppression is to find the places within ourselves that block love and to remove those blocks. Everything counts, and every encounter, every person, every single time we are compelled to turn to hate is an opportunity for us to dissolve the parts that keep us small, that keep the nightmare of intolerance and judgment alive.

Once in early sobriety I recorded a podcast called *Hell Is Other People,* in which I talked about all the bullshit we encounter on the path toward sobriety. I was trying to help normalize the pain of those encounters for other people going through it, but I wish I'd taken it further, to talk about how every single hellish encounter of my life was meant to teach me how to love more generously and wholly. If things had gone differently, if my life had been easy, if only truly kind and helpful people dotted the timeline of my existence, I would never have been as stretched as I have been to find compassion for all people, all beings. I would never have understood how the end of the story could possibly be love.

14

People Who Need People

The opposite of addiction is connection.

—JOHANN HARI

O ne of the great ironies of sobriety, or any path of significant evolution, is that it fractures your existing support systems and connections at the exact time you need people the most. This is because you are breaking out of countless social pacts that say, *I will stay a miserable stuck piece of shit if you will,* or because while you were drinking, you broke them with your socially unacceptable, dicked, selfish ~~disease~~ behavior. Let me repeat that so it sinks in: Recovery is the period of time when you will need people the most.

Connection is literally our lifeblood as *Homo sapiens;* it is our capacity to socially cooperate that explains why Sapiens and not Neanderthals cover the earth and why we were able to evolve. We have survived because a hundred thousand-ish years ago our brains prioritized connection and cooperation with one another, and that prioritization allowed us to thrive and do things like kill sabertooth tigers, build villages and trade networks, farm the land, colonize, and wipe out the poor Neanderthals. In just seventy thousand years, we were able to fan out from a few small tribes in Africa and inhabit every corner of the globe. It wasn't because of the size of our brains but because our brains are built to connect us to one another, to cooperate with one another to accomplish impossible tasks.

In 2015 Johann Hari, author of *Chasing the Scream,* posited that the opposite of addiction is connection. Everyone went apeshit. Seemingly every single person in my network sent me his article—and subsequent TED Talk—because it was such a radical notion: that we are sick with addiction because we are disconnected. At first I was appalled at the intrinsic reductionism in that statement—it felt like an invalidation of everything we were just starting to understand about the pathology of addiction in the wake of developments in neuroscience, and too simple of an answer. Only, as I've come to understand more about addiction, I've found the position that addiction is an outgrowth of disconnection to be far more encompassing of the complex nature of addiction (and why so many of us suffer from it), and the rest to be somewhat reductionist. We aren't just guzzling wine because of, say, our dopamine; we're getting absolutely shitfaced because to exist in a world where our labor is our value, where families and communities are disappearing, where a Kardashian's contouring trick gets more attention than detention camps on our borders, where we look for jobs that pay our rent over jobs that feed our soul, is to barely exist; is to be disconnected from any sort of meaning and value.

In *The Globalization of Addiction,* Bruce Alexander suggests that addiction is a symptom of a free-market, capitalist society, which prioritizes money and materialism above all else. In our singular pursuit to make money, we deprioritize connection to our purpose as individuals, each other, and our culture. When we lose this connection—this essential belonging to ourselves and a community—for the sake of making ends meet or making it big, we become nothing more than hungry ghosts, existing to fill a void through consumption and materialism that will never be filled by these things. Alexander argues that the void can be filled only through psychosocial integration, or the reconciliation of a person's "vital needs for social belonging with their equally vital needs for individual autonomy and achievement."

In other words, capitalism causes disconnection, and disconnection causes addiction.

Maybe this seems like a tangent, or some radical anticapitalist perspective that has nothing to do with an argument for why we need people. It's not. The root of what is wrong in our society is that we have lost both our power as individuals and our connection to one another. To seek to regain these things is not to argue for socialism; it is to argue for lives where we are singular and autonomous individuals who are free to express our truest nature, while simultaneously feeling we are part of something larger than ourselves. We need to claim our uniqueness and our individuality, and we need to belong not despite this individuality but because of it.

So much of this book is about finding and claiming who you are, of standing in the flavor that is you and standing proud. This chapter isn't about that; it's about both navigating the loneliness and isolation the quest for self-actualization requires, and then finding the places where you belong while maintaining and pursuing the fullest expression of who you were made to be.

ISOLATION

I loathe the word *isolation*. In the recovery world, isolation is the monster under the bed, the thing haunting and hunting you that must be avoided at all costs. And I get why that is, I get how deeply tied addiction is to feeling cut off, disenfranchised, alone on this plane: Socially isolated beings (and lab rats) will use drugs to plug their loneliness hole. But isolation can also be part of what saves you, what breathes you, what makes your bones. To me, isolation is an almost inextricable and necessary part of recovery, yet it's often weaponized against us as if it's part of our drinking problem or maybe the cause of it: *You're isolating again, aren't you? Don't you know that's dangerous?*

The flip side to isolation—solitude—is meant to be the good kind of isolation, like the Thoreau version. Solitude is the kind of alone you're *supposed* to want, that you perhaps seek out through socially endorsed means, like a solo backpacking trip to Machu Picchu. If you ask people to define the difference between the two things, to explain why one is wrong and one is right, they'll say something like: Isolation is a negative, lonely state of being that is typically not entered into by choice, while solitude is a positive, full state, meant to be embraced. But that doesn't explain the times in my life when I felt the loneliest, when I felt the most cut off from the world and *not* by choice, where I hated the depth of my disconnection, my aloneness—my *isolation*—that I now look back on and think of as the most wonderful, expansive, gut-wrenching, and *positive* parts of my life, while some of my moments of solitude have been the most negative. Freud said, "One day in retrospect, the years of struggle will strike you as the most beautiful." This was true for me— today, in retrospect, those terrible, lonely years of breaking apart and coming together again—in isolative solitude—strike me as the most beautiful.

Getting sober was, at the beginning, as isolative as the addiction itself. When I stopped drinking the first time, I was kind of alone, and during my second attempt at sobriety, I was *entirely* alone. My loved ones had no idea what I was doing (try explaining that you're "working on sobriety" while still slamming Pinot, people will really get that), and because of their reactions when I broke my sobriety, I really didn't want them to. When it came to my friends, I didn't want to tell them I was trying to quit drinking again, either—and for the most part, it didn't seem like they wanted me to. In so many ways, I had no one, because there was no one I really trusted with the truth. So I started telling strangers the truth.

I told a massage therapist that I needed help, and when she showed me genuine kindness and care, I asked her to come to my home for future treatments. When I found a psychotherapist I liked, Leah, I started to tell her the complete and whole truth, or at least most of it. I worked at a health care company, and because many of my friends were health care providers, I shared my process with them in business meetings; sometimes I even made appointments with them just to talk. I joined a coaching program and told the woman leading it I was trying not to drink—turned out her husband was sober, and he and I talked. I told one of my best friends I was trying to get sober because I knew her dad was a decades-long card-carrying member of AA, and he and I talked, too. And by the time I was ready to actually quit drinking again, what I had somehow done was collect a team of individuals who were on my side. And yet I don't think I remember a period of my life where I felt more cut off from the world.

People often ask me, "How did you do it alone?" And I think, *Oh my God, I was never alone.* I see Leah and Mark and Sally and Geoff and Fran and Susan and my second therapist, a dude who was awful, but nonetheless still right there on Team Holly. I see Annalee, who took me on a hike with her friends when I needed it, and her dad, Andre, who talked with me about his twenty-plus years of sobriety with so much love and kindness and compassion I thought I might die. I see Ashley, who gave me the mantra that would change my life, and her husband, who was the first sober person I ever talked to. I see the acupuncturist I would schlep to once a week in Chinatown, and Rusty Wells, who taught my Sunday yoga classes, and Amy, who packed me bowls of pot and told me about her sober friends and also her friends who had died from drugs. I see Shawn, who let me commandeer our work meetings to talk about *May Cause Miracles* and how awful *Us* magazine really is. I see Steph Snyder and Kia Miller, who were with me night after night on my computer teaching me yoga, and Gabby Bernstein, whose voice carried me through day after day as I consumed her guided meditations. I see Allen Carr, who yelled at me about how bad alcohol is in his masterpiece of a book, and all those other authors from the early days whose books would forever change my life.

And this list here? This is only a list of those who were with me *before* I stopped drinking. When I truly embraced the fact that I had a problem, which wasn't until after I quit the third and final time, the list grew exponentially. I went to AA for a short period, and even though I didn't make friends through it or work the program or even like it, you'd better believe that sitting with people who were like me, who were going through what I was going through, was everything.

Because I was being honest with people in my life, and telling everyone that I had a problem with alcohol (and I mean *telling everyone*), I was even more socially supported and not isolated. In Italy sitting with my friend Geoff and his sister Jenny and her husband Tim, drinking my cappuccino as they sipped their Sicilian white, we actually talked about my drinking, and whether it was hard being in Italy without wine. We didn't pretend there wasn't a new normal happening. I started to talk about my drinking at dinners and networking events, and I made my first sober friend at a business lunch because of that. I found connection, and from there it just kept growing.

Which is all to say, I don't know how I would have done any of this without isolation, without loneliness, without solitude. I also don't know how I would have done any of it without people, without connection.

Keys to Dealing with Isolation in Recovery

On a call recently, a student from my school asked me if it was okay to both like and hate her isolation. She'd just left a long-term partnership, she was alone for the first time in a long time, and she found herself wanting to decline all invitations, to sit in her hot, sticky loneliness, to explore this newfound version of herself she'd somehow always and never known. I understood her predicament—if loneliness was anything to me in early sobriety, it was desperately confusing. I understood what it felt like to know you need people, to want to connect with people, yet to absolutely not want anything to do with people; to be by yourself, to crave being by yourself, to feel like something is terribly wrong with you because it feels so painfully lonely, or because you aren't supposed to like lonely.

Early in my recovery and not long after I quit my job, I went to Italy for a few months to be alone with myself and figure out what mattered most to me. Since I went there to be alone, I found it increasingly interesting that I spent my time texting the man I was fucking back home, or using dating apps, or dating Italian men I wasn't that into, or—instead of staring at a piece of art or architecture—scanning the throngs of tourists for someone, *anyone,* to hang out with me and keep me from myself.

Inevitably, I would find someone to fill that space, and then maybe even moments into our date, our walk, our conversation, I would want out; to just be by myself. And so I would run. It makes absolutely no sense, but also it does—because we need connection, but first we need to connect with ourselves. Such is the tension we navigate. A quote I found at the time by Brendan Francis was key: "At the innermost core of all loneliness is a deep and powerful yearning for union with one's lost self."

There is no map for this; no special set of instructions that will prevent you from feeling like an alien alone on a foreign planet. I can only offer you the things I learned along the way, that would have helped me understand how to be by and with myself, while seeking connection with others.

YOU WILL FEEL LONELY

You are not on a mission to save the princess, you're on a mission to save yourself—you don't go with a team, you go with yourself. Loneliness isn't some block on the path, it's the whole damn path, and if you're feeling it, that means you're doing it right.

YOU NEED PEOPLE

Hear me on this: *You. Need. People.* We humans are biologically designed to connect with one another, and from the moment we are born into this world, our development as humans— emotionally, intellectually, physically, spiritually—is contingent on how we connect. That said, most of us who struggle with addiction also have pathologies in the area of connection, meaning that from a young age something malfunctioned in the area of connection—from not being held enough, to being separated from our parents, to being abused, and so on. It is imperative that you find people with whom you have genuine connections as you recover. The building of relationships *is* the building of ourselves. If this contradicts what I just said about loneliness, that's only because everything in recovery is a contradiction— you just need to learn how to hold two opposing thoughts at once.

YOU NEED CARE TEAM PEOPLE

You will need individuals in your life who count as a support team: people who can tether you, who bring different things to the table. Start collecting people who know what you are going through, whom you can be honest with, who root for you, who can help you. They can be a sponsor in AA, a therapist, a coach, or someone who's been down the path you're on. Get massages and acupuncture. Go to yoga classes with teachers who care about their students and get to know them. Go to meditation groups or alternative types of recovery groups, like SMART Recovery or Refuge Recovery. Go to your doctor for your annual checkup and get them on board with your goals. Go to a church or synagogue or mosque and talk to the priest/rabbi/imam. We have *so many resources* and *so many people* willing to be of service to us. Find them. Ask them for help.

YOU NEED PEER PEOPLE

I didn't have peer people for nine-plus months of my early recovery. I went to my first AA meeting after my last drink, and I didn't make a single friend there. I didn't start to make real peer connections until I went through Kundalini yoga teacher training, six months sober, and while the Kundalini folks weren't sober, they were on the same path as me, and that counted for a lot. When I did finally start accumulating sober friends, I was more than ten months sober and over a year into the journey of attempting sobriety, and this was through a Meetup I started.

From there it just grew . . . fewer not-sober friends, more sober friends. I found them in as many ways as you can imagine.

ONE PERSON IS MORE THAN ENOUGH

Many of us think we need a sea of people, a village; oftentimes that thought comes from an idea of what is socially acceptable— social proof of how worthy or cool or normal or likable you are is often tied up with how popular you are, how many friends you have, how many plans you make, how many likes you get on your #tbt on Instagram. I spent the first three decades of my life fighting to be popular and palatable and liked, for my social calendar to be full. Part of my recovery was letting that part of me die, of learning that my self-worth isn't dependent upon how many people text me in a day, or whether or not I have plans on a Friday night. These days I am enough, regardless of how many people I know or call me a friend. When you are searching for your people, don't look for quantity, look for quality. Sometimes just one quality person can be enough—one good strong relationship that acts as your anchor is more than many of us get.

Most of the time, an anchoring relationship like this is one with a therapist or a coach. Mine was with my therapist, Ann. She showed up one day at my Kundalini teacher training, and after a series of events conspired to bring us together, she agreed to be my therapist and soon became the bedrock I needed while I found my footing and grew my own root system. She was in my corner—consistently, without fail—and because I trusted her so much, because I felt so seen and heard and felt by her, I was able to do some of the hardest things I've ever had to do in my life. I may have had a lot of people rooting for me, but Ann was everything, and if I had had only her in that first year, it would have been enough.

REFRAME ISOLATION AND LEARN TO BELONG TO YOURSELF

Before I quit drinking, when my life was increasingly marked by a need to stay home and pump alcohol and Netflix and takeout and cigarettes and pot in and out of my body (in isolation), it had also been marked by a need to say yes to everything—every happy hour, party, dinner invitation, work event, concert. I had such an innate sense of FOMO, it didn't even matter if I wanted to do the thing—I never said no. It was like a rubber band of a balancing act: I'd pull too hard in one direction (overextending myself socially), then snap back in the other direction (drug-induced catatonia, at home, by myself).

Before sobriety, I was never actually *with* myself. I was either avoiding myself in a crowd of other people, or running away from myself chemically. Recovery was the first time in my life that I found comfort in my own company. And in that space, that oh-so-sacred space of isolation and solitude, I found God within me. As my old world fell away, before the new one rose up to meet me, I found myself. And the most miraculous thing of all—I found that I *liked* this person.

I had finally reached the point where it no longer mattered what other people thought—what I thought became more important. By some stroke of magic, I began to find love for this fledgling girl who had almost lost it all. Learning how to be with her—in isolation—and not be drunk, high, or bingeing, was one of the most important parts of this journey. This isn't to say that it didn't hurt or that I wasn't lonely. But it was also a rite of passage into selfhood that I'd never before experienced, never before allowed myself to experience. Before sobriety, I thought only losers hung out by themselves. After sobriety, I learned that only people who truly know themselves can be with themselves in solitude. Perhaps the difference between isolation and solitude is that we have to go through isolation to truly experience and own the fullness that is solitude.

A BALANCE MUST BE STRUCK

Your recovery needs to have some semblance of balance, which is in itself a subjective idea. Only you will know the right mix for you—which people, what kind of space and solitude, friends now or later. Only you know what your special mix of recovery is, how it's going to look, how many people will be included, and how much time you will spend alone, reacquainting yourself with those long-forgotten parts. Create a recovery with the people and things that will help *you* get to where you need to go, rather than the mix that others think you need, or the mix that our image-driven society tells you you need.

How to Make Friends in Sobriety

A few years into recovery, I did something that I'm more comfortable doing now than I ever imagined I would be: I met a woman for coffee who I'd scoped off the internet. Like all first dates that originate on the web, we had that first moment of awkward *Is that you?* recognition as we tried to match selfies to real-life faces. We settled into some small talk based on the little pieces we already knew of each other, but because we were both in recovery, in a flash we were talking about our sex lives, our depression, our art, how terrifying it was to meet new people while sober. Time flew by. As I was walking back to my apartment, I couldn't help but text my mom the big news: *I made a new friend!*

This is not an abnormal occurrence anymore. These days I make friends easily and celebrate some of the deepest connections of my life; some old, of course, but most of them new, post-sobriety friendships. My postdrinking people see me and understand me and know me and get me and love me, dark and light parts and all. If I am rich in any way, it is rich in community.

It wasn't always this way.

My first year of sobriety tested almost every friendship I had. There were some people who left immediately because our relationship was really only about alcohol. Some friendships unspooled a little more slowly as I began to value and prioritize different things, or as I became a different person, or because just maybe I became a person with standards. There were some friendships that I'd had for years, good friendships, where all of a sudden we had nothing left to say.

One night at a café with one of my oldest, best mates, who I'd never been able to get enough of, I found myself counting the minutes; we had nothing in common anymore. Over a year into my sobriety, I asked another friend if she didn't want to hang out with me anymore because I didn't drink, and she reminded me that it wasn't just me who was allowed to change. Most of the friendships that had sustained me for the better part of my adulthood fell away, and the ones that remained were in total reformulation as I was reformulating. Nancy Levin once wrote, "Honor the space between no longer and not yet," and I almost believe she wrote that for what happened to my friendships in sobriety.

This is not an uncommon experience. When we get sober, we tend to lose or outgrow some of the relationships that sustained us, but we also brush up against the very harsh reality that because addiction is stigmatized and most of us recover in silence, there are huge barriers to finding a new community. And if you're like me and you skip the AA scene, the barriers are further compounded. Here are some tips, tricks, and resources to help you overcome these barriers and start forming your new friend-family.

Look for Friends That Align with Your Spirit, Not Your Sobriety

One of the keys to expanding my community has been that I don't look for sober as a qualifier—I look for whether our life paths are aligned. Not everyone who is seeking the things I am seeking, or who cares about the things I care about, is sober. And that's okay, because sober isn't the most important thing about me. My love of photography, social justice, writing, meditation, yoga, reading, addiction advocacy, inappropriate humor, entrepreneurship, metaphysics, risk-taking, Italy, music, creativity, and so on, are what really make me come alive, so friendships founded in a shared interest of these things tend to be highly rewarding. I look more for the richness that someone has to offer and whether they see and value me than whether they abstain from booze. Oddly enough, most of the people I attract these days, based on this principle of spirit alignment, either don't drink or don't place a high value on it.

Put Yourself Out There

Jane Sarasohn-Kahn, a health care economist, is one of the individuals who helped get my company, Tempest, off the ground. She's also one of my dearest friends. We came to know each other after I spoke at a professional networking event, and a woman who thought we might have a lot to talk about introduced us via email. Jane had just published a piece in *HuffPost* calling attention to women's growing reliance on wine and opioids to get by. Some months later we met in real life at an event where I was volunteering. After that real-life meeting, I asked Jane for help with my business, risking rejection. A few months after she said yes to that request, I was running around Florence, Italy, with her and her family.

Today Jane and I muse about what life will be like when we are both living in Italy and are neighbors, and she is one of the most important humans in my world. Had I never put myself out there at that networking event, had I never run with the introduction, had I never volunteered at that other event, had I never asked Jane for help, had I not said yes when she asked me to come to Florence while I was in Rome—*had I not so many things*—I wouldn't have her as one of my people. And so it goes with so many of my other love stories: if I hadn't asked for a phone number, sent an email, gone to that brunch by myself, gone to *that party* by myself (yep, I've gone to parties by myself), traveled by myself, or said yes to countless terrifying things, I would have missed out. We must take risks in order to further our lives and expand our worlds.

Consider Ditching Your Anonymity

From the moment I stopped drinking, I talked about it. At first, I talked in my small real-life circles—to my friends, people at work, my family. That didn't do much for me in the way of making new friends—if anything it *cost* me friends—but it did allow me to start owning who I was. A few months into sobriety, I started talking about it in conversations with people at professional networking events, and at one in particular I spoke to a group of women about it. Out of the ten ladies present, one was also in recovery, and my speaking up gave her courage to speak up as well and claim her own sobriety, which is the story of how I made my first sober friend.

Soon afterward I came out on my Facebook page and my LinkedIn profile. Coming out on social media allowed people I already knew who had suffered the same issues to find me (and find me they did, lots of them). Eventually, my story was passed on outside of my immediate network, and strangers got in touch with me to tell me they were sober, too. Ditching my anonymity was akin to sending up a flare in the middle of a black sky—the right people saw it, and from that many friendships were seeded. Bonus? People who suffered not from addiction but from other stigmatizing conditions or who also had big secrets came out of the woodwork. My courage to tell my truth gave many other people courage to tell theirs. Ursula Le Guin said, "We are volcanoes. When we women offer our experience as our truth, as human truth, all the maps change. There are new mountains." Me sharing my story changed the map, created new mountains, and those mountains are the ground on which so many connections, relationships, and love affairs have bloomed.

Use Instagram

Unbelievably, Instagram has one of the better communities out there for sober folk. You can search hashtags like #sober, #sobriety, #soberlife, #teetotaler, or any combination of words dealing with recovery and sobriety, and find post after post from others who are walking the same path as you. I've made dozens of friendships through Instagram, some of which have translated into the deepest and closest real-life friendships I've ever had. If you are hesitant about coming out on your regular profile, create a second one specifically for the purpose of being part of the sobriety community; you can do this anonymously or under your real name. Then engage and comment and follow and post and join. Like anything else, what you put into it, you'll get out of it, and your risk will equal your reward.

Try Meetup

Meetup.com is an online forum that enables people who share interests to find one another and meet in person. There are all sorts of Meetups, for everything from yoga to hiking to professional networking to coding to baking, and a large number of sobriety-themed Meetup groups with hundreds or thousands of members. Simply go online and search your local area for such groups, using terms such as *sober, sobriety,* or *nondrinkers.* If you can't find a group close to you, think about starting one. I started a Meetup called Sobriety Club for Girls (now defunct) and hosted meetings at my apartment. They were awkward as hell (because I am socially anxious and I hate hosting anything), but they were also where I met my second, third, fourth, fifth, and sixth sober friends. Alternatively, you can use Meetup to find individuals with other shared interests. For instance, if you search for *meditation, hiking, outdoors, knitting,* or *running,* you're likely to encounter folks who don't center their lives around a bar.

Activism, Volunteering, Actively Giving a Shit

We're living in a time when so many ideas, institutions, and people are threatened that the sheer overwhelm can easily halt us. Where do we even start? The great news is that by volunteering for something, anything—for a national political movement or your local library—you're contributing to a greater, positive cultural shift. Get on mailing lists, or follow community organizations and organizers on social media. If you've never been to a protest, check one out. Being with other people who care—especially strangers—can be a collective catharsis. Protests can make you feel less alone: just show up, see what's happening, and see if anything resonates. You can join groups on issues that directly affect you, or show support for those that seemingly don't. That's a step into allyship, and a way to demonstrate solidarity with friends, neighbors, and people you don't know (yet). All these actions, tiny or big, feel good because they're all steps toward our collective freedom. If you feel moved to stand up or give back, do something about it.

Go to Personal Development Retreats and Workshops

In the last few years, I've participated in lots of yoga, meditation, and personal development workshops and retreats. I've yet to leave one without a phone number, and many times I've forged bonds that have turned into fulfilling relationships. If you don't know where to start, you can look to SheRecovers, Esalen, Kripalu, Spirit Rock, or Omega Institute, or look up your local yoga studio to see if they are hosting any events or workshops. If you follow a spiritual teacher of some kind, look at their website to see if they are offering any sort of workshop or talk, or sign up for their email list to stay abreast of upcoming events.

I've also gone to a number of antiracism workshops that I would count as not just "personal development" but "societal and cultural development." As a white woman, part of my awakening has included a growing awareness of my privilege and an active education in dismantling the ways I contribute to the oppression of black, brown, and indigenous people. It's the job of white women (and white men) to undo this discrimination, the same way it's the job of men to undo toxic masculinity. My friend Rachel Cargle is a prolific teacher who holds lectures throughout the country (and has an incredibly engaged community on Instagram and Patreon). You can also find chapters of the antiracist groups White People for Black Lives (WP4BL) and Showing Up for Racial Justice (SURJ) throughout the country. When you are at these types of events, strike up conversations, stay vulnerable, and exchange phone numbers. I promise you, this is how you find your people. It's how I've found many of mine.

Look for Sobriety-Specific Events or Dry Bars

Unlike when I stopped drinking, today there are a number of organizations—and even bars without alcohol (what!)—that cater to the sober lyfe. This movement is in its infancy, so the events are somewhat hard to chase down if you don't live in a big city, but that's not always the case—people are, after all, sober everywhere. In New York City, there are Club Soda events (started by my friend Ruby Warrington, author of *Sober Curious*), Listen Bar (a pop-up alcohol-free bar), and The Getaway (a bar in Brooklyn that serves nonalcoholic cocktails). There are sober Meetups for people of color, women, the LGBTQIA community, and many other intersections of identity. My friend Josh Hersh started Meetups for queer introverts (called Qalm) that has Meetups all over the nation; Sans Bar, which was founded in Austin, Texas, by Chris Marshall, sponsors booze-free pop-up bars across the country; Day Breaker, started by another friend of mine, Matt Brimer, hosts early-morning sober dance parties before work. And my company, Tempest, sponsors in-real-life events, too (jointempest.com). There will undoubtedly be more; people are sick of drinking, and people need people, so we can expect a lot more of these types of events and alcohol-free establishments.

Talk to the Ones You Stalk

Some of my closest friends have come about through my stalking of them, or their stalking of me, on the internet. If you see someone online that lights your fire and who you feel you might want a relationship with, go for it. You might start by complimenting their work, or even offering to help their cause. You have nothing to lose by reaching out.

Participate in Recovery Meetings

I would be remiss if I didn't mention that many people I know on this path have made friends within the rooms of AA or within the rooms of other in-person recovery groups, as well as various online recovery forums. In-person meetings (besides AA) include SMART Recovery, Refuge Recovery, and Women for Sobriety. Online there are Women for Sobriety, Soberistas, In The Rooms, Integral Recovery Fellowship Meeting, SMART Recovery, and Refuge Recovery. There are many Facebook pages dedicated to recovery such as She Recovers, Sober Senorita, *The Temper* (Tempest's media publication dedicated to dismantling the narrative around alcohol), and Tempest. There are also other types of recovery modalities that incorporate meditation and yoga, such as Y12SR or Eight Step Recovery. Be brave enough to try as many of them as you can. Even if a meeting or online forum turns out not to be your jam, there is always the possibility of making friends.

Patience and Perseverance Pay

Lastly, just remember all good things take time. That means giving yourself space to be alone as you ground yourself in recovery and not demanding an immediate banging social life and circle of besties; that means giving your friends time to adjust to the new you (or time to go away); that means giving yourself time to explore new avenues of knowing people; that means giving yourself time to seed things that may flower into big, beautiful relationships. Hang in there, keep trying, keep faith, and most important, let it happen in due time. Because it will. Your people are out there, you just need to find them.

15

What Do You Do for Fun
If You Don't Drink?

Tell me, what is it you plan to do with
your one wild and precious life?

—MARY OLIVER

In August 2015, I sat across the dinner table from a strikingly
handsome American man eight years my junior. We were in
Rome at a restaurant, eating pizza and fried things and drinking
fizzy water and macchiatos, and I was wearing this tight little
dress, sans underwears. We were on our fifth date in as many
days and had been to flea markets and risked our lives crossing
the *autostrada* on foot with bags of cured meat and we'd sat
above the Roman Forum at midnight talking about God and
met for dates at various Bernini sculptures and kissed in front of
the place Julius Caesar was murdered. I'd laughed so hard in his
presence, I peed myself a little. Twice.

So when he asked me what I did for fun—me "being sober
and all"—I was a little perplexed. Our five days of extreme living without drinking, smoking, and drugging flashed before my
eyes. "Off the top of my head? I travel to foreign lands by myself
to observe countless objects of art, history, and culture, eat fried
food, drink coffee at midnight, and sometimes I go on dates

with younger men and leave my underwear at home." He laughed. "Right." And then he asked again, "But seriously . . . ?"

A week later, off the Gulf of Naples, swimming in *nostre mare* after dark with another man who was staying in the room next to me—under the full moon in eighty-degree weather—the same question came up.

"Okay," he said, "I have a question. I hope this doesn't sound rude. But if you don't drink, smoke, or do drugs, what the hell do you do for fun?"

"This," I said. "*This.*"

I understand this question more than I understand most questions about sobriety. I understand it because I get exactly where it comes from and I understand exactly why people ask and I understand why it seems so incomprehensible. I understand it because it was *my* question. How do you vacation in Mexico without tequila, eat dinner without wine, brunch without champagne, party without shots? How do you *live* without the distinct pleasure of being silly drunk?

Prior to October 2012, if you had asked me to describe what I imagined sobriety looked like, I would have said something that sounded like a fart noise while pointing two thumbs down. A life without alcohol might as well have been a death sentence of boring. A life half lived with half smiles that smelled like Clorox bleach.

What I have discovered on this side of the bar scene is the exact opposite. Instead of the boring life I'd anticipated before quitting booze, my life without alcohol is where my actual living began. *Nothing* was as half-lived, forced, sad, or redundant as an existence that required alcohol to have fun. It is a perpetual Groundhog Day to be trapped in the bar scene, with options limited to those that include alcohol, and an increasing prioritization of the alcohol over socializing. I didn't need booze before I found it, and my life today is lived as if it never existed.

Removing alcohol does not remove options—it creates more of them. By no longer consuming a depressant that fuels your anxiety, an anesthetic that limits the depth of your feelings, a neurotoxin that impairs brain function to the point of forgetting the best parts of the night, and a poison that requires a long recovery period postconsumption, you are choosing to have fun.

What I Do for Fun Now That I Don't Drink

Normal Things

NORMAL THINGS ARE FUN! This one shocked me. I had forgotten the simple pleasure of reading a book, going to a movie, riding a bike, sitting down to a meal, hiking a trail, or driving in a car with my family. Toward the end of my drinking life, these things seemed torturous—I either avoided them or tried to incorporate alcohol to make them more interesting.

This is not uncommon. Remember, drinking artificially activates the pleasure center of our brains, causing above-normal levels of dopamine to be dumped into our systems. Over time the brain compensates for this overstimulation, trying to reestablish homeostasis by effectively dulling our ability to receive pleasure from *normal* things (or anything besides alcohol). So we aren't motivated to do the things that would normally bring us joy, and when we do them, we don't get as big a hit of pleasure, or any at all. Removing alcohol, and allowing time to pass so my system could normalize, has allowed me to genuinely enjoy the most mundane activities.

Act Like a Kid

When I was fifteen, my best friend and I would rollerblade to Goomba's Pasta and get buckets of fettucine Alfredo. We'd stay up all hours playing board games, making home videos with my dad's camcorder, and acting like fools. I remember when we started drinking and going to parties how quickly we denounced our previous existence. "What kind of losers were we?" we'd remark to each other, horrified that we'd ever been reduced to relying on our own innate ability to enjoy life. How did we possibly have fun without getting drunk at weekend parties and letting creepy young men stick their fingers in our vaginas in some random kid's parents' room, or lying next to a toilet with the spins?

I was led to believe that my childlike wonder would die off as I matured; I bought into a narrative that tells us the only way to have fun after a certain age is to get totally hammered, or at least a good buzz going. There came a point where what truly brought me joy—being with my friends and letting my inhibitions go naturally, allowing myself to be absorbed in the moment—was no longer socially acceptable. Drinking and debauchery were sold to me as what adults do, as the only way adults really have fun; it was embarrassing to *not* drink, to *not* party, and I know that because I made fun of people who didn't.

This is the lie of alcohol.

It tricks us into giving up things that actually bring us pure joy in exchange for a drug that accompanies 90 percent of all college campus sexual assaults, that will kill one in ten of us, that makes us disconnect from one another, that causes us to forget entire parts of nights we deem "just so fun." We go from being able to naturally act like kids to thinking the only time we get to access this state is when we're a few drinks in.

In 2010, sitting with my closest people at a friend's wine bar, we tried to make a list of things we could do without alcohol and were totally stumped. *What did we do before this?* We decided to go shoot guns at a range, and afterward we ended up at a bar, and not because we couldn't have fun in each other's company, but because we'd all bought into the myth that alcohol was necessary to let loose, to enjoy ourselves, to be weird. To be like kids. Quitting drinking revealed to me the lie I'd so hungrily lapped up at fifteen, which was that our natural capacity for wonder, awe, and absorption leaves us. It doesn't. That stuff never leaves us. It is always there; we just have to remember to engage with it.

Sobriety has been an intentional reconnection to this silly, weird, childlike part of myself. One of the first Christmases I spent sober, I invented a game called Holly Crab Hands and chased my niece around with crab legs extending out of my sweater screaming, "I am Holly Crab Hands!" On my first girls' trip I convinced my five best friends to play hide-and-seek, and we capped off the night by playing dress-up and recording a music video. I have run through fields, rolled down hillsides, and skipped through streets. I've played chase, freeze tag, dress-up, more board games than I care to admit, bought a trampoline for my cubicle at work, and took up rollerblading. If it sounds fun, immature, or ridiculous, I'm into it. If I get to make a fool of myself, or act like myself, or act like a five-year-old, or embarrass a five-year-old, I am into it.

Get Your Introvert On
I had always thought because I love people/love knowing a lot of people/love being around people/come alive around people, that I was by nature an extrovert (and scored as one on the Myers-Briggs Type Indicator as well: ENFJ). And so for my en-

tire life, I forced myself into a big social life, thinking that was who I was. I felt deeply inadequate if I wasn't out doing something on a Friday night, flawed if I wasn't part of a big group, and guilty for wanting alone time. What I've found on this side of things is that while I love my friendships and people, I'm also exhausted by them. When I gave myself the chance to actually spend time alone (without drinking), I found I preferred it to groups of people, crowds, and parties. Fun for me is doing yoga at home by myself, snuggling up with a few hundred books, turning up the music, and having a dance party of one.

I now get that this is who I am and what I need, and I don't apologize for being introverted. Being alone doesn't equal loser, it equals healthy, regenerative, and thrilling (yes, thrilling). Being alone also doesn't negate or lessen my extrovert tendencies. I know my social life awaits whenever I need it, I know I can still put on some heels and red lipstick and be fabulous in a crowd; I know that if someone calls me on a Monday and asks what I did all weekend and I say, "Read three books, took five baths, drank tea, meditated, and sang to my cat," all it means is that I partied the way I needed to party.

Embrace Your Radical Crone

In addition to reconciling my introversion, I've also accepted the part of me that is an old cat lady. In *Rise Sister Rise*, Rebecca Campbell discusses the four archetypes we cycle through each month, or the four stages of womanhood: the Maiden, the Mother, the Wild Woman, and the Crone. Metaphorically, the maiden is preovulation, the mother is fertile, the wild woman is premenstrual, and the crone is menstruating. Again, that's metaphorical—you don't have to have a vagina or a period or identify as a woman to know these stages.

The crone has been through it all, doesn't take shit, and

doesn't give fucks. She is the wise one, the one who cuts straight to the chase. She also, quite specifically, doesn't do something because she's *supposed* to; she does what she *wants* to. This translates to many different things for me: It looks like going to bed at nine or even eight (when I want to), wearing what I want to wear (scarves and loose fabrics and flat comfy orthopedically supporting shoes but also sometimes stilettos), staying in, telling people to turn down music that's too loud, asking for what I need without being embarrassed, being me without apologizing. Crone me loves my bed and baths and quiet evenings with just a few people; she likes cats and hats and sunscreen and walking slowly and saying no and not responding to electronic communications; she definitely has no clue how to use Snapchat. Sometimes Crone me passes gas in front of other people because Crone me would much rather suffer judgment and disgust than the pain of holding in a fart. That kind of stuff. We are all the things; we are innocent maidens and givers of life and wild, angry beasts, and we are absolutely little old ladies who prefer mint tea to mint juleps.

Create
In that space between the life I was swimming from and the life I was swimming toward, I had a lot of time to fill, and also a somewhat preternatural drive toward creation. In early sobriety, I started with a set of crayons, printer paper, and an Instagram account, filling my time with mindless drawing and coloring (stick figures mostly), photography and filtering (this was when Instagram was fun). As time expanded without the numbing agents, as the world became more vivid and big, so too did my need to express my creativity.

I started getting more adventurous in my clothing, and more dedicated to my photography, and one day—out of a desperate need to speak out—began a secret blog so I could write (which is how I found my agent, Rebecca, which is why you are holding this book). Today a large part of my fun comes from creation. I get completely absorbed in writing, taking photos and editing them, creating the vision of my company, Tempest. I work with our marketing team on brand design and our product team on software design and development, our instructional design team on content and course creation—and on and on. Equally, I get lost in researching addiction and harnessing that information into something that feeds my work and my message. I create every day, and typically, that is the bulk of my work. Creating is more than fun—it is total and complete absorption.

As an aside, some people posit that addiction is a response to suppressed creation. In the Gospel of Thomas, Jesus says, "If you bring forth what is within you, what you bring forth will save you. If you do not bring forth what is within you, what you do not bring forth will destroy you." I believe that some of my own sickness arose because I spent a majority of my time creating things that didn't matter to me (like spreadsheets) and suppressing the parts of me that wanted so badly to come out (my voice, my art, my opinions). Which is to say, creating isn't just about fun, it's also about saving your life.

See the World with New Eyes

As Jen Sincero wrote in her book *You Are a Badass,* "We're on a planet that somehow knows how to rotate on its axis and follow a defined path while it hurtles through space! Our hearts beat! We can see! We have love, laughter, language, living rooms, computers, compassion, cars, fire, fingernails, flowers, music, medicine, mountains, muffins! We live in a limitless Universe overflowing with miracles! The fact that we aren't stumbling around in an inconsolable state of sobbing awe is appalling. The

Universe must be like, 'What more do I have to do to wake these bitches up?'"

One of the biggest side effects of sobriety is that you begin to see the world with new eyes. For me, this started simply. One day as I was walking down the street, I noticed the clouds moving across the sky. I was downtown on a crowded street, and I stopped and stared up, mouth agape, looking around like, *Do you all see these clouds?!* I felt like Will Ferrell in *Elf* when he goes to New York for the first time. I stopped looking two minutes ahead and began moving through my life with total awe for the magic that surrounded me every day, the wonder that is this world. How we got here, how miraculous it is that we make it through a day, how insane it is that we are a tiny dot within an infinite Universe, what a privilege it is to be alive. I've pulled my car over on the middle of the freeway to take a picture of the sky, stood up in a convertible *while I was driving* in Hawaii so I could film it, and done many stupid, seemingly pointless things so I could eat the world as it is.

In 2016, when I moved to Los Angeles—a place I've always hated—I fell in love with the graffiti, dried-up canals, desert, and suburban sprawl. Even the traffic looked different, like some kind of dystopian performance art. L.A. hadn't changed, but I certainly had. It is a really, *really* big deal to live in a place you have reverence for. Even if it's covered in concrete and people shit on the street, it can be beautiful. Sobriety, if it is anything, is paying attention, seeing the wonder and the beauty around us that we so easily sprint by on our way to the next thing. And this is more than fun; this is actually living.

Take Risks

One of the more appealing aspects of drinking was that it enabled me to do wild, risky things. My favorite memories were of risking arrest for public nudity or having sex in a weird place, the times I would tell someone how I really felt about them or something they did, the times I would steal a cup I liked from a restaurant or sneak a joint at a work event, the times I would get on a stage to do the Kid 'n Play (I'm old, that was a thing). While these things were ridiculous, they made me feel alive. I love breaking rules, I love thrill, I love being bad.

On this side of things, I've kept the same spirit, only without the need to be bombed to do it. Things like quitting my job with no real plan eons before I was ready, blogging to the world the most private parts of my existence, starting a company with zero clue, having opinions that are decidedly in the margins of popular opinion, traveling with no itinerary, hopping on motorcycles with strange men in foreign countries, asking for things I'm afraid to ask for, dancing terribly in front of people. I live from a place of "Why not?" and this newfound sense of right-minded risk-taking—as in risk-taking I am fully in control and aware of—has led to some of the more fantastic moments of my life and given me major courage and freedom.

For those of us who feel we satisfied our rebellious streak through brown liquids and late drunk nights, we need to reconnect with our idea of rebelliousness. We all fear losing that part of us that makes us feel alive or strong or maybe more like men. When I first started coaching clients and they would inevitably ask about losing their edge in sobriety, I would tell them I got that edge from dancing sober, telling the truth, and so on; and then as I learned more, I graduated to saying that sobriety in itself is rebellious—which it is. It's far more subversive and hardcore to not do what everyone else is doing than to go along with the pack. As Mark Twain said, "Whenever you find yourself on the side of the majority, it is time to pause and reflect." So those were my answers for a while; it's a wild rebellious thrill to dance sober, and it's rebellious in and of itself to not drink. But then in 2018, I started connecting rebelliousness and sobriety a bit differently.

In the wake of the 2016 election and the rising, palpable anger of women in the United States, I started to question things I'd never questioned before and think in ways I'd never thought. I thought of the men who put their hands on my thigh tattoo as if I were their prize cow, or how insane it is to believe that it's my job to protect myself from rape and sexual assault (to dress a certain way so as to not invite it, for example), or how many times I demurred unwanted advances, or smiled when some rando told me to smile, or maybe even got a rush from being catcalled on the street.

I thought specifically of a time in 2017 when I met an older man, a college professor, in a rose garden on the Aventino and how we'd gotten to speaking and how fun it was to have someone to practice my Italian with. Ten minutes into our conversation he put his hand in my lap and suggested we go to dinner. I thought about how nervous I was, how polite I was, how much care I took to not embarrass him or make him feel uncomfortable; it never occurred to me that I wasn't the one responsible for bearing that weight, but women are trained to do just this. We are polite and kind and soft, and we smile as we are violated hundreds of different ways; his comfort is always our responsibility, and ours doesn't quite matter. He harms us, and we manage the embarrassment. It's our duty.

When I walked away from that encounter, I held two ideas in my mind. The first was that perhaps I'd invited it—asked for it—by wearing my short shorts and talking to him. The second was: *Fuck all men.*

Recall from Chapter 6 where Carol Flinders tells us, "To say what one wants, go where one likes, enjoy whatever pleasures one can afford, and most of all, to *be* somebody—[these are things] that have normally defined male privilege." I wondered: Why couldn't I say what I wanted to, which was "You fucking pig. A woman talking to you isn't an invitation to put your hand where her vagina is, or to even assume she wants to have dinner with you." I wondered: Why couldn't I even go to a goddamn *rose garden* without feeling like I was prey in an open field?

But then something happened, the #MeToo movement, and then I found Rebecca Solnit, and I finally understood that to exist as a woman isn't an invitation, which changed everything. I'd been growing tired of street harassment and clapping back for some time, but then I got bolder, stopping when it happened and looking the man in the face and asking him why, or telling him *shame on you.*

I also began noticing how much I moved around men in the world, and I wondered: what would happen if I forced them to move around me? So I tried an experiment: one where I wouldn't move when walking and coming toward a man; I would move for women, obviously, and disabled men and older men, but I made a point to absolutely not move when walking toward an able-bodied white man.

I realized how little men moved around women even when they are forced to. I was bulldozed and body-checked a number of times. This one time, again in Rome (I'm there a lot, and I walk a lot when I'm there), I was walking down a sidewalk, and a man was coming toward me. He was on his cell phone, totally unaware of anything around him, though he did see me. I held to my path, and he did too, until we were stopped face to face; a total standoff. It lasted about five seconds before he finally conceded, extending his arms out in a gesture like an usher: *After you, ma'am.* It was a win, and not because I got my way, but because at that moment I stopped allowing myself to be second in a world that constantly reminds me I am, telling me if I do something like this, then I'm an aggressive, angry man-hater.

It's 2020, and I speak up when I'm being tone-policed instead of getting quieter. When women write me letters telling me I'm mean and egoic and angry, I don't put it in a sack and carry it around like it's mine, because it isn't, not anymore. I use my voice, even if it is shaky, even if it is sometimes too angry. I don't let people convince me that I'm not kind because I am holding a ground that so many women before me were murdered or tortured or imprisoned for holding, or trying to hold. I am keenly aware of the ways women are oppressed or patronized or subordinated, and I no longer give into it; or at least, I try very hard not to. I also try very hard not to let it stay with me; it is a balance of being big and small.

I wouldn't call this "fun," but I did call whiskey neats and trying to drink like men "rebellious and edgy" and therefore some twisted idea of fun. I call this what happens when you fully denounce a substance that is marketed to you to keep you from your power, or when you show up for this life with clear eyes and see all the ways you've been held down by yourself and by society. The ultimate act of rebellion, and the real delicious one, is served up from the courage you summon to exist in the world as an equal, as a human claiming their space.

Be Yourself

Just for a moment, sit and think about all the things you're terrified of people finding out about you, or of the things you do behind closed doors that you would never let out, or the things you would be humiliated having to do in front of an audience. What if everyone saw your body as it was, or your face without makeup? What if you had to sing in front of an audience, or dance in front of one, or speak in front of one? What if people knew how you can't stop texting this one person you dated or that you [insert whatever private, shame-filled thing you do here].

I spent thirty-three years avoiding looking at myself, thinking that if I looked too closely, what I would find would destroy me. I thought my tastes were wrong, my style immature, and my opinions too strong. It was only a matter of time before I would be found out as the pathetic thing I believed myself to be. As you can imagine, this was not fun.

John Dupuy says, "The disease of addiction has become the adventure of creating our highest and best selves," and for me, this is 100 percent true. My path has not been to simply abstain from alcohol, it has been to journey through the layers of self-hate, and the discovey of a most authentic being pulsing below— the adventure of becoming Holly.

And the shocker? I actually *like* what I found buried down there. I *like* myself. I like my tastes, style, preferences, opinions, movements, and peculiarities. I like the books I read, the clothes I wear, the music I listen to, my dry wit, my big hearty man-laugh, my maniacal drive, my deformed big toe, my big messy heart, my big messy life. All of it. And because I'm the person I spend the most time with, this means I get to spend a lot of time with a person I dig. As you can imagine, this is fun.

Everything You Did Before, Minus the Boring Stuff
In *The Easy Way to Control Alcohol*, Allen Carr suggests that everything we can do drunk we can also do sober, and that we don't have fun because of alcohol, we have fun because of what we are doing and who we are with. In a point that hit home, he says that if we need to drink to do something, we probably shouldn't be doing it anyway.

Carr encourages people to get out there immediately and

confront their social life head on. I don't agree with this; I know plenty of people who needed to stay away from their social lives—or places, events, and people deeply connected to their drinking—for a time while they healed. Only you truly know what is right for you; it was right for me to confront it with a deep sense of curiosity. I went on as if nothing had changed, and attended events I would have normally attended—parties, nights out at bars, business trips, company events, dinners, concerts, and so forth. However, I didn't go into any of it with a sense of deprivation; I didn't tell myself it wouldn't be as fun or that it'd be weird or that I'd have the sense that I "didn't get to" drink anymore. I stayed present and witnessed both how it felt to be sober and also to measure how much fun people were *really* having after a few drinks. Turned out that staying out until four a.m. with drunk people wasn't exactly how I wanted to spend my time.

For me, going home sober at the end of the night and waking up without a hangover felt like the most wonderfully delicious thing I'd ever experienced. When you think for years that you're supposed to drink, then realize you don't have to drink or play the same game everyone else seems to be stuck in, it is the sweetest, most liberating feeling. Now I don't do things I don't want to do, or spend time with people I don't want to spend time with. This may sound like common sense, but to me it was a revelation.

When we use booze as a crutch, we tell ourselves almost anything can be made interesting. Except we are typically using booze to make it through things we wouldn't do otherwise. I absolutely loathe baseball, large parties, and clubs, but with alcohol those things were made bearable—because I was anesthetizing myself to make them bearable. And spending time with people I didn't have anything in common with was the same; I was able to do it because I was drunk, not because the relationship was rewarding or the person became more interesting after a few drinks.

When you take alcohol out of the picture, you get really clear about what things you actually enjoy, what people fill you up. You get more time, because you aren't wasting it doing things you don't want to do, and you get clear on what actually tickles your pickle, or which people you can laugh with without having to use drugs. In other words, you get choices back, and those choices are endless and wonderful.

DATING SOBER

The first date I went on sober was with someone I met on Tinder, and we met at a bar. I didn't clue him in beforehand to the fact that I didn't drink; I just showed up to a bar and ordered a Diet Coke. Two things stand out to me. The first: how terribly awkward first dates really are when you're fully conscious through the entire thing. The second: it wasn't a big deal that I didn't drink. We never saw each other again, but it had nothing to do with the fact that I was sober. I didn't date that first year of sobriety because I wasn't that into it.

The second man I dated was Luca, who I also found on Tinder; we went out sometime around my one-year soberversary. Again, I didn't tell this man that I didn't drink before we went out; I just didn't drink on our first date, and that led to an easy and natural conversation about sobriety. We dated multiple times over the course of about fifteen months, and my sobriety didn't seem to be a problem, until I was turned off by his hangovers, until one night he admitted that it wasn't that I didn't drink, but rather how much my not drinking made him feel shameful about his own relationship with alcohol. Still, we met up in Rome a few weeks after that admission, where he arrived to meet me *five thousand miles away from our home* only to tell me over pasta in Trastevere that he'd stopped in Brussels on his way to meet me, and gotten back together with his ex-girlfriend; he'd told her he was going to Rome to meet a friend, and I told him to go fuck himself.

After that, I started to tell men I was sober before we met, and while I want to say that *of course* the sobriety factor thinned my options and made some of them run for the hills, I also want to say: good, because what women need more of from men is for them to show what pieces of shits they can be *before* we give them any of our time. Sobriety has been a filter, not a defect.

But there's that word: defect, which is the exact thing I thought of myself as I plunged forward into sobriety. If I thought before recovery that I was absolutely unlovable, that was only a fraction of the undesirableness I imagined for myself in my new life as someone who'd certifiably struggled with substance addiction. Who could love someone this broken? Who would? These were thoughts that consumed me at some point that don't even register anymore: If sobriety is anything to me, it's a badge of survival, a symbol of what I used to do, what I no longer do, and telling people I don't drink is one of my favorite pastimes.

I went through so much in such a short time; wanting to date, hiding my sobriety, shoving it in their faces. Struggling with my worth, considering myself a liability, discovering that my perceived weaknesses were actually sources of power. Mostly though, dating sober has taught me to show up as myself, and exactly as myself, and that I am a prize, a Khaleesi, a woman to be earned.

If you're getting sober for the first time, and you're the kind of person who still has to date, first, my sympathies, because dating is truly awful. Next, my excitement, because through the process of trying to find someone, you will end up collecting more pieces of yourself. Finally, my hope, because here is the part of your dating life where you no longer date to find someone to fill the emptiness; you look for someone to share the fullness that you both already are.

SOBER SEX

The first time I ever let a man kiss my clit, had someone's fingers inside me, saw a penis, put my mouth on a penis, let a penis enter my sacred virginal parts—that is to say, the first time I did *anything* sexual—I was drunk, or high, or both. I lost my virginity at seventeen, a month shy of my eighteenth birthday, on Christmas Eve. I was plied with a twenty-two of Newcastle, a joint, and while I wasn't so obliterated as to not remember it, I was fucked up enough to be able to do it. In the years that followed, while not every sexual encounter was lubricated with alcohol, absolutely every first encounter was, and most of the subsequent encounters required it. Which is to say, almost all my sex was the fuzzy kind.

And thank God for that, because if there was one thing I didn't know how to do, it was to be around men, or have sex with them men, or suck their dicks, without putting on a show. I was an actress, one who moaned at the exact right moments and faked orgasms to get it to stop and withstood the jackrabbit thump so favored among men who have absolutely no idea—or care for—how to please a woman. Which was fine by me because I didn't have sex to be pleasured; I had sex to please.

When I stopped drinking alcohol, I also stopped having sex, and not just with men but with myself, too. Meditation, exploring the astral plane, thinking about Jesus, taking pictures, crying in the bathtub, looking at the sky and running through fields, researching addiction, finding myself: these things were what mattered. An orgasm, which I didn't have for the entire first year, didn't.

But then one day in late 2013, the desire came back, along with a new skill: I could orgasm for *minutes* at a time—a howling, screaming, endless rip of pleasure—which was not discovered through any sort of intercourse, but the course of remembering I could masturbate. To say that I started to desire sex again would be an understatement, because I was insatiable, in a way I had never even imagined I could be insatiable. The term "walking sex" might have been a term used to describe myself, and by might I mean did. I was an orgasm waiting to happen.

The first man I slept with in sobriety—someone I'd only met because my friend had shagged him and we'd started following each other on Instagram—was a target the second I saw his big bear face on social media. I knew we would have sex, and I knew it would be good. After a few weeks of incessant texting and DM'ing, he came over to my apartment, tore my clothes off, pulled my tampon out, and put his glasses on: he told me he wanted to have a better look at my pussy. Then I basically starred in my own porno, and not the kind I'd grown up on where it's all about the size of John Holmes's dick, but the kind of pornography where the star of the show was just me and my desires. This was new.

Whereas before sobriety I couldn't stand to be seen with my clothes off, or let anyone give me pleasure without feeling the need to repay it; whereas before—when I was mostly drunk through the whole thing—sex was shameful and words like *pussy* were even more so; whereas in every single sexual encounter I'd been in prior to this moment in my thirty-fourth year of life, I'd focused on looking fuckable, fucking good, and being the prop for his pleasure; in this first sober sexual encounter of mine, there wasn't any of that. It was, for the first time in my life, entirely about me and what I wanted.

I wish I could tell you that this was the case in every encounter thereafter, but it wasn't. I've had terrible partners, and selfish partners, and the kind of partners that still make me want to contort myself into a mirage of female fuckability. I've been jackrabbit-thumped and choked and I've had men who *turned on ESPN instead of cuddling with me.* In other words, sobriety hasn't prevented me from having terrible sex with terribly inconsiderate, ill-equipped, emotionally unavailable, clueless, selfish men, because LORD, they are out there, and they are abundant, and good luck dodging them. But what I have had, most notably, is a severely escalating awareness of what it feels like to be left out of the equation of your own sexuality, and an escalating inability to put up with it. Here is the time in my life when: I walk out on bad sex, I ask for what I need, and his ego does not hold more value than my comfort, or what I'm willing to put up with.

This is a story not of how awkward it is to be fully present for the sound of your queef, or the slapping noise that sex actually makes, or what your naked skin and naked humanity really feel like in the presence of another person, and you are, maybe for the first time, *present.* This is not even a story about sex. It is the story of my sexuality, and sobriety is the story of how I came to own it. This is the story of reclamation.

The story of sex, postaddiction, is as wide and deep and varied as we are. Some of us will come through sobriety and find that it opens the door for more questioning—of our sexual orientation, or our gender, or both. Some of us will find that we have never wanted to be monogamous, or that maybe we don't ever want to have sex again. Others of us, and a good number, too, will have thicker layers to peel back. For survivors of sexual assault that have any sort of sexual trauma, sober sex might reopen every wound you've ever tried to deny, or maybe it's even impossible—this is a thing that happens, too. Maybe you married your college sweetheart and all you've ever known is the drunk version of each other, and maybe you don't know where to go from here, and maybe you never will. Perhaps you no longer want to have sex with your partner, or perhaps you've found—as so many of my friends have—the fact that your partner still drinks is a barrier to your sexual attraction. I could go on.

Whatever it is, sober sex, or even the lack of sex in sobriety, is like all other things: another offering, another way for you to find your way home to you.

16

Activism, Sobriety, and the True Resistance

It is no measure of health to be well adjusted to a sick society.

—JIDDU KRISHNAMURTI

Not long after I quit my corporate job, I started working with a career coach, and she had me do a "future-self meditation." It's exactly as it sounds: you close your eyes and imagine yourself at some point in the future, and this focused meditation reveals the things you need to know now about where it is you're going. I landed twenty years in the future, where a present-day, thirty-four-year-old me descended in a field somewhere near the Northern California coastline. I walked through dry grass and knocked on the door of a home that looked more like it belonged in the Hamptons. The woman who opened the door was a fifty-four-year-old version of myself, in a blue collared shirt. She invited me in for coffee to answer my questions. I wanted to know the important things, like did I get married? Answer: *Yes, he's in the other room.* Did I go to Italy that summer, or did I travel to Central America? Answer: *You go to Italy, and then you keep going back.* Did I do the work in the world that I set out to do? To this question there was no answer, just the vision of an older me staring back, and the woman I saw had lived through wars. Her bones were made, her energy stoic and sattvic. When I left her in the future and came back to 2014, my coach Zoe asked me what I learned. I replied, "I go to Italy, and I spend my life fighting for social justice."

There was something so absolutely desperate in me when I got sober, a calling and a purpose like I'd never known. I couldn't think about anything else than how broken the field of addiction recovery was. That my insurance didn't cover the treatments I needed. That doctors who prescribe addictive drugs aren't trained in addiction medicine, but attend Twelve Step meetings as part of their medical residency. That people who are sick, who need help, are given prison sentences instead of care. That humans who are labeled addicts and alcoholics are treated as hopeless and worthless, liars and cheats, and are stripped of their dignity and force-fed treatments many of them don't want, that don't even work. That the Rehab Industrial Complex—a $35 billion industry—mostly lines the pockets of the people who exploit desperation. So much was absolutely wrong with the entire picture, and I was obsessed with fixing it. To me, at the time of that future-self meditation—and what I knew then about the recovery space—this was so clearly a social justice issue.

But then as it goes, I started to dig deeper, and larger truths revealed themselves to me. It wasn't just the Rehab Industrial Complex, or just addiction, it was how deeply these two things were tied to the Prison Industrial Complex. That America is home to nearly a quarter of the world's incarcerated people, and 80 percent of them are incarcerated for drug-related offenses, was suffocating to learn about, but was just the tip of the iceberg that is our century-old, all-out assault on illicit drug consumption. The American War on Drugs—which began, unofficially, as early as colonization with the policing of Native Americans' ceremonial use of peyote, and continued with the policing of Chinese immigrants in the West for using opiates—was racist at its root. Not only did it make all drug use illicit around the globe during the twentieth century (save alcohol and tobacco, two very white, profitable American chemicals), and establish American control and policing in almost every country, but it also became the most weaponized racist tool post Jim Crow. The War on Drugs is what underwrites anti-blackness, a fact demonstrated by: our treatment of opiate addiction (a white health problem) and crack addiction (a black crime); the jailing of black Americans for drug-related charges at nearly *ten times* the rate of white Americans; the cash bail system (cash bail is frequently set higher for black individuals, who are the targets of racially profiled pretext stops and held on bail they can't afford); and the proportion of black and brown people incarcerated relative to their representative proportion in the general population. This all comes into view when you stand back, but can also be seen when you zoom in, say, on Fox News, where in the same week it broadcast a story criminalizing Botham Jean (a black man murdered in his own home by his white cop neighbor) for having a small amount of pot in his home, and another story glorifying Peter Thiel (a rich white man) for his $12 billion stake in Tilray, a pot company.

Over the past seven years, a picture has developed for me, not unlike one of those FBI evidence boards with the red string connecting all the crime bosses. It's not just the way women have been sold whiskey as our power suit, or how the citizens of Low- to Middle-Income Countries are targeted by Big Alcohol and ritually sacrificed for profit. It's so much more. It's the relationships between the alcohol industry and the government. It's the ties between the War on Drugs, racism, addiction, and the for-profit prison system. It's unchecked capitalism and the resultant surging rates of addiction, and who profits from it, and who loses their freedom and their lives because of it. It's Big Pharma and its ties to the Mental Health Industrial Complex, or Big Pharma and its role in the exploding epidemic of opiate deaths, or Big Pharma and the ever-increasing rates of depression diagnoses that are only outpaced by the ever-increasing rates of the pharmaceuticals we pop to alleviate that depression. It's a government that outspends on the persecution and jailing of drug users, pushers, and traffickers, while it scrambles to contribute resources to the healing from addiction. It's the links between NCAAD, AA, and other governmental institutions that front as the arm of public safety—as measures meant to heal and curb addiction—while the government profits directly *from* the proliferation of addiction. It's the push to legalize pot in the name of white profit, while untold numbers of black and brown folks languish in our jail system for the most minor pot offenses, or the black and brown humans who are forever withheld the right to vote, gain meaningful employment, or even secure housing because of a criminal record for a crime that was only a crime because powerful white men hadn't yet figured out a way to profit from it.

The web is spun thick and wide and deep, and we are all caught in it. We live in a very, very sick society, one that rewards those who make the rules, write the definitions, and then change them at a moment's notice. Example: "John A. Boehner, the former speaker of the House, once stood second in line for the presidency and staunchly against legalized marijuana. Now you can find the longtime Republican standing before a wall-size photo of the Capitol, making an online infomercial pitch for the cannabis industry," *The New York Times,* June 3, 2019.

At the time of that future-self meditation, it felt like a stretch to say out loud that addiction was a social justice issue—even though I knew in my gut it was one. I hadn't made the connections I have now between pervasive social issues and addiction. I hadn't read about Harry Anslinger—the first head of the Federal Bureau of Narcotics (what is now the DEA)—and how his racist agenda fueled a relentless persecution of black jazz musicians, most notably Billie Holiday. My belief that addiction was an issue of social injustice stemmed from my most basic understanding of things like the lack of treatment options for those suffering from addiction, or the way we are dehumanized. Listening to a mother talk about her "junkie daughter," or my own relative talk about her friend's "addict grandson"—in that way we are conditioned to talk about the sickest, most vulnerable people in our orbit as problems to be fixed or liabilities to be handled or criminals to be locked up—ripped something in me. I started out with a complete and heartbreaking rage over how we treat (and don't treat) people suffering with addiction, and only because I was one of them. Which is to say, maybe it felt like a stretch to call it a social justice issue because it also felt so *personal.*

So I started out railing against the label *alcoholic,* the rights of individuals to choose treatment other than AA, the oppressive nature of imposed anonymity, and the marketing tactics employed to ensnare women. It felt like a radical act: to be sober and be seen, to suggest there was another way to heal from addiction, to call out drinking culture or call out Goop for promoting it. But then I kept pulling the thread, and I was naturally led to the other realities I'd been privileged to ignore, or be ignorant of, and addiction and recovery emerged as the mother of all social justice issues—tied to sexism, racism, classism, ableism, capitalism, and homophobia. It intersects every system, and every systematic oppression.

As I became more educated, I couldn't help but stitch these issues together on social media, something white women applauded me for as I spoke in the wake of the 2016 election about misogyny and rape and its ties to alcohol-centric culture. I got little to no pushback as I posted Rebecca Solnit quotes, or my own #MeToo story, or spoke about alcohol as a rape drug, but when I started to learn more about the racism inherent in the War on Drugs, or about restorative justice, or Black Lives Matter, or racism at all, and talk about those issues on social media, I found that some of the same women who applauded me for making connections between the alcohol industry and rape culture could not abide me talking about racism or white privilege. Some white women voiced their displeasure at my taking what seemed to be a hard right turn from addiction: "I wish you'd stick to sobriety." I received letters of dismay for this perceived departure from my topic, my cause, my calling; I'd lost my center, or as one person put it, "gone marginal." Another told me I'd dirtied the sobriety movement with talk of "identity politics," and by that, they meant I'd confused or dirtied the movement by including identities other than white ones, or straight ones, or cis ones. Enough people couldn't yet understand that speaking about racism (or sexism, or homophobia) *is* talking about sobriety.

If you are a white, hetero, cis woman, and you are in recovery, you are expected to participate in a recovery modality that is built to break down male privilege, and discounts the thing that has made you sick, which is existing in a culture that is sexist to its core. In order to heal, we must claim our voice and our power, take up space, build an ego, stop apologizing, get our needs met, and go against almost everything we've been conditioned to be, which is small and pleasing and subservient. If you are a white, hetero, cis woman, perhaps you understand that if you try to heal in a space that denies your lived experience—a space in which it is unsafe to speak of the things that have held you down and out of power, or the rape you endured, or the way your husband beats you—you will not heal. And if you are a woman of color or any other oppressed identity, and you try to heal in a space that denies your lived experience—of the micro-aggressions you metabolize daily, of the murder of your people by racist cops who operate above the law, of the disenfranchisement you face for the color of your skin or your sexual orientation, of the constant threat of harassment and bullying and murder because you're trans, or nonbinary, or queer—you will not heal.

Recovery is a social justice issue not just because of all the aforementioned links to capitalist society or the Prison Industrial Complex, but because to exist for so many of us *is* political when your very identity is politicized. We are sick not because we live within a bubble where only alcohol is the problem, where only opiates are the problem; we are sick because of our experiences living in a *system* that is the problem, and if recovery dismisses any single one of our experiences, it is not recovery. It is perpetuation of the same exact sickness.

If recovery is anything, it's the first step on the path to radical self-awareness. We begin to tell the truth to ourselves for the first time in our lives, connect to our essential way of being, develop a deep self-compassion, and an appreciation of our fullest individual expression. We learn to own a power we could not otherwise claim, and we become, to a large degree, un-touchable, not only transcendent of old patterns of self-abuse but equipped to transcend external systems of abuse as well. When we free ourselves from the bonds of addiction, and claim a power we could not otherwise, and turn this power into action, we become, in name, an activist. We become part of the momentum and legacy already in motion by other radically awakened, liberated folks, which in turn forms into collective action. In other words, radical self-awareness is the root of our collective liberation. This does not mean that we have to be sober, or in recovery, or perfect, to be activists; this means we have to do the work of dismantling self-abuse and build from there; the revolution is not outside us, it's within us.

I write these final words on June 28, the anniversary of the Stonewall Riots in New York, where a group of queer and trans people fought back against the harassment of the LGBTQIA community by the NYPD. In this case, the revolution started in a bar. In my own case, the revolution started in a bar, too—I had to begin somewhere, and for me it was confronting my addiction. Our revolutions don't rise out of peak experiences; they emerge when we're smacked down, robbed of our spirit, angry, oppressed. Revolution is a reaction to violence, and it is generative, in that revolution calls forth a latent power that resides in each of us that's been waiting its whole life to burn the fucking system to the ground.

Recovery is the resistance. Here is where you start.

Acknowledgments

Sobriety has nothing on what it takes to write a book. I mean that with all due respect, and simply from my own perspective of levels of hard; I think perhaps it was the sobriety that enabled this book to become.

I started outlining the concept for this book in 2016, and I started writing the proposal in October 2017. Between that time and now, so much has happened it hardly seems like I was even there at all. I turned forty; I lost part of my hearing; I fund-raised multiple rounds of capital for Tempest; I lost some of my most important relationships, and I gained some of them back. I made some of the richest friendships of my life; my company grew from two employees to thirty; I moved to New York; I became a first-time homeowner; I got a cat. The making of this book has happened because of and despite of these things—and only because of the countless ways I was supported by the best humans that grace this fine earth. This is my attempt to thank some of them, in no particular order.

To Rebecca Gradinger, my agent, who believed in me in a way I dreamed someone could believe in me and my work. You are a fucking angel, the mightiest little beast, and one of my dearest friends. Thank you for making this happen. To my editor Tricia Boczkowski, my sack-dress twin, my bambina, thank you for putting up with my prima-donna shit, for editing with your keen eye, your brilliant wit, and your kind heart, and walking this mess of a neophyte through the maze that is publishing. I LOVE YOU, and to boot: *I love that I can break all the rules in this section.* To Whit Frick, thank you for seeing something in me, for believing in me and the potential of this book, for fighting for my work and my voice, for creating the home that is Dial Press and inviting me into it. To the whole team at Random House, Chris Brand, Rachel Willey, Aubrey Martinson, Avideh Bashirrad, Susan Kamil, Robert Siek, Benjamin Dreyer, Brianne Sperber, Emily Isayeff, Maria Braeckel, Susan Corcoran, Barbara Fillon, and Leigh Marchant. To Steph Dolgoff, my princess, thank you for your edits and for knowing my voice and keeping it close to your heart as you worked; thank you for your intelligence and your grace and your willingness to go on this ride with me.

To Sarah Lidgus, this book would not be possible without you and your tireless, maniacal commitment to me, my work (our work), and these pages. For loving me through the disaster that some parts of this process were and bringing me coffee and Zazie and reminding me that I could do it. For that one time when I was wearing all the crystals. For your edits, and your edits, and your edits, and your edits on your edits, and your patience, and your voice. For existing. Don't forget: This is your book, too, honey. Just like your baby is my baby. (At least 10 percent both ways.) To DL Grant, for your edits and voice and call-ins on the hardest things, for existing and staying and figuring things out with me. You are a miracle and I love you to the end. To Tracy Murphy, my not-jerk-jerk, my apple, my love: thank you for reminding me EVERY FUCKING DAY that I am worthy, that I am good, that I am doing it, especially when I forget. Thank you for reminding me of every-thing I need to be reminded of. Thank you for existing, and finding me, and loving me. Thank you for reading everything I send to you and always telling me it's great, even when it's not. To Mary Vance for being with me since the beginning, for your contributions and edits to this book; you are my queen, and I could never have done this without you. To Kim Kokoska, I will never forget our first meeting or what it meant that you were willing to take a risk on this girl and this idea: You are family. To Whitney Combs, for your contribution to this book, to this work, to our Tempest family; for signing on before there was anything to sign on for. I love you so much it hurts.

To the white cis male trifecta who made me, me: To Jeff DeFla-vio, there are too many things to thank you for; it's an impossible task, my darling. The most vivid memory I have: you on the night I got my test results back, at my door with flowers, standing by me in my darkest as you do so well. Thank you for making what is, possible. I love you without limit. To Steve Schlafman, honey, you have no idea how much of an impact you have made on everything that exists; so much of this is only because you believed in me, and listened to me, and championed for me before anyone else could or would. You are made of the stuff that makes this world magical; you are my brother, my friend, and everything I could have dreamed to find on this path. To Tim Schwartz, I still remember our first call, and every single thing you have done for me from that day in 2014 through now. Thank you for not letting me quit even though I wanted to time and again, for giving of yourself— and always—so effortlessly and freely to make so many things come true; thank you for being in my corner, for *believing* in me the way only you can, and growing up with me.

To Megan Carrier, honey, there will never be enough words to express what you are to me and what amount of gratitude I have for you existing, for your believing, for your sacrificing, and for making what is come into existence. I will never stop reminding you that this is yours, because it is. Thank you for being my family, my sister, my cheerleader, my emotional support peacock, for the thousands of ways you have birthed things into existence, for your unwavering love and support. For making Tempest, Tempest. You are a miracle; this would not have happened without you.

To Laura McKowen, what the fuck do I even say to you? I can't do it. I can only tell you that if I had never found you, if you had never found me, if we hadn't done the things we did together, and jumped off cliffs together, and screamed and made noise and broken all the rules; if we hadn't believed in each other, I cannot imagine what my life would be. You made me into the woman I am, and watching you become the woman you are has been one of the treasures of my life.

To Mom, for giving me my life, for showing me what life and persistence and being a true warrior is; for your example, and your sacrifice, and your wild belief in me even when there was no reason to believe; for your forgiveness, for your unconditional love, for your heart and your resilience. Watching you these last few years grow into who you've become, watching you always evolving and changing and surprising me, is such a gift. You are such a gift, and I don't know how the hell I got so lucky to be your daughter. I am so proud of you, so in love with you, so honored to be your descendant, to find myself becoming more of you each day. To Heather Whitaker, oh, bitch, how many times did I wish for a different sister? I mean, if we're being honest, and we are, it was plenty. Only, somehow you're my air, a thing I would cease to be without. Watching you become a mom and become your own person as I've become mine has revealed the ultimate truths to me about who you are and how you have made me into me; I love you so much it chokes me. To Sam Leon, I love you forever and thank God you exist; thank you for being an early fan, a secret reader of Hip Sobriety, a champion in my corner, my brother in every sense of that word. To Samaria, Elia, and Kooka Leon, my babies, you wonderful perfect people, one day you'll understand how much you saved Auntie's life. You are my pride and joy, my beautiful reward for existing; I cannot wait to see how you conquer this world, how you leave your mark.

To Azita Nahai, who showed up at all the right times because soul contracts, thank you. Thank you for peeling me off the floor a thousand times, for knowing what I know before I know it, for holding the ground while I grow, for saying the words that always need to be said, for being my sister in every sense of the word. I am so in love with you.

To Cath Gray, for being my travel wife, for going first in this book writing thing and showing me how it's done, for your grace and kindness and unwavering support, for your brilliance and your spirit and your friendship and your edits; growing old with you is one of the things I look forward to the most in this world.

For the employees of Tempest: to all of you who sacrifice so much to make this thing real, who have taken such a personal mission and made it their own, who have built not just a company, but a world vision of my dreams; you are my fucking family. Thank you for everything you've given to this, and to me, and to our students. Thank you for showing up every day with your broken hearts and your love of this world and its inhabitants; you are the best people I know in the world and I am so fucking proud of what we've done, and what we're doing.

To Sutian Dong and Will Quist: for holding my hand week after week, and making Tempest what it is. I am forever grateful. To Zal Bilimoria, David Lee, Dave Morin, and Parke and Coran Capshaw, Anarghya Vardhana, Dan Levitan, Pete McCormick, the folks of Maveron, for taking the ultimate gamble.

To Geoff Hyde, Tariq Mizra, and Danielle Coulter for taking care of me and letting me live on your couches in those early days.

To Sally Ward and Georg Wien for making your home my home

through the years; for giving me a place to land always, and a meal; for being my champions and my family.

To Jane Sarasohn-Kahn, for being the first one to jump in and back me, for encouraging me to do what I had to do, for making this thing a thing. I love you. Grazie.

To Stephanie Snyder. You are my teacher, the living embodiment of everything I have buried in me that I'm still digging out, of everything good in this world; thank you for existing, for your work, for living in example. Thank you for saving my life.

To Scott Stabile, for coming back in this lifetime after our torrid love affair in some previous life to hold my hand and remind me, and the world, of its beauty.

To Ann Dowsett Johnston, for going first, for your friendship and guidance, for your courage, for your support and unyielding belief in me and my work. You are a miracle, your courage gave me mine.

To Court and Ber, for understanding I needed to run fast and furiously ahead; for understanding me, period; for being the true responsibility bears.

To Albie, for coming in during the final stretch, for seeing in that way I never imagined any man could.

To TXL. Thank you for wildness, for staying, for your perplexing ability to show up when I've given you every reason not to, for being an impossible asshole and an impossible genius with a larger than life heart. For making me, or at least being the thing I made myself against. I love you fiercely.

And finally, to every student, every community member, every reader, and every person who has been a supporter of my work, of our work: You are the point. You are always the point.

Notes

vii   "There is nothing stronger": Hannah Gadsby in *Hannah Gadsby: Nanette*, directed by John Olb and Madeleine Parry (Guesswork Televsion, 2018), https://www.netflix.com/watch/80233611?trackId= 13752289&tctx=0%2C0%2Cc9577f44-0b83-4656-809f-86bea76da77c -7511882%2C%2C.

INTRODUCTION

8   Between 2002 and 2012: F. Grant, S. P. Chou, and T. D. Saha, "Prevalence of 12-Month Alcohol Use, High-Risk Drinking, and *DSM-IV* Alcohol Use Disorder in the United States, 2001–2002 to 2012–2013: Results from the National Epidemiologic Survey on Alcohol and Related Conditions," *JAMA Psychiatry* 74, no. 9 (2017): 911–23.

8   One in ten: M. Stahre et al., "Contribution of Excessive Alcohol Consumption to Deaths and Years of Potential Life Lost in the United States," *Preventing Chronic Disease* 11 (2014): 130293.

8   from 2007 to 2017: Jayne O'Donnell, "Alcohol Is Killing More People, and Younger. The Biggest Increases Are Among Women," *USA Today*, November 16, 2018.

CHAPTER 1: THE LIE

11   "Addiction begins with": Jean Kilbourne, *Can't Buy My Love: How Advertising Changes the Way We Think and Feel* (New York: Simon & Schuster, 1999), 234.

19   "imperialist white-supremacist": bell hooks, *The Will to Change: Men, Masculinity, and Love* (New York: Washington Square Press, 2004), 17.

CHAPTER 2: TOXIC EYELINER AND GOOP COCKTAILS

23   "What we must": Jean E. Swallow, *Out from Under: Sober Dykes and Our Friends* (San Francisco: Spinsters, Ink, 1983), x.

24   National Council on Alcoholism and Drug Dependence's twenty-six-point questionnaire: "Alcohol Abuse Self-Test," National Council on Alcoholism and Drug Dependence, https://ncadd.org/learn-about -alcohol/alcohol-abuse-self-test.

25   "Wonderful and joyous!": Cheryl Strayed in "The Past Is Present," an episode of the *Dear Sugars* podcast, March 11, 2016, https://www .wbur.org/dearsugar/2016/03/11/dear-sugar-episode-forty-six.

26   "Ethanol, also commonly": "Ethanol," Wikipedia, https://en.wikipedia .org/w/index.php?title=Ethanol&oldid=905555648.

27   The global wellness economy: "Wellness Now a $4.2 Trillion Global Industry—with 12.8% Growth from 2015–2017," Global Wellness Institute, October 2018, https://globalwellnessinstitute.org/press -room/press-releases/wellness-now-a-4-2-trillion-global-industry/.

28   skyrocketing rates: Rene Wisely, "Doctors Are Seeing More Alcoholic Liver Disease in Young Adults," University of Michigan: Michigan
.   Medicine Blog, January 22, 2019, https://healthblog.uofmhealth.org /digestive-health/doctors-are-seeing-more-alcoholic-liver-disease -young-adults.

29   Goop Health Summit: Riley Griffin, "Goop Is Making a Killing Off Women Who Want More Than a Doctor's Advice," Bloomberg, March 18, 2019, https://www.bloomberg.com/news/articles/2019-03-18 /gwyneth-paltrow-s-goop-is-cashing-in-on-booming-wellness -market.

29   in a French bistro: "How Morley Safer Convinced Americans to Drink More Wine," CBS News, August 28, 2016, https://www .cbsnews.com/news/how-morley-safer-convinced-americans-to -drink-more-wine.

30   likely to underestimate: T. Stockwell, J. Zhao, and S. Macdonald, "Who Under-Reports Their Alcohol Consumption in Telephone Surveys and by How Much? An Application of the 'Yesterday Method' in a National Canadian Substance Use Survey," *Addiction* 109 (October 2014): 1657–66, doi.org/10.1111/add.12609.

30   "When you tally up": Keith Humphreys, "People Severely Underestimate—or Lie About—How Much They Drink," Cut, June 9, 2014, https://www.thecut.com/2014/06/people-underestimate-how -much-they-drink.html.

30   drink a lot more than we think: "America's Alcoholism Awareness:

"What We Don't Know About Alcoholism," Alcohol.org, https://www
.alcohol.org/guides/americas-alcoholism-awareness.

30 *even one glass of wine*: R. Burton and N. Sheron, "No Level of Alcohol
Consumption Improves Health," *Lancet* 392, no. 10152 (September
23, 2018): 987–88, https://www.thelancet.com/journals/lancet/article
/PIIS0140-6736(18)31310-2/fulltext.

30 "The states of withdrawal": Judith Grisel, *Never Enough: The
Neuroscience and Experience of Addiction* (New York: Doubleday,
2019), 41–47, esp. 43.

31 Disrupts sleep: Denise Mann, "Alcohol and a Good Night's Sleep
Don't Mix," WebMD, January 22, 2013, https://www.webmd.com
/sleep-disorders/news/20130118/alcohol-sleep#1.

31 seven REM: William Porter, *Alcohol Explained* (self-pub., 2015),
49–57.

32 three to four days: Ibid., 52–53.

32 release of cortisol: Annie Grace, *The Alcohol Experiment* (New York:
Avery, 2018), 35; Grisel, *Never Enough*, 43–46.

32 It's one of the worst drugs: Meredith Watkins, "The Connection
Between Anxiety and Alcohol," American Addiction Centers, June 18,
2019, https://americanaddictioncenters.org/alcoholism-treatment
/anxiety; Mark Hay, "All the Reasons You Shouldn't Drink When
You're Depressed," Vice, June 20, 2018, https://www.vice.com/en_us
/article/mbknav/all-the-reasons-you-shouldnt-drink-when-youre
-depressed.

32 any other toxins waiting to leave our system: Sara Gottfried, *The Brain
Body Diet* (New York: HarperOne, 2019), 56–58.

32 our body fat, or adipose tissue: Alex Fergus, "How Toxins in Your Diet
Are Making You Fat," AlexFergus.com, n.d., https://www.alexfergus
.com/blog/how-a-toxins-are-making-you-gain-fat-toxic-diet.

32 also affects the central nervous system: Gottfried, *Brain Body Diet*,
297.

33 it anesthetizes the body: Porter, *Alcohol Explained*, 99.

33 only beverage on the market: Joseph Stromberg, "This Is Why Alcohol
Doesn't Come with Nutrition Facts," Vox, March 14, 2015, https://
www.vox.com/2014/11/12/7195573/alcohol-nutrition.

33 Causes facial redness: Porter, *Alcohol Explained*, 100; Emily Laurence,
"What's the Deal with That Post-Drinking Red Face Flush?" Well +
Good, April 30, 2019, https://www.wellandgood.com/good-food
/red-face-from-alcohol.

33 "neurological sledgehammer": Grisel, *Never Enough*, 80–102.

34 adrenal glands: Mark Mathews, "The Centerpiece of Alcoholism,"
Health Recovery Center, January 12, 2016, http://info.healthrecovery
.com/hrc-blog/the-centerpiece-of-alcoholism.

34   higher rates of cancer: Gottfried, *Brain Body Diet,* 268.
34   raises estrogen levels: Amy Shah, "How Much Booze Do You Have to Drink to Mess with Your Hormones?" Mind Body Green, n.d., https://www.mindbodygreen.com/articles/is-drinking-alcohol-bad -for-hormone-balance.
34   breast cancer alone: "Alcohol and Cancer Risk," NIH National Cancer Institute, n.d., https://www.cancer.gov/about-cancer/causes -prevention/risk/alcohol/alcohol-fact-sheet; *IARC Monographs on the Identification of Carcinogenic Hazards to Humans,* World Health Organization International Agency for Research on Cancer Monograph 96 (2018): 418–86, https://monographs.iarc.fr/wp -content/uploads/2018/06/mono96-6B-06.pdf.
35   risk of breast cancer: "Drinking Alcohol," Breastcancer.org, https://www.breastcancer.org/risk/factors/alcohol.
35   mouth and throat, esophagus: Peter Russell, "Drinking Alcohol Linked to 7 Types of Cancer," WebMD, July 22, 2016, https://www .webmd.com/cancer/news/20160722/alcohol-seven-types-cancer#1.
35   Causes premature aging: Jodi Sawyer, "How Fast Can Alcohol Age You?" DoctorOz.com, n.d., https://www.doctoroz.com/blog/jodi -sawyer-rn/how-fast-can-alcohol-age-you.
35   Destroys the microbiome: "Single Episode of Binge Drinking Linked to Gut Leakage and Immune System Effects," National Institutes of Health, May 14, 2014, https://www.nih.gov/news-events/news -releases/single-episode-binge-drinking-linked-gut-leakage-immune -system-effects; D. Coyle, "8 Surprising Things That Harm Your Gut Bacteria," Healthline, June 19, 2017, https://www.healthline.com /nutrition/8-things-that-harm-gut-bacteria.
37   Trump Fatigue Syndrome: Lee Drutman, "How to Combat Trump Fatigue Syndrome," Vox, May 17, 2017, https://www.vox.com /polyarchy/2017/3/7/14844120/how-to-fight-trump-fatigue-syndrome.
37   "extremely anxious": "Managing Stress Related to Political Change," American Psychological Association, February 2017, https://www.apa .org/helpcenter/stress-political-change.
37   "very or somewhat significant": J. F. Harris, "Trump May Not Be Crazy, but the Rest of Us Are Getting There Fast," Politico, October 12, 2018, https://www.politico.eu/article/us-president-donald-trump -may-not-be-crazy-but-the-rest-of-us-are-getting-there-fast/.
38   number-one date rape drug: Andrea Fox, "What Is the Most Common Date Rape Drug?" EfficientGov, April 4, 2018, https://efficientgov .com/blog/2018/04/04/what-is-the-most-common-date-rape-drug.
39   sexual assaults involve alcohol: Antonia Abbey et al., "Alcohol and Sexual Assault," *Alcohol Research and Health* 25, no. 1 (2001): 43–51.
39   college campus rape: "Sexual Assaults on College Campuses Involving

Alcohol," Alcohol.org, October 22, 2018, https://www.alcohol.org
/effects/sexual-assault-college-campus.

39 intimate partner violence: Buddy T., "Drinking Can Bring Out
Violence in All Types of Relationships," verywellmind, April 7, 2019,
https://www.verywellmind.com/drinking-alcohol-increases-physical
-violence-62655.

39 violent crimes overall: Harold Pollack, "Alcohol Is Still the Deadliest
Drug in the United States, and It's Not Even Close," *Washington Post*,
August 19, 2014.

39 Women who drink before: Ann Dowsett Johnston, *Drink: The
Intimate Relationship Between Women and Alcohol* (New York:
HarperCollins, 2013), 78.

39 experience sexual assault: Ibid., 80.

39 over three million deaths worldwide: "Management of Substance
Abuse," World Health Organization, n.d., https://www.who.int
/substance_abuse/facts/alcohol/en.

39 *The Handmaid's Tale*: Madison Roberts, "*Handmaid's Tale* Wines
Pulled After One Day Amidst Fierce Backlash Over 'Rape-Themed'
Marketing," *People*, July 12, 2018.

CHAPTER 3: IS ALCOHOL HAVING A "CIGARETTE MOMENT"?

41 "It's easier to": Dan Evon, "Did Mark Twain Say 'It's Easier to Fool
People Than to Convince Them That They Have Been Fooled'?"
Snopes, December 29, 2016, https://www.snopes.com/fact-check
/did-mark-twain-say-its-easier-to-fool-people-than-to-convince
-them-that-they-have-been-fooled/.

43 "A great deal": Bernays quoted in A. M. Brandt, *The Cigarette Century:
The Rise, Fall, and Deadly Persistence of the Product That Defined
America* (New York: Basic Books, 2007), 86.

44 By 1954, 45 percent: Ibid., 507.

45 colonizers carried it over: Lisa Grimm, "Beer Mythbusting: The Truth
About Pilgrims, Adjuncts, and Prohibition," Serious Eats, November
12, 2012; updated August 9, 2018, https://drinks.seriouseats
.com/2012/11/beer-myths-corn-pilgrims-first-beer-thanksgiving
-lager-prohibition-history.html.

45 We think drinking alcohol: Mark Forsyth, *A Short History of
Drunkenness* (New York: Three Rivers Press, 2017), 38.

46 alcohol-related liver failure: Paul Chisholm, "A Spike in Liver Disease
Deaths Among Young Adults Fueled by Alcohol," Shots: Health News
from NPR, July 18, 2018, https://www.npr.org/sections/health
-shots/2018/07/18/630275042/a-spike-in-liver-disease-deaths-among
-young-adults-fueled-by-alcohol.

46 height of cigarette consumption: Brandt, *The Cigarette Century*, 5.

47   Today nearly 70 percent: "Alcohol Facts and Statistics," National
      Institute on Alcohol Abuse and Alcoholism, https://www.niaaa.nih
      .gov/alcohol-health/overview-alcohol-consumption/alcohol-facts
      -and-statistics.

47   a $1.5 trillion industry: "Alcoholic Beverages Market Expected to
      Reach $1,594 Billion, Globally, by 2022—Allied Market Research," PR
      Newswire, April 5, 2017, https://www.prnewswire.com/news-releases
      /alcoholic-beverages-market-expected-to-reach-1594-billion-globally
      -by-2022---allied-market-research-618354513.html.

47   sixteen companies: "Exposing Big Alcohol," IOGT International,
      https://iogt.org/the-issues/advocacy/exposing-big-alcohol/.

47   three million people a year: "Management of Substance Abuse," World
      Health Organization, n.d., https://www.who.int/substance_abuse
      /facts/alcohol/en.

48   "We've opened seven": Olly Wehring, " 'Africa Is Asia in 15 to 20 Years
      from Today'—just-drinks speaks to Pernod Ricard CEO Alex Ricard,"
      just-drinks, February 19, 2019, https://www.just-drinks.com
      /interview/africa-is-asia-in-15-to-20-years-from-today-just-drinks
      -speaks-to-pernod-ricard-ceo-alex-ricard_id127811.aspx.

48   "The Chinese domestic": "Say What? Actual 'Big Tobacco' Quotes,"
      Australian Council on Smoking and Health, n.d., https://www.acosh
      .org/resources/big-tobacco/say-what-actual-big-tobacco-quotes.

48   The history of the cigarette: The following discussion is drawn from
      Brandt, Cigarette Century.

50   7.1 million people die: "Tobacco: Key Facts," World Health
      Organization, May 29, 2019, https://www.who.int/news-room
      /fact-sheets/detail/tobacco; "The Toll of Tobacco Around the World,"
      Campaign for Tobacco-Free Kids, https://www.tobaccofreekids.org
      /problem/toll-global; Brandt, Cigarette Century, 14.

50   Consolidation of the alcohol market: Iain Gately, Drink: A Cultural
      History of Alcohol (New York: Gotham Books, 2008), 418–19.

51   While in 1938: Ibid., 419; "Traditional Media Advertising Spending
      on Alcoholic Beverages in the United States in 2016, by Category (in
      million U.S. dollars)," Statista, https://www.statista.com
      /statistics/748562/alcoholic-beverage-ad-spend-category-us.

51   losing 3.3 million: "Management of Substance Abuse," World Health
      Organization, n.d., https://www.who.int/substance_abuse/facts
      /alcohol/en.

51   recognized Joe Camel: J. R. DiFranza et al., "RJR Nabisco's Cartoon
      Camel Promotes Camel Cigarettes to Children," JAMA 266, no. 22
      (Dec. 11, 1991): 3149–53.

51   Anheuser-Busch introduced: Gately, Drink, 459.

52 fewer than 100,000: "Alcohol Facts and Statistics," National Institute on Alcohol Abuse and Alcoholism, n.d., https://www.niaaa.nih.gov /alcohol-health/overview-alcohol-consumption/alcohol-facts-and -statistics.

52 surging death tolls: "Global Status Report on Alcohol and Health 2018," World Health Organization, 45, 304, https://iogt.org/wp -content/uploads/2018/09/WHO-GSR-Alcohol-2018.pdf.

52 The big sixteen: "Exposing Big Alcohol," IOGT International, https://iogt.org/the-issues/advocacy/exposing-big-alcohol/.

52 such as Uganda: "Uganda Bans Alcohol Sold in Sachets," BBC, June 3, 2019, https://www.bbc.com/news/world-africa-48476168.

53 Big Alcohol consolidated: "The Structure of the Beverage Alcohol Industry," International Center for Alcohol Policies, Report no. 17, March 2006, https://www.hri.global/files/2011/07/25/13.4_ICAP _-_Structure_of_the_Beverage_Alcohol_Industry_.pdf.

53 "We are governed": Edward Bernays, *Propaganda*, 3rd rev. ed. (New York: Ig Publishing, 2005), 37.

53 "engineered consent": Edward Bernays, "The Engineering of Consent," March 1, 1947, reprinted at https://doi.org/10.1177 /000271624725000116.

54 "How can we get women": Edward Bernays, *Biography of an Idea: The Founding Principles of Public Relations* (New York: Open Road Integrated Media, 1965), Kindle loc. 7692 of 19116.

54 "Women! Light another Torch": Ibid., Kindle loc. 7699.

55 women would close the gap: M. Roser and H. Ritchie, "Smoking: Correlates, Determinants & Consequences," Our World in Data, https://ourworldindata.org/smoking#correlates-determinants -consequences.

57 fantastically successful: Ibid.

57 men are drinking less: A. White et al., "Converging Patterns of Alcohol Use and Related Outcomes Among Females and Males in the United States, 2002 to 2012," *Alcoholism Clinical and Experimental Research* 39, no. 9 (September 2015): 1712–26, https://onlinelibrary .wiley.com/doi/abs/10.1111/acer.12815.

60 "There are some": Quoted in Brandt, *Cigarette Century*, 115.

60 cigarette use continued to rise: Ibid., 337.

60 it wasn't until: Ibid., 237.

60 Tobacco Industry Research Committee: "Tobacco Industry Research Committee," Tobacco Tactics, n.d., https://www.tobaccotactics.org /index.php/Tobacco_Industry_Research_Committee.

60 "There is not enough": Brandt, *Cigarette Century*, 197.

61 "produce and sustain scientific": Ibid., 160.

62 Eugenics is the "science" of breeding: James Whitman, *Hitler's American Model: The United States and the Making of Nazi Race Law* (Princeton, N.J.: Princeton University Press, 2017), 7–8.

62 only those with bad genes: Brandt, *Cigarette Century,* 178.

62 "biologically defective persons": Gately, *Drink,* 401.

63 RCPA couldn't find funding: Joe Miller, *US of AA: How the Twelve Steps Hijacked the Science of Alcoholism* (Chicago: Chicago Review Press, 2019), 19–21.

63 the efforts of Alcoholics Anonymous: Ibid., 27–101.

65 sexual assault and violent crimes: Antonia Abbey et al., "Alcohol and Sexual Assault," *Alcohol Research and Health* 25, no. 1 (2001): 43–51; Buddy T., "Drinking Can Bring Out Violence in All Types of Relationships," verywellmind, April 7, 2019, https://www .verywellmind.com/drinking-alcohol-increases-physical -violence-62655.

65 got to the crux: Leandra Medine, "Tell It to Me Straight: Is Wine Ruining Me or Saving Me?" Man Repeller, June 20, 2018, https://www .manrepeller.com/2018/06/is-wine-good-for-you.html.

65 literally no amount: Burton and Sheron, "No Level of Alcohol Consumption Improves Health."

CHAPTER 4: THERE IS NO SUCH THING AS AN ALCOHOLIC

67 "Our deep collective": Grisel, *Never Enough,* 82.

78 about 70 percent of adults: "Alcohol Facts and Statistics," National Institute on Alcohol Abuse and Alcoholism, https://www.niaaa.nih .gov/alcohol-health/overview-alcohol-consumption/alcohol-facts -and-statistics.

79 64 percent of people: K. Krisberg, "What's in a Word? How Language Affects Public Health: Research Shows Word Choices Can Influence Well-being, Treatment," Nation's Health, April 2018, http:// thenationshealth.aphapublications.org/content/48/2/1.1.

80 2 percent of our GDP: J. Kendall, "Study: U.S. Beer Industry Creates More Than 2 Million Jobs," Brewbound, May 24, 2017, https://www .brewbound.com/news/study-u-s-beer-industry-creates-2-million -jobs.

80 the opioid epidemic, which claims: L. Scholl et al., "Drug and Opioid-Involved Overdose Deaths—United States, 2013–2017," *Morbidity and Mortality Weekly Report* 67 (2019): 1419–27, http://dx .doi.org/10.15585/mmwr.mm675152e1external icon.

81 Ninety percent of: M. Esser et al., "Prevalence of Alcohol Dependence Among US Adult Drinkers, 2009–2011," *Preventing Chronic Disease* 11 (2014): 140329, http://dx.doi.org/10.5888/pcd11.140329.

85 "I believe the person": Koch quoted in Thomas Szasz, *Ceremonial*

Chemistry: The Ritual Persecution of Drugs, Addicts, and Pushers (New York: Anchor Press, 1974), 231.

85   Today around 20 percent: W. Sawyer and P. Wagner, "Mass Incarceration: The Whole Pie," Prison Policy Initiative, March 19, 2019, https://www.prisonpolicy.org/reports/pie2019.html?c=pie&gclid =EAIaIQobChMIvJWj7Ii-4gIVGIrICh3HjgrfEAAYASAAEgLmEfD _BwE.

85   around 3.3 million people: "Management of Substance Abuse," World Health Organization, https://www.who.int/substance_abuse/facts /alcohol/en.

85   450,000 people died: *World Drug Report 2018: Executive Summary Conclusions and Policy Implications,* United Nations Office on Drugs and Crime (Sales No. E.18.XI.9), 1, https://www.unodc.org/wdr2018 /prelaunch/WDR18_Booklet_1_EXSUM.pdf.

CHAPTER 5: THE RIGHT QUESTION

87   "I'd say the": Catherine Gray, "Is It Time to Ditch the Label Alcoholic?" Temper, n.d., https://www.thetemper.com/is-it-time-to -ditch-the-term-alcoholic/.

89   twenty licit and illicit drugs: D. J. Nutt, L. A. King, and L. D. Phillips, "Drug Harms in the UK: A Multicriteria Decision Analysis," *Lancet* 376, no. 9752 (November 1, 2010): 1558–65, https://doi.org/10.1016 /S0140-6736(10)61462-6.

89   40 percent of people: David Sheff, *Clean: Overcoming Addiction and Ending America's Greatest Tragedy* (New York: Mariner Books, 2013), 81–82.

92   "chronic, relapsing brain disease": Quoted in Marc Lewis, *The Biology of Desire: Why Addiction Is Not a Disease* (Philadelphia: PublicAffairs, 2015), 5.

93   "like all habits": Ibid., 33.

93   "overwhelming involvement with": Bruce Alexander, *The Globalization of Addiction: A Study of Poverty of the Spirit* (Oxford: Oxford University Press, 2008), Kindle loc. 1080 of 15778.

93   opposite of connection: Johann Hari, *Chasing the Scream: The First and Last Days of the War on Drugs* (New York: Bloomsbury, 2015), Kindle loc. 5742 of 15778.

93   "My definition of addiction": J. Lavitt, "Dr. Gabor Maté on the Trauma Underlying the Stigma of Addiction: An Interview," Fix, December 12, 2017, https://www.thefix.com/dr-gabor-mate-trauma-underlying -stigma-addiction-interview.

94   The choice theory: Lewis, *Biology of Desire,* 7.

94   The self-medicating: Ibid., 2.

94   The disease model: Lance M. Dodes, *The Sober Truth: Debunking the*

Bad Science Behind 12-Step Programs and the Rehab Industry (Boston: Beacon Press, 2014), 24–28.

95   and the classification: Lewis, *Biology of Desire,*13.

95   The learning model: Ibid., 27–46.

95   The dislocation model: Alexander, *Globalization of Addiction,* Kindle loc. 1121–426.

96   "10 percent of humans": Sheff, *Clean,* 96.

100 genetic predisposition: M. Schuckit, "A Brief History of Research on the Genetics of Alcohol and Other Drug Use Disorders," *Journal of Studies on Alcohol and Drugs,* supp. 17 (2014): 59–67, https://www.ncbi.nlm.nih.gov/pmc/articles/PMC4453498/.

101 When dopamine floods: "Alcohol and Dopamine," DrugRehab.com, https://www.drugrehab.com/addiction/alcohol/alcoholism/alcohol-and-dopamine/.

101 necessary for survival: Kevin McCauley et al., *Pleasure Unwoven* (Salt Lake City: Institute for Addiction Study, 2009), DVD.

102 a hedonic set point: Ibid.

102 corticotropin-releasing factor: Ibid.

102 lose their effectiveness: Ibid.

103 a triune brain: "The Triune Brain," Science of Psychotherapy, October 26, 2016, https://www.thescienceofpsychotherapy.com/the-triune-brain/.

103 In alcohol addiction: R. Goldstein and N. Volkow, "Dysfunction of the Prefrontal Cortex in Addiction: Neuroimaging Findings and Clinical Implications," *Nature Reviews Neuroscience* 12, no. 11 (October 20, 2011): 652–69, https://www.ncbi.nlm.nih.gov/pmc/articles/PMC3462342/.

CHAPTER 6: AA WAS CREATED FOR MEN

106 "The path of renunciation": Irigaray quoted in Carol Lee Flinders, *At the Root of This Longing* (San Francisco: HarperCollins, 1998), 68.

108 brainchild of Bill Wilson: Ernest Kurtz, *Not God: A History of Alcoholics Anonymous* (Center City, Minn.: Hazelden, 1979), 7–36.

109 When it was founded: Gabrielle Glaser, *Her Best Kept Secret* (New York: Simon & Schuster, 2013), 85–88.

110 "To Wives": *Alcoholics Anonymous: The Story of How Many Thousands of Men and Women Have Recovered from Alcoholism* (New York: Alcoholics Anonymous World Services, 1939, 2001), 104–21.

110 The original title: Glaser, *Best Kept Secret,* 85.

110 Marty Mann: Ibid., 86; M. McClellan, "Who Was the First Woman in Alcoholics Anonymous, and Why Do We Care?" Points: The Blog of the Alcohol & Drugs History Society, May 13, 2011,

https://pointsadhsblog.wordpress.com/2011/05/13/who-was-the
-first-woman-in-alcoholics-anonymous-and-why-do-we-care/.
110   the first Black group: B. White, "The Color and Character of AA,"
Selected Papers of William L. White, January 26, 2018, http://www
.williamwhitepapers.com/blog/2018/01/the-color-and-character-of-aa
.html.
110   A 1979 history of: Kurtz, *Not God*, 3.
111   "If we take Bill Wilson's": Charlotte Kasl, *Many Roads, One Journey:
Moving Beyond the 12 Steps* (New York: HarperCollins, 1992), 18.
111   "Step 1. We admitted": *Twelve Steps and Twelve Traditions* (New York:
Alcoholics Anonymous World Services, 1989).
112   Twelve Traditions: Ibid.
113   rejects those who use: Katrine Jo Andersen and Cecilie Maria
Kallestrup, "Rejected by A.A.: How the 12 Step Program and Its
Decades-old Philosophy Are Exacerbating the Opioid Crisis," *New
Republic*, June 27, 2018.
114   Sigmund Freud was responsible: Kendra Cherry, "Freud's Id, Ego, and
Superego," verywellmind, July 5, 2019, https://www.verywellmind
.com/the-id-ego-and-superego-2795951.
117   all religious and spiritual traditions: Flinders, *At the Root*, 61–81.
118   "I realized that": Ibid., 83.
118   "Women, on the other": Ibid., 84.
118   "they are terms": Ibid.
118   "find your voice": Ibid., 85.114.
119   evangelical Protestant: "Oxford Group," Wikipedia, February 25, 2019,
https://en.wikipedia.org/w/indexphp?title=Oxford_Group&oldid
=885083123.
119   At least 73 percent: U.S. Department of Health and Human Services,
*National Survey of Substance Abuse Treatment Services (N-SSATS):
2016: Data on Substance Abuse Treatment Facilities* (Rockville, Md.:
Center for Behavioral Statistics and Study, 2017), 22, https://www
.dasis.samhsa.gov/dasis2/nssats/2016_nssats_rpt.pdf.
119   our criminal justice system: Kara Dansky, "Jail Doesn't Help Addicts.
Let's Stop Sending Them There," ACLU Blog, October 17, 2014,
https://www.aclu.org/blog/smart-justice/mass-incarceration
/jail-doesnt-help-addicts-lets-stop-sending-them-there; "Incarceration, Substance Abuse, and Addiction," Center for Prisoner Health
and Human Rights, n.d., https://www.prisonerhealth.org/educational
-resources/factsheets-2/incarceration-substance-abuse-and-addiction/.
119   medical doctors go to: Jan Hoffman, "Most Doctors Are Ill-Equipped
to Deal with the Opioid Epidemic. Few Medical Schools Teach
Addiction," *New York Times*, September 10, 2018.

CHAPTER 7: QUITTING LIKE A WOMAN
121 "We know what": Glennon Doyle-Melton, *Love Warrior* (New York: Flatiron Books, 2016), 10.
122 So I left: Tempest, www.jointempest.com.
129 John, a therapist: John Dupuy, *Integral Recovery: A Revolutionary Approach to the Treatment of Alcoholism and Addiction* (Albany: State University of New York Press, 2013).
129 Ken Wilber's Integral Theory: Ken Wilber, *The Integral Vision: A Very Short Introduction to the Revolutionary Integral Approach to Life, God, the Universe, and Everything* (Boston: Shambala, 2007).
136 People are kicked: W. White, C. Scott, M. Dennis, and M. Boyle, "It's Time to Stop Kicking People Out of Addiction Treatment," *Counselor* 6, no. 2 (2005): 12–25, https://dbhids.org/wp-content /uploads/2015/07/2004-Possible-Resource-Papers-StopKickingPeople OutofAddictionTreatment.pdf.
137 "transcending and including": Ken Wilber, *A Brief History of Everything* (Boston: Shambala, 1996), 7.

CHAPTER 8: WORKING WITH OUR CORE BELIEFS
140 both big and small: Chödrön quoted in Courtney E. Martin, "Big and Small at the Same Time," On Being, February 19, 2016, https://onbeing.org/blog/big-and-small-at-the-same-time/.
144 "the technical term": Bessel van der Kolk, *The Body Keeps the Score: Brain, Mind, and Body in the Healing of Trauma* (New York: Viking Penguin, 2014), 95.
158 "Until your knees": Marianne Williamson, *A Return to Love* (New York: HarperCollins, 1992), 12.
165 Life Practice: Dupuy, *Integral Recovery*, 119.
166 three main strategies: Rick Hanson, *Buddha's Brain: The Practical Neuroscience of Happiness, Love, and Wisdom* (Oakland, Calif.: New Harbinger Books, 2009).
168 "You end up loving": Michael Singer, *The Untethered Soul: The Journey Beyond Yourself* (Oakland, Calif.: New Harbinger Books, 2007), 126.

CHAPTER 9: HOW TO QUIT ALCOHOL WHEN YOU'VE NEVER STUCK TO A DIET
170 "Where we think": Mohr quoted in Frank Bonomo, "10 Powerful Lessons from My 30-Day Fitness Integrity Challenge," FrankBonomo Coach.com, August 30, 2018, https://www.frankbonomocoach.com /blog/2018/8/30/10-powerful-lessons.
177 about 2 percent of body mass: M. Raichle and D. Gusnard, "Appraising the Brain's Energy Budget," *Proceedings of the National*

Academy of Sciences 99, no. 16 (2002): 10237–39, https://www.ncbi
.nlm.nih.gov/pmc/articles/PMC124895/.

178   three components necessary: Charles Duhigg, *The Power of Habit:
Why We Do What We Do in Life and Business* (New York: Random
House, 2014), Kindle loc. 1078–1535 of 16098.

180   *hyperarousal* and *hypoarousal*: Charlotte Tomaino, *Awakening the
Brain: The Neuropsychology of Grace* (New York: Atria Books, 2012),
124–33.

CHAPTER 10: BREAKING THE CYCLE OF ADDICTION

186   "Anyone who thinks": Hay quoted in Sarah Wilson, *First, We Make the
Beast Beautiful* (New York: HarperCollins, 2017), 194.

206   I came up with a method: Judson Brewer, *The Craving Mind: From
Cigarettes to Smart-phones to Love—Why We Get Hooked & How We
Can Break Bad Habits* (New Haven, Conn.: Yale University Press,
2017), 30–13.

208   deep learning: Daniel Coyle, *The Talent Code: Greatness Isn't Born. It's
Grown. Here's How* (New York: Bantam Dell, 2009), 4–6, 17–19,
30–33.

CHAPTER 11: GET AT THE ROOT

209   "When I realized": Katie Bickell, "How to Mother Yourself in
Recovery—According to a Mom," *Temper*, https://www.thetemper
.com/how-to-be-your-own-mother-in-early-recovery-according-to-a
-mom/.

211   "When children are": Marianne Williamson, *The Gift of Change:
Spiritual Guidance for a Radically New Life* (New York: HarperCollins,
2004), 232.

212   "As a mother you are": Kelly Brogan, *A Mind of Your Own: The Truth
About Depression and How Women Can Heal Their Bodies to Reclaim
Their Lives* (New York: HarperCollins, 2016), 265.

213   It seeks wholeness: Van der Kolk, *Body Keeps Score*, 217.

214   "completing process": Peter A. Levine, *Waking the Tiger: Healing
Trauma* (Berkeley, Calif.: North Atlantic Books, 1997), 85–97.

215   Addictive patterns: "PTSD and Addiction: The Connection Between
Trauma and Drug Addiction," American Addiction Centers, June 11,
2019, https://americanaddictioncenters.org/ptsd.

216   two different types of trauma: Elyssa Barbash, "Different Types of
Trauma: Small 't' versus Large 'T,'" *Psychology Today*, March 13, 2017,
https://www.psychologytoday.com/us/blog/trauma-and-hope/201703
/different-types-trauma-small-t-versus-large-t.

216   EMDR: Van der Kolk, *Body Keeps Score*, 248–62.

216 emotional freedom technique, or EFT: Ibid., 264.
217 somatic experiencing or SE: Ibid., 217–19.
217 neurofeedback uses: Ibid., 309–29.
219 Susanna Barkataki: "Susanna Barkataki," Susannabarkataki.com.
231 stabilize your blood sugar: Mathews, "The Centerpiece of
     Alcoholism."

CHAPTER 12: NAVIGATING THE SOBER ILLUMINATI

235 "Simply because we": https://secularaaoz.org/relevant-quotes-for
     -secular-aa.
240 medication-assisted treatment (MAT): Andersen and Kallestrup,
     "Rejected by A.A."
246 prescriptions given to her: Cat Marnell, *How to Murder Your Life: A
     Memoir* (New York: Simon & Schuster, 2017).
247 "The story of my body": Roxane Gay, *Hunger: A Memoir of (My) Body*
     (New York: HarperCollins, 2017), Kindle loc. 72 of 2761.
253 During Brett Kavanaugh's: Megan Garber, "The Pernicious Double
     Standards Around Brett Kavanaugh's Drinking," *Atlantic*, September
     28, 2018.
254 "The story of Cassandra": Rebecca Solnit, *Men Explain Things to Me*
     (Chicago: Haymarket Books, 2014), 103.

CHAPTER 13: HELL IS OTHER PEOPLE

256 "For a seed to": https://www.goodreads.com/quotes/1013836-for-a
     -seed-to-achieve-its-greatest-expression-it-must.
260 "When your soul awakens": John O'Donohue, "The Question Holds
     the Lantern," *Sun Magazine*, https://www.thesunmagazine.org
     /issues/407/the-question-holds-the-lantern.
262 "The people who": Kasl, *Many Roads, One Journey*, 322.
264 the first step for women: Ibid., 320–24.
264 "Life will give": Eckhart Tolle, *A New Earth: Awakening to Your Life's
     Purpose* (New York: Penguin, 2005), 41.
266 "The important thing": https://www.goodreads.com/quotes/15639
     -the-important-thing-is-this-to-be-able-at-any.
273 "You come to the point": Martin Luther King, Jr., "Loving Your
     Enemies," sermon delivered at Dexter Baptist Church, November 17,
     1957, https://kinginstitute.stanford.edu/king-papers/documents
     /loving-your-enemies-sermon-delivered-dexter-avenue-baptist
     -church.
273 "Defense is the": https://twitter.com/byronkatie/status
     /391367054185357313.
274 "When the urge arises": Shantideva, *The Way of the Bodhisattva: A*

Translation of the Bodhicharyāvatāra (Boston: Shambala, 1997), Kindle loc. 1521–34 of 4846.

274   a log of wood is: Pema Chödrön, *Bodhisattva Mind* (Louisville, Colo.: Sounds True, 2006), audiobook.

274   "Nothing real can": Helen Schucman, *A Course in Miracles* (Mill Valley, Calif.: Foundation for Inner Peace, 2007), x.

274   "She said she": https://www.instagram.com/jennadewan/p/9pIjv8jtE0/?hl=en.

CHAPTER 14: PEOPLE WHO NEED PEOPLE

277   "The opposite of addiction": Hari, *Chasing the Scream*, Kindle loc. 5742 of 7946.

277   connection: Johann Hari, "The Likely Cause of Addiction Has Been Discovered, and It Is Not What You Think," *HuffPost*, January 20, 2015 (updated April 18, 2017), https://www.huffpost.com/entry/the-real-cause-of-addicti_b_6506936.

278   a free-market, capitalist society: Alexander, *Globalization of Addiction.*

279   "vital needs for social": Ibid., Kindle loc. 1130 of 15778.

289   "Honor the space": Nancy Levin, "Is It Time for a Graceful Exit?" Nancy Levin Blog, June 24, 2015, https://www.nancylevin.com/is-it-time-for-a-graceful-exit/.

292   "We are volcanoes": Rebecca Solnit, *The Mother of All Questions* (Chicago: Haymarket Books, 2017), 18.

CHAPTER 15: WHAT DO YOU DO FOR FUN IF YOU DON'T DRINK?

297   "Tell me, what: Mary Oliver, "The Summer Day," Library of Congress, https://www.loc.gov/poetry/180/133.html.

299   Remember, drinking artificially: McCauley et al., *Pleasure Unwoven.*

302   four stages of womanhood: Rebecca Campbell, *Rise Sister Rise: A Guide to Unleashing the Wise, Wild Woman Within* (New York: Hay House, 2016), 114–19.

304   "We're on a planet": Jen Sincero, *You Are a Badass: How to Stop Doubting Your Greatness and Start Living an Awesome Life* (Philadelphia: Running Press, 2013), 36.

306   "Whenever you find yourself": C. Cannon, "Putting Words in Mark Twain's Mouth," Real Clear Politics, December 10, 2012, https://www.realclearpolitics.com/articles/2012/12/10/fake_twain_quotes_and_other_hazards_of_twitter_116376-3.html.

307   "To say what one wants": Flinders, *At the Root*, 83.

310   "The disease of addiction": Dupuy, *Integral Recovery*, 7.

310   everything we can do: Allen Carr, *The Easy Way to Control Alcohol* (London: Arcturus, 2003).

CHAPTER 16: ACTIVISM, SOBRIETY, AND THE TRUE RESISTANCE

319   That doctors who prescribe: Hoffman, "Most Doctors Are Ill-Equipped to Deal with the Opioid Epidemic."

319   That people who are sick: Dansky, "Jail Doesn't Help Addicts. Let's Stop Sending Them There." "Incarceration, Substance Abuse, and Addiction," Center for Prisoner Health and Human Rights, https://www.prisonerhealth.org/educational-resources/factsheets-2 /incarceration-substance-abuse-and-addiction/;"The Fallout Legal Consequences of Alcoholism," American Addiction Centers, June 18, 2019, https://americanaddictioncenters.org/alcoholism-treatment /legal-consequences.

319   That the Rehab: Arjun Sethi and Cate Graziani, "Stop the Treatment Industrial Complex," Politico, March 9, 2016, https://www.politico .com/agenda/story/2016/03/stop-the-treatment-industrial -complex-000061; Dan Munro, "Inside the $35 Billion Addiction Treatment Industry," Forbes, April 27, 2015, https://www.forbes.com /sites/danmunro/2015/04/27/inside-the-35-billion-addiction -treatment-industry/#7a16304917dc.

319   80 percent of them: "Mass Incarceration," ACLU, https://www.aclu .org/issues/smart-justice/mass-incarceration; Christopher Wren, "Drugs or Alcohol Linked to 80% of Inmates," New York Times, January 9, 1998; "The Drug War, Mass Incarceration, and Race," Drug Policy Alliance, January 2018, http://www.drugpolicy.org/sites /default/files/drug-war-mass-incarceration-and-race_01_18_0.pdf.

319   The American War on Drugs: Alexander S. Dawson, The Peyote Effect (Oakland: University of California Press, 2018), 44–54; Szasz, Ceremonial Chemistry, 75–87; Frederic Block, "Racism's Hidden History in the War on Drugs," HuffPost, March 5, 2013; Dale Gieringer, "The Opium Exclusion Act of 1909," Counterpunch, February 6, 2009, https://www.counterpunch.org/2009/02/06 /the-opium-exclusion-act-of-1909/.

320   all drug use illicit around the globe: Fernando Esquivel-Suárez, "The Global War on Drugs," Global South Studies, https://globalsouth studies.as.virginia.edu/key-issues/global-war-drugs; Graham Boyd, "The Drug War Is the New Jim Crow," ACLU Blog, July–August 2001, https://www.aclu.org/other/drug-war-new-jim-crow; Michelle Alexander, The New Jim Crow (New York: New Press, 2010).

320   underwrites anti-blackness: T. Santoro and J. Santoro, "Racial Bias in the US Opioid Epidemic: A Review of the History of Systemic Bias and Implications for Care," Cureus 10, no. 12 (December 2018): e3733, https://www.ncbi.nlm.nih.gov/pmc/articles/PMC6384031/; M. Bebinger, "Opioid Addiction Drug Going Mostly to Whites, Even as Black Death Rate Rises," All Things Considered, NPR, May 8, 2019,

https://www.npr.org/sections/health-shots/2019/05/08/721447601
/addiction-medicine-mostly-prescribed-to-whites-even-as-opioid
-deaths-rose-in-bla; B. Pearl, "Ending the War on Drugs: By the
Numbers," Center for American Progress, June 27, 2018, https://www
.americanprogress.org/issues/criminal-justice/reports/2018/06/27
/452819/ending-war-drugs-numbers/; J. Sherman and L. Abrams,
"The Bail System is Racist and Unjust. It Needs to Be Reformed," Real
Clear Policy, August 17, 2018, https://www.realclearpolicy.com
/articles/2018/08/17/the_bail_system_is_racist_and_unjust_it_needs
_to_be_reformed_110764.html.

320   zoom in, say, on Fox News: @Fox4, Twitter, September 13, 2018,
https://twitter.com/FOX4/status/1040361795519541249; "Search
Warrant's Findings Released in Botham Jean's Apartment," Fox 4
News, September 13, 2018, http://www.fox4news.com/news
/search-warrant-marijuana-found-in-botham-jeans-apartment-after
-deadly-shooting; H. Abdurraqib, "The Media Can't Justify Botham
Jean's Killing. But They're Trying," BuzzFeed News, September 25,
2018, https://www.buzzfeednews.com/article/hanifabdurraqib
/botham-jean-amber-guyger-police-brutality; Charles Mudede,
"Fox News Attempted to Demonize Unarmed Black Man Killed by
Dallas Cop in His Own Apartment," Stranger, September 14, 2018,
https://www.thestranger.com/slog/2018/09/14/32327223/fox-news
-attempted-to-demonize-unarmed-black-man-killed-by-dallas-cop
-in-his-own-apartment; Thomas Barrabi, "Marijuana Stock Backed by
Peter Thiel Surges on US Import Approval," Fox Business, September
19, 2018, https://www.foxbusiness.com/markets/marijuana-stock
-backed-by-peter-thiel-surges-on-us-import-approval.

320   women have been sold whiskey: Rupert Steiner, "Whiskey Giant
Pernod Ricard Winning Over Women as Sales Roar," Market Watch,
February 12, 2019, https://www.marketwatch.com/story/whiskey
-giant-pernod-ricard-winning-over-women-as-sales-soar-2019-02-12;
Pierre Andersson, *Global Hangover: Alcohol as an Obstacle to
Development* (Sweden: IOGT-NTO International Institute, 2008),
23–33.

320   It's the relationships: "Alcohol Beverage Industry Economic Impact,"
https://fourloko.com/alcohol-beverage-economic-impact/; R. Rabin,
"Federal Agency Courted Alcohol Industry to Fund Study on Benefits
of Moderate Drinking," *New York Times*, March 17, 2018.

320   It's the ties: Ari Melber, "Presumed Guilty: How Prisons Profit Off the
'War on Drugs,'" MSNBC, August 14, 2013, http://www.msnbc.com
/msnbc/presumed-guilty-how-prisons-profit-the; Alexander, *New Jim
Crow*.

321   It's unchecked capitalism: K. Lee, "Capitalism Makes Us Crazy: Dr.

Gabor Maté on Illness and Addiction," Truthout.org, June 1, 2013, https://truthout.org/audio/capitalism-makes-us-crazy-dr-gabor-mate -on-illness-and-addiction/; Alexander, *Globalization of Addiction*; D. Courtwright, *The Age of Addiction: How Bad Habits Became Big Business* (Cambridge, Mass.: Belknap Press of Harvard University Press, 2019); Naomi Klein, "Johann Hari & Naomi Klein: Does Capitalism Drive Drug Addiction?" Democracy Now, March 11, 2015, https://www.democracynow.org/2015/3/11/johann_hari_naomi _klein_does_capitalism.

321   It's Big Pharma: Robert Whitaker, *Mad in America: Bad Science, Bad Medicine, and the Enduring Mistreatment of the Mentally Ill* (Philadelphia: Perseus, 2002); Robert Whitaker, *Anatomy of an Epidemic: Magic Bullets, Psychiatric Drugs, and the Astonishing Rise of Mental Illness in America* (New York: Broadway Books, 2010); Andrea Tone, *The Age of Anxiety: A History of America's Turbulent Affair with Tranquilizers* (Philadelphia: Basic Books, 2009); Szasz, *Ceremonial Chemistry*; Barry Meier, "Origins of an Epidemic: Purdue Pharma Knew Its Opioids Were Widely Abused," *New York Times*, May 29, 2018; Chris McGreal, "Johnson & Johnson Faces Multibillion Opioids Lawsuit That Could Upend Big Pharma," *Guardian*, June 23, 2019, https://www.theguardian.com/us-news/2019/jun/22/johnson-and -johnson-opioids-crisis-lawsuit-latest-trial; Daniel Oberhaus, "Risky Drugs Are Being Marketed to People with Mental Health Issues," Vice, August 15, 2017, https://www.vice.com/en_us/article/a33gbe /risky-drugs-are-being-marketed-to-people-with-mental-health -issues; Robert Whitaker, "The Downside of Meds," Boston.com, May 10, 2010, http://archive.boston.com/news/health/articles /2010/05/10/robert_whitaker_talks_about_the_downside_to _psychiatric_meds/.

321   It's a government: German Lopez, "The War on Drugs, Explained," Vox, May 8, 2016, https://www.vox.com/2016/5/8/18089368 /war-on-drugs-marijuana-cocaine-heroin-meth; Bushauna Freeman, "Government Spending on Drug Control: Are the Priorities Right?" University of Pennsylvania Leonard Davis Institute SUMR Blog, August 15, 2016, https://ldi.upenn.edu/sumr-blog/government -spending-drug-control-are-priorities-right.

321   It's the links: Miller, *US of AA*, 27–101; "Alcohol Tax Revenue," Tax Policy Center, https://www.taxpolicycenter.org/statistics/alcohol-tax -revenue; "Beer, Wine & Liquor: Annual Lobbying," Opensecrets.org, https://www.opensecrets.org/lobby/indusclient.php?id=N02.

321   It's the push: Kristen Clarke, "Cannabis Industry Shouldn't Expand Until We Fix Marijuana's Racial Inequities, Injustices," *USA Today*, February 22, 2019; Maria Paz Gutierrez, "(Legally) Selling Weed While

Black," an episode of *Code Switch Podcast,* September 22, 2017, https://
www.npr.org/sections/codeswitch/2017/09/22/551888824/-legally
-selling-weed-while-black; Mary Papenfuss, "Ocasio-Cortez Slams
the 'Racial Injustice' of the Cannabis Business as White Men Profit,"
HuffPost, February 15, 2019, https://www.huffpost.com/entry/ocasio
-cortez-diverity-cannabis-industry_n_5c676fcce4b05c889d1f6cfc.

321   "John A. Boehner, the former": Elizabeth Williamson, "John Boehner:
From Speaker of the House to Cannabis Pitchman," *New York Times,*
June 3, 2019.

322   Harry Anslinger: Johann Hari, "The Hunting of Billie Holiday: How
Lady Day Was in the Middle of a Federal Bureau of Narcotics Fight
for Survival," Politico, January 17, 2015, https://www.politico.com
/magazine/story/2015/01/drug-war-the-hunting-of-billie-holiday
-114298.

325   Stonewall Riots: "How the Stonewall Riots Changed the Course of
History," All That's Interesting, August 11, 2015, updated January 3,
2019, https://allthatsinteresting.com/stonewall-riots.

ABOUT THE AUTHOR

Holly Whitaker is the founder and CEO of Tempest (formerly Hip Sobriety). With years of experience in the field of health care service and tech, she created her company in 2014 and established an alternative recovery community online with the tools, resources, and education to combat addiction. She lives in Brooklyn with her cat, Mary Katherine.

ABOUT THE TYPE

This book was set in Minion, a 1990 Adobe Originals typeface by Robert Slimbach (b. 1956). Minion is inspired by classical, old-style typefaces of the late Renaissance, a period of elegant, beautiful, and highly readable type designs. Created primarily for text setting, Minion combines the aesthetic and functional qualities that make text type highly readable with the versatility of digital technology.